POINT AND FIGURE CHARTING

WILEY TRADING

POINT AND FIGURE CHARTING

The Essential Application for Forecasting and Tracking Market Prices

Second Edition

Thomas J. Dorsey

John Wiley & Sons, Inc.

New York • Chichester • Weinheim • Brisbane • Singapore • Toronto

Copyright © 2001 by Marketplace Books. All rights reserved.

Published by John Wiley & Sons, Inc.
Published simultaneously in Canada.

This publication is designed to provide accurate and authoritative information in regard to the subject matter covered. It is sold with the understanding that the publisher is not engaged in rendering professional services. If professional advice or other expert assistance is required, the services of a competent professional person should be sought.

ISBN 0-471-41292-9

Printed in the United States of America.

10 9 8 7 6 5 4 3 2 1

ACKNOWLEDGMENTS

It's been five years since the first edition of *Point and Figure Charting* was printed. The first edition was a success beyond any of our expectations. The success and consistency of sales over the years assures us that this method is the right method for most investors. Dorsey, Wright & Associates' client base has grown significantly over these years. One of the things that make this company so solid is the lack of turnover in our employees. This is extremely important in this business because it is a never-ending learning process. My two top analysts, Tammy DeRosier and Susan Morrison, have been here virtually since the company began. They both now have 14 years' experience using this method of analysis. Tammy and Sue both have developed ways of evaluating stocks with new twists on the old indicators. Sue has done in-depth research on Relative Strength that you will benefit from in this new edition. I looked over at Sue recently and said, "You've shifted gears again with respect to understanding the markets." In other words, she had shifted up to a much higher understanding about the investment process. The guidance she was providing our professional customers had reached new levels of excellence. It's like the world chess master Bobby Fischer rising to absolute mastery of the chess game. It took years of dedication and hard work to reach the level where he played for the world title against Boris Spasky of Russia. Bobby Fischer won in what turned out to be one of the greatest matches ever. This is what I meant by my comment to Susan. Tammy has just as much experience. This is why virtually no turnover of the analysts at Dorsey, Wright has kept us on the leading edge of technical analysis. The accumulated years of experience in technical analysis at Dorsey, Wright exceeds 100 years.

Susan, Tammy, Jay, and my partner Watson Wright have become world-class Wall Street Technical Analysts as have our other analysts Kevin Depew and Paul Keeton. Steve Raymond works the same magic with Mutual Funds. Mike Moody and Harold Parker, our Portfolio Managers at Dorsey, Wright Money Management, are two of only about 150 Chartered Market Technicians in the world. They, too, are world-class portfolio money managers. The Dorsey, Wright & Associates (DWA) Internet site/investor productivity system is the largest and most comprehensive site of its kind on the Internet. Jay, a backbone of the company, spearheaded this system from day one when it started as a dial-in bulletin board more than six years ago. Our dial-in bulletin board preceded the Internet by a couple of years. Jay has kept us on the leading edge of technology since we came online with our first charting system. When Jay is out, the whole system falls on the shoulders of Jay's assistant, Justin Knight. And, none of this work would get done without Nancy Emig, our office manager, who is one of the best new additions to our team. It took us a while to find the right person to handle the complexities and stress of the job, and Nancy fits the bill perfectly. At DWA, once you come, you do not leave. We all keep working hard to get better and better. It is an "all for one and one for all" atmosphere.

All of our analysts write a daily 20-page research report. This translates into approximately 250 reports per year, or 5,000 pages of original research. Our phones are open to all our clients for person-to-person consultation during the day. The reports are written in between phone conversations to professionals. On average, each analyst handles a minimum 30 calls per day. This is what makes our team that much more incredible. Writing the report takes tremendous creative thinking and writing capabilities. This daily research must be logical, organized, and easy to understand, yet complex enough to make money in today's changing economy. The key to our success at DWA has been our ability to empower others to become all they can be at the investment process.

Revising this book took on an added dimension as there were many new things to talk about. As Tammy, Sue, and I worked on this project, we realized that we had experienced firsthand one of the most dynamic bull markets and now one of the most painful technology meltdowns in history. Revising this book became a collaborative effort. Tammy and Sue have done some ground-breaking research in Relative Strength that is discussed in this book, and both analysts use these concepts to brilliantly manage a sizable portion of our Corporate Profit Sharing account. These are the concepts outlined in this book.

My thanks go out to the whole team at Dorsey, Wright for continually striving for excellence each and every day. They are in my opinion, the greatest team of professionals ever assembled on Wall Street. You are about to read a blockbuster of a book.

THOMAS J. DORSEY

CONTENTS

Chapter 1

INTRODUCTION

Point and Figure Charting: A Lost Art

The Point and Figure method is not new by any stretch of the imagination. It is, however, a lost art simply because most investment professionals and individual investors have lost sight of the basics that cause fluctuations in the prices of securities. In today's rapidly evolving technologies, the irrefutable law of supply and demand has been all but forgotten. In the end, the only thing that will outlive technological change and that is truly sustainable is the transcendent competence of an individual's workmanship. New methods of security analysis continue to crop up capturing the ever-expanding curiosity of the investment public. It seems everyone is searching for the Holy Grail, yet few are willing to become a craftsmen at the investment process. So many are looking for a computer program that will define the winning trades each day without any effort from the investor or professional who has ultimate responsibility for the portfolio of stocks. A long time ago when I was a stockbroker at a major firm on Wall Street, I learned there is no Holy Grail. The key to success in this business, and any business for that matter, is *confidence.* According to my dictionary, confidence means "firm belief or trust; self-reliance; boldness; assurance." In the securities business, the key term in the definition is *self-reliance,* and it is the one trait most investors and stockbrokers lack. Investors today are increasingly averse to making their own decisions, which is why the mutual fund business has grown to record levels. Those who have taken

1

control of their own investments have done so without much in the way of training and education in the investment process. The irony is that 75 percent or more of professional money managers never outperform the broad stock market averages. Nevertheless, most investors look at the stock market as an enigma. It confounds them that the market reacts in what seems to be an illogical pattern. Increased earnings expectations should result in price appreciation of the underlying stock, right? Not necessarily. In many cases, the opposite takes place. In the year 2000, we saw exactly that. Stocks with great fundamentals collapsed under their astronomical valuations. Companies like Lucent Technologies declined from 80 to the single digits. Major firms on Wall Street were in love with the stock's fundamentals at 80. Lucent's only problem was not in the company itself but in its customers' ability to pay for the products they had purchased from Lucent. This information did not show up in the fundamental research until the stock had collapsed. It did, however, show up in the Point and Figure chart. Those who were well versed in evaluating the supply-demand relationship of the stock saw trouble early on.

Now it is the year 2001, and over the past six years my confidence in this methodology has increased tremendously. While nothing in the method has changed an iota, how we use it has expanded and grown. We have developed some new indicators, many based on the Bullish Percent and Relative Strength concepts covered in the first edition, and have found new ways to use many of the old indicators.

In the past five years, we have gone through some of the most volatile markets anyone has seen. Negotiating the markets in this volatile and changing economy points up the need for an operating system to guide investors. This book provides that operating system. The old paradigm of buying quality stocks with real products and visible earnings has gone right out the window. At least the media and most investors think so. In the late 1990s, the mantra on Wall Street was, forget earnings they aren't important, only revenues are important. We heard 22-year-old CEOs suggesting that the old line companies, the backbone of the United States, "just don't get it." Well, the crash of the dot-com companies that thought they "got it" has awakened Americans to a market that both gives and takes away. At this writing, the

22-year-old CEOs "didn't get it." Investors have come to realize that real wealth is made in the stock market. They have also come to realize that the market can take it away just as fast. Attention to the bottom line is now back in vogue as investors recognize that net earnings are in fact important. In the latter part of the 1990s, firms attempted to create brand names by simply throwing millions of dollars into advertising. Companies were trying to create solid brand names in one month that took companies like Procter & Gamble 40 years to create. Some companies even sell products below cost, with the expectation of making up the difference in advertisement revenues.

This all came to roost in the second quarter of 2000 when the Nasdaq stocks literally melted down in a matter of a few weeks. All of a sudden, the market that once valued The Street Dot Com (TSCM) at 71 now valued it at 3. Microstrategy (MSTR) once traded as high as 330 and at this writing has fallen to 14. The highflier Priceline.com was as high as 165 and is now 5. How quickly the market corrects overexuberance, as Alan Greenspan warned. The highfliers were not the only ones that were hit in 2000; some stocks, many New York Stock Exchange names, hit their peaks in 1998 and are just beginning to show signs of life again. Quality companies like Eastman Kodak, Cisco Systems, Polaroid, Procter & Gamble, AT&T, Worldcom—the list goes on and on—have seen their stock prices cut in half or worse. There was basically nowhere investors could hide. It was an interesting market from April 1998 to March 2000 in which the indexes did fairly well while the stocks underlying them were killers. This happens when an index is controlled by a handful of stocks like the Dow Jones, Nasdaq, and the S&P 500. It is so easy for an index to be pushed and pulled by the top tier stocks while the vast majority of stocks underlying the index are struggling at best.

You know what concept never wavered once during this treacherous period? It was the irrefutable law of supply and demand. In almost all the cases cited, the charts foretold trouble down the road. In later chapters, I point out how these supply-and-demand indicators "saw" this crash coming and told us the risk was high. We were then able to get our clients out of harm's way. We have once again gone through a market condition never seen before. The Internet has injected change into the whole game on Wall Street. Barriers to entry to dot-com businesses are nil on the Net, and that freedom brings tremendous competition. The playing field is being leveled every day. The one constant that has not changed in over 100 years is supply and demand and the Point and Figure method of analyzing markets.

What Do Investors Today Have in Common with 18-Year-Old Bungee Jumpers?

The answer is, no fear. Over the past decade, investors came to believe that buying the dips is the key to success: Stocks always come back, don't panic, just buy more. Some people leveraged their homes to put money in the stock market. This kind of situation never ends well, and in the year 2000 it didn't. The crash in Nasdaq stocks caught just about everyone off guard, and massive losses were generated buying the dips, averaging good money after bad. I don't believe investors have broken this habit yet, but they are certainly bowed.

The "buy every dip" mentality is what I call *false courage*. False courage is confidence you may feel when under the influence of alcohol or drugs. It dulls the senses and gives you the confidence to do things you otherwise would not consider. A friend of mine, Cornelius Patrick Shea, used to say, "My pappy use to tell me the 'sauce' makes ya say things ya don't mean and believe things that ain't true." The "sauce" for investors consisted of the seemingly never ending rise in highflying tech stocks. It was so intoxicating that investors were "saying things they didn't mean (buy 1,000 more) and believing things that weren't true (revenues are increasing with no end in sight)." During the latter part of the 1990s and first quarter of 2000, investors were enamored with the seemingly never-ending ascent of the stock market and in particular the Nasdaq. The media aided this belief with the ceaseless chant of zero inflation and endless increases in worker productivity due to technological advances. Because of their intoxication, investors kept taking more risks through leverage in high volatility stocks beyond any rational measure. I even had a broker call me up with a story of how her aunt was not allowed to use margin at her firm because of her advanced age (she was 80). Do you know what she did? She took a second mortgage out on her house, put it in her stock account, and continued trading. In essence, she skirted the brokerage firm's margin requirement and margined the account anyway. I wonder how she fared after the crash of March 2000, May 2000, and November 2000? She may have lost her house.

Many investors have forgotten that having a logical, organized, well-founded method of investing in the markets is the only way to success. Haphazard, overleveraged, methodless investing will always lead to disaster, just as it did in 2000. The Nasdaq not only corrected, it headed south like a migrating bird. Its decline was so swift that, in a matter of weeks it had lost 37 percent from its high, and that even masked what happened to so many stocks. Many individual stocks lost 80 percent or more of their value. Investors with a whole portfolio of high-tech/high-wreck Internet and technology stocks may not see the light of day in their accounts for many years to come. The average gain in the stock market over the past 80 years is around the 10 percent level. If an investor loses 50 percent of his portfolio value, that portfolio will have to rise 100 percent to get back even. How long will that take at an average 10 percent per year? About seven years. If an investor bought at the top in 1973 and rode the market down, it took 7½ years to get back even. Can you wait 7½ years to get your money back if you ride a bear market down as the media and mutual funds suggest you should do? If your answer is no, then you are ultimately interested in risk management, which is what this book is all about.

I was in a store the other day purchasing a new laptop computer to write this book. I got into a conversation about investing in the market with the head of the computer department. He was having a hard time understanding what I did. I told him that successful investing requires an operating system like the one in every computer. The computer's operating system allows it to effectively read and run all the software products. Operating systems like Windows 98 simply provide a set of instructions that tells the computer how to run. Without an operating system, software cannot run on the computer. Investing is the same. Investors must have an operating system firmly in mind to work from, before they can accomplish anything.

This operating system is the core belief in some method of analysis an investor both understands thoroughly and embraces wholeheartedly. It's like getting religion on Wall Street. At some point, all successful investors have to find some church on Wall Street that they can attend every week. Many investors subscribe strictly to the fundamental approach of investing. This method only delves into the internal qualities of the underlying stock. It does not take into consideration timing entry and exit points in that stock, and above all, supply and demand imbalances. Other methods of analysis might involve astrology, Fibonnaci retracement numbers, Gann angles, waves, cycles, candlestick charts, bar charts, or any other method you are willing to embrace. At Dorsey, Wright, we only subscribe to one irrefutable method—the law of supply and demand. If you want to go back to the basics, with a methodology that has stood the test of time, in bull and bear markets, and is easy enough to learn whether you are age 8 to 80, then you are reading the right book. This operating system will carry you through your investment endeavors, from stocks and mutual funds to commodities.

Why Does This Method Make Sense and Where Did It Originate?

We humans have certain limitations when coping with rapid decision making. Most investors find it difficult to think through the complex decisions they need to make about equities. The problem is not that we have too much information. The problem is managing and processing this information. It is like a fire hose of information that hits us in the face every day. The question is how to control that massive information flow and break it down into understandable bits that we can use to make effective decisions. In essence, we have decision overload.

To help you organize this information, we have some powerful tools (see our Web site: www.dorseywright.com). The simplest example of how information is organized is the telephone. We have an ability to remember three or four numbers in succession easily but seven is difficult. This is why our phone numbers are divided up in threes and fours. The pound sign and the star sign on the phone were there for years with no apparent function. Now we routinely use them. They had no function when they first appeared on phones, but the phone companies knew that eventually there would be a use for them in managing information. Similarly, Charles Dow found a way to organize data back in the 1800s. He was the first person to record stock price movement and created a method of analysis called *Figuring* that eventually led to the Point and Figure method described in this book. The Point and Figure method of recording stock prices is simply another way of organizing data.

At the turn of the twentieth century, some astute investors noticed that many of Dow's chart patterns had a tendency to repeat themselves. Back then, there was no Securities and Exchange Commission; there were few rules and regulations. Stock pools dominated the action and outsiders were very late to the party. It was basically a closed shop of insiders. The Point and Figure method of charting was developed as a logical, organized way of recording the imbalance between supply and demand. These charts provide the investor with a road map that clearly depicts that battle between supply and demand.

Everyone is familiar with using maps to plan road trips. When we drive from Virginia to New York, we start the trip on I-95 North. If we don't pay attention to our navigating and inadvertently get on I-95 South, we are likely to end up in Key West, Florida. To prepare for a journey with your family to New York from Virginia, you need to familiarize yourself with the map, check the air in your car's tires, begin with a full tank of gas, and make sure the children have some books and toys. In other words, plan your trip. Most investors never plan their investment trip. The Point and Figure method of analyzing supply and demand can provide that plan. Nothing guarantees success, but the probability of success is much higher when all the possible odds are stacked in the investors' favor. Somewhere along the road, you may be forced to take a detour, but that's okay as long as you stick to your original plan. This book will outline the best plan for financial success when you are investing in securities.

When all is said and done, if there are more buyers in a particular security than there are sellers willing to sell, the price will rise. On the other hand, if there are more sellers in a particular security than there are buyers willing to buy, then the price will decline. If buying and selling are equal, the price will remain the same. This is the irrefutable law of supply and demand. The same reasons that cause price fluctuations in produce such as potatoes, corn, and asparagus cause price fluctuations in securities.

Two methods of analysis are used in security evaluation. One method is *fundamental analysis.* This is the method of analysis familiar to most investors. It deals with the quality of the company's earnings, product acceptance, and management. Fundamental analysis answers the question *what* security to buy. Technical analysis is the other basic method. It answers the question *when* to buy that security. Timing the commitment is the crucial step. Fundamental information on companies can be obtained from numerous sources. There are many free Internet sites that deal strictly with fundamental analysis. The technical side of the equation is much more difficult to find because few securities professionals are doing quality technical analysis that the average investor can understand. This book is designed to teach you how to formulate your own operating system using the Point and Figure method, coupled with solid fundamental analysis.

Why You Should Use Point and Figure Charts

Although the investment industry is overloaded with different methodologies to evaluate security price movement, the Point and Figure method is the only one I have found to be straightforward and easy to understand.

The charts are made up of X's and O's. Recording the movement of a security using this method is very much like recording a tennis match. A tennis match can last 12 sets. Each player can win a certain number of sets, but the final count determines which player wins the match. In the Point and Figure method, we are only interested in the culmination of the match, not the winner of the underlying sets. The patterns this method produces are simple and easy to recognize—so simple that I have taught this method to grade schoolers in Virginia. I have always maintained that simple is best.

The concept underlying the method must be valid. Supply and demand is as valid and basic as it gets. I am not criticizing the validity of other methods; it's just that most people can easily understand supply and demand because it is a part of everyday life. Why not make it a part of your everyday investing?

The greatest market indicator yet invented was developed by A.W. Cohen in 1955. It is called the *New York Stock Exchange Bullish Percent Index.* We have used it for many years with great success. In that time, we have refined it as the markets have changed, but the basic philosophy is still intact. I have devoted a whole chapter of this book to a discussion of this indicator. Our sector rotation method, which is explained in another chapter, is a derivative of the Bullish Percent concept. Once you learn these basic principles, your investing confidence will increase tremendously. You will soon find yourself acting rather than reacting to different market conditions. This method changed my life, and it can do the same for anyone who takes the time to read this book and then implements the investing principles contained therein.

In the Beginning

It took me years of operating in a fog in the brokerage business before I came across the Point and Figure method. I started my career at a large brokerage firm in Richmond, Virginia, in late 1974. When training new employees, the firm focused primarily on sales. As trainees, we were drilled in the philosophy that the firm would provide the ideas and our responsibility was to sell them. The first four months at the firm we devoted to study. Every potential broker must pass the Series 7 examination to become registered with the New York Stock Exchange. The course was extensive—covering everything from exchange rules and regulations to complicated option strategies. Once we had passed the exam and completed five weeks of sales training, we were ready to be unleashed on the public.

As in any other profession, experience counts a lot, and we were severely lacking in that area. The market had just gone through what seemed to be a depression, losing about 70 percent of its value. Prospecting for new accounts was a difficult task at best, but those of us who survived spent the next four years building a book of business and learning by trial and error. Each morning, we had mounds of new recommendations from New York to sift through, all fundamental. We were not allowed to recommend any stocks our firm did not have a favorable opinion on; the rule was no thinking on our own—it could cause a lawsuit. Our job was to sell the research, not question it.

Over the years, we had some tremendous successes and some spectacular failures, definitely not a confidence builder. In my spare time, I kept searching for some infallible newsletter writer. This search, however, only proved that the newsletter writers were better at selling newsletters than at picking stocks. The ship was basically rudderless, but we forged ahead. Now, almost 21 years later, nothing much has changed in the way business is done. There are some new bells and whistles and fad investments, but the backbone of the industry continues to be equity recommendations based solely on fundamental analysis. During my tenure at that firm, I specialized in option strategies. Options were relatively new, having been first listed for trading in April 1973. I spent much of my time studying this investment tool, and in 1978 I was offered the opportunity to develop and manage an options strategy department at a large regional brokerage firm home-based in the same town. It was an irresistible challenge, so I embarked on this new adventure.

Overnight, my clientele changed from individual investors to professional stockbrokers. I was now responsible for developing a department that would provide options strategy ideas to a salesforce of 500 brokers. At this moment, I had to be totally honest with myself. Just how much did I really know about the stock market? I knew that my success at selecting the right stocks to support our options strategies would ultimately determine the success or failure of my department. The answer to that question was startling.

After four years of working as a successful stockbroker, I had very little knowledge about selecting stocks on my own, much less evaluating sectors and the market itself. I was used to doing what the firm directed. The one thing I did know was that relying on any firm's research was likely to be hit or miss. Developing a successful options strategy department meant I would have to find someone who was adept at stock selection.

During my search for a stock picker, one name continued to crop up: Steve Kane, a broker in our Charlotte branch. I contacted Steve and explained my new adventure to him and offered him a position in my department. He decided to join me. My grand plan was that Steve would provide the stock, sector, and market direction; and I would provide the option strategies to dovetail his work.

As any craftsman would, Steve brought along his tools, which consisted of a chart book full of X's and O's on hundreds of stocks and a Point and Figure technical analysis book written by A.W. Cohen (this book is no longer in print). The basic principles of the Point and Figure method were first published in 1947, the year I was born, and the book was called *Stock Market Timing*. Each week, Steve would fastidiously update these charts of X's and O's and use them to make his stock selections. Over the first year, Steve did very well. Stocks he selected to rise generally did. Stocks he felt would decline generally did. His calls on the market and sectors were also very good. The team was working well, and best of all, we were self-contained. We were a technical analysis and options strategy department rolled into one. We weren't always right, but we were more right than wrong and, most important, we had a plan of attack.

Just as things were looking good, a specialist firm on the New York Stock Exchange offered Steve a job with the opportunity to trade their excess capital. It was an offer Steve could not refuse, and I supported his decision to go. I found myself back in the same predicament that I had been in a year earlier. Rather than try to find someone else who understood the Point and Figure method of technical analysis that I had become accustomed to, I decided it was time to learn it myself.

Steve explained the basics to me and recommended I read his closely guarded copy of A.W. Cohen's book. That weekend I started reading it, and after the first three pages, my life changed. All the years of operating in a fog, searching for answers, and believing it was all too complicated to learn, came to an end. What I found in the first three pages made all the sense in the world to me. I knew in that moment what I would do for the rest of my life. This was the missing link that all brokers needed to effectively service their clients. We now operate the only Stockbroker Institute in the United States, and it is the culmination of my dream that night. We have trained hundreds of stockbrokers in this method and watched their confidence and client profits climb through the roof. We have also held our first Individual Investor Institute in concert with Virginia Commonwealth University, and the auditorium was packed. Something right is going on here.

On Taking Risks in Life[*]

There are many similarities between the principles in sports and the psychology of the stock market. I am a world record holder in powerlifting, and in my endeavors to improve my lifts, I learned a lot from Judd Biasiotto's articles in *Powerlifting* magazine. I have gotten to know Judd personally, and we see so many similarities between our two businesses that we have written articles together. In fact, we will soon publish a book together that explains how some of the psychological aspects of sports competition can be applied to investing.

When Judd was working with the Kansas City Royals baseball team, his roommate, Branch B. Rickey III, met a guy who was willing to let us buy into a condominium project being constructed in Florida. The deal was that we could purchase up to 10 condominiums at a price of 10,000 each. At the time, 10,000 was a pretty good chunk of money, but the deal was extraordinary. If everything went as planned, there was a good chance we could double or triple our money in no time. Still there was a risk—there always is a risk. Because it was beachfront property, the taxes were very high. Unlike Branch, I did not have the money to invest long term. I would have to borrow the money at a fairly high interest rate and then hope that I could turn the property over in a short period. Otherwise, I would lose a lot of money. In the end, I decided not to do the deal. Of course, you know the end of the story already. The property is now worth anywhere from $500,000 to $1 million.

Yes, I could have been living in the Bahamas relaxing on the beach, but I failed to take the risk. There is one thing I'm certain of—if you don't have the guts to put yourself on the line now and

---

[*]This section was written with the assistance of Judd Biasiotto, PhD.

then, your chances of success are limited. To reach the top, athletes—or anyone else for that matter—have to know how to live on the edge. They have to enjoy the elements of risk and a little danger. I'm not talking about taking needless, senseless, incalculable risks, like running with the bulls in Pamplona or attempting a 500-pound dead-lift when your personal best is 300 hundred pounds; such actions prove nothing except that you have the brain of an infant. What I'm talking about is intelligent, calculated risk-taking in which the risk in question has a legitimate cost-reward relationship.

This really speaks to the business of investing. You have to be a risk-taker to even survive in this business, much less flourish. Every time you buy a stock, you are risking your hard-earned money. If you are a broker, you are risking your clients' hard-earned money. If you can't operate in a high-risk environment, then the business of investing is not for you. I have met many investors and brokers who just couldn't make a buy decision for fear of losing their or their clients' money. It's good to have a healthy dose of trepidation in this business of investing money. That way you don't make stupid mistakes, but freezing only causes you to miss great opportunities. There is a big difference between having a healthy respect for risk and allowing risk to paralyze your thought processes. Many investors and brokers simply can't deal with market volatility. A fine line exists between managing risk and being controlled by risk. The stock market is not a place for the faint of heart. To reach the pinnacle in the personal or professional investment field, you have to learn to live on the edge, to enjoy the element of risk and danger—at least to a reasonable degree.

Look back through time and you'll find that people who had the courage to take a chance, who faced their fears head on, were those who shaped history. The people who played it safe, who were afraid to take a risk, well, have you ever heard of them? I love what Theodore Roosevelt said about this very issue:

> It is not the critic who counts, not the man who points out how the strong man stumbles or where the doer of deeds could have done them better. The credit belongs to the man who is actually in the arena, whose face is marred

by dust and sweat and blood, who strives valiantly, who errs and comes up short again and again because there is no effort without error and shortcomings, who knows the great devotion, who spends himself in a worthy cause, who at the best knows in the end the high achievement of triumph and who at worst, if he fails while daring greatly, knows his place shall never be with those timid and cold souls who know neither victory nor defeat. (*Powerlifting,* June 1999)

Roosevelt's words remind me of this business of investing, and how many critics are out there ready to pounce on your every misstep although they never step into the ring, never actually put their reputation or their money on the line. In the case of a professional, these critics never lose one minute of sleep because they are worried about other peoples' well-being.

Do you see yourself in the preceding quote? Those of you who are reading this book are the people in the ring. You are here to learn this method to better help you fight the battle. You realize that nothing is perfect and at times you will err and err again; but quit, you will never do. As time goes on, you will begin to intuitively understand things in the market that used to baffle you. Eventually, you will reach craftsman status. The critics will continue criticizing because that is what they do best. Just turn the television on to any financial station and you will come away with gibberish. Once you nail down these principles of analysis, you will have no need for business periodicals or financial TV.

I remember vividly my broker years. My face was marred and bloodied many times but I was in the ring trying, striving for excellence. I just didn't have a plan back then. What a difference this information and way of thinking would have made if they had been available to me when I was a broker. Mix this with my enthusiasm and dedication to excellence and the combination is unbeatable. Many of you have already done this, and it makes me feel so good to see so many of you actually making a major difference out there in your own and others financial well-being.

Theodore Roosevelt was right, the credit goes to you the investor or broker who is actually in the arena, who at times comes up short again and again but in the end experiences triumph. This is why I wholeheartedly recommend you learn these methods and manage your money yourself. Win or lose, be the one in the ring where the action is. Make the decisions, take the calculated risk, live. Don't find yourself at the mercy of others or at the end of your career having ridden the bus and looked out the window, watching others reach greatness. It's all here for the taking. You just have to want it. Sports are full of great physical specimens, but there is a real shortage of athletes who are willing to play their game with reckless abandon, and athletes who are willing to put themselves and their careers on the line. Those who do are usually the ones at the top.

The truth in that last line inspires me. If you're not willing to risk, you have no growth, no change, no freedom. And when that happens, you are no longer involved in living; for all practical purposes, you have no life. You're dead, but you just don't know it. So risk, for goodness sake. Be a part of life. You have the power to be or do anything you want. You can produce miracles if you have a mind to. You have the magic, you just have to tap into it. Get in touch with it, make things happen, live—journey to the stars, push on to new galaxies. If you don't, you will never know your greatness!

Chapter 2

POINT AND FIGURE
FUNDAMENTALS

Many investors are familiar with charts of some kind or other, whether from school or reading newspapers or magazines. Point and Figure charts were developed over 100 years ago and have stood the test of time. We've even added a new dimension to the history of their effectiveness in negotiating all markets. That new dimension is the Internet craze. So when I say they have withstood the test of time, I mean right up through today. And, I'm even more confident now about this method than I have ever been.

I have taught this method of technical analysis in many seminars and classes. I have even taught it to schoolchildren as young as 12 years old. One reason this methodology is so teachable is that it is based on supply and demand. The law of supply and demand governs the movement of prices in stock, or anything else for that matter. If there are more buyers than sellers willing to sell, prices rise; on the other hand, when there are more sellers than buyers willing to buy, prices decline. These imbalances in supply and demand, and nothing else, cause prices of stocks to move up and down. When you cut through all the red tape and obfuscation on Wall Street, you are left with the raw facts of supply and demand. Fundamental changes in the underlying company's outlook can cause this imbalance, but it is the imbalance nonetheless that causes the stock to move. Don't get me wrong. I am not saying fundamental analysis is not important: It is the first line of defense. I want any stock I buy to be fundamentally sound. I love to start with a list of fundamentally sound stocks before I begin to evaluate the supply-and-demand relationship of the stocks. Keep that firmly in mind as we go forward. The problem with fundamentals is they change ever so slightly early on and this change is rarely picked up on the fundamental analyst's radar screen. The investors who truly understand these nuances begin to cast their vote on the stock early on and this causes the supply-demand relationship to change. This change is then picked up on a Point and Figure chart, which in turn tips off the astute investor of an imminent change in the underlying stock's direction.

The Point and Figure method of analyzing stock movement was designed simply as a logical, organized way of recording this battle between supply and demand. The word *organized* is the key. A basic road atlas would be difficult to use if the actual lines depicting the roads and interstates were missing. It is the same in the stock market business. Looking at an endless list of High-Low-Close quotations on any particular stock can be equally confusing. When these quotations are organized in a logical fashion, however, the battle between supply and demand becomes much more evident. The Point and Figure chart simply shows whether supply or demand is winning the battle. We use various chart patterns and trend lines to guide our buy-and-sell decisions. These patterns are covered in detail in later chapters as is market and sector analysis.

A tennis match is a helpful analogy in describing this battle between supply and demand. Consider a match between tennis greats, Jimmy Connors and John McEnroe. Let's call demand Jimmy Connors and supply John McEnroe. Their tennis match consists of various sets. The sets in this tennis match are similar to the Point and Figure chart moving back and forth, changing columns of alternating X's and O's. This seemingly random movement in the Point and Figure chart is similar to the seemingly random changes in sets the players win during the tennis match. Eventually, Connors or McEnroe wins enough sets to emerge victorious in the match. Likewise, only when the match between supply and demand is completed can we get a handle on which way the stock is likely to move. The Point and Figure chart considers the sets that are played as market noise and not worthy of inclusion in the decision-making process. In the short run, stock prices move about randomly but eventually demand or supply takes control and a trend begins. In this book, I refer to tennis and football in explaining many of the market indicators and stock chart patterns you are about to learn. Let's play ball!

The Basic Tenets of a Point and Figure Chart

We will begin with the basics of maintaining your own chart. It only takes a few minutes each day to update 20 or 30 charts by hand but why bother when we have a Web site that does all the work for you on over 8,000 stocks a day? It does help in gaining a strong feeling for the process if you maintain a few by hand each day. We have a broker client who updates over 400 each day by hand and would never give up that process no matter what. At Dorsey, Wright, positions in the firm's profit-sharing account are charted by hand each day. It gives a feel that one cannot get any other way. Most investors, however, don't have that time available after market hours, and thus the Internet is a valuable time-saver. If you should choose to maintain charts by hand, all you would need is a financial page providing the high and low prices of stocks each day. If you have a computer with a phone modem, you will be in technical analysis heaven these days.

The Point and Figure chart uses only the price action of the stock—volume is not a consideration. Volume will have to show up in the chart patterns because there will be no movement of the stock unless there are more buyers than sellers willing to sell or more sellers than buyers willing to buy. Much of the volume in stocks today is related to option strategies that have nothing to do with a bet on the direction of the stock. You would be amazed at how much is option related. Remember, we are only interested in the battle between supply and demand. Two letters of the alphabet are used in this method of charting, "X" and "O." The X represents demand. The O represents supply. The key to this method is how the chart moves from one column to the next. For the purposes of this book, we will use the 3-point reversal method. As you become more adept, you may want to choose other reversal points. At my company, however, we never deviate from the three-box method described in this section: We keep it simple.

Figure 2.1 shows a basic chart that gives you an idea of what the Point and Figure chart looks like. Talking about the X and O reminds me of a seminar I held in Minneapolis one day. A beautiful woman in her 70s came up to me after the seminar and told me how her husband had gained new vigor and enthusiasm for life now that he charted all their stocks every day. (They had attended two other seminars I had held in Minnesota and had read my book.) She went on to tell me how she also helped him manage their considerable portfolio. She said with a smile, "He handles the hugs and I handle the kisses." What a wonderful story! I could, in fact, write a book devoted to stories of people who became successful investors when they embraced this operating system.

The chart pattern is formed by alternating columns of X's and O's. The only way a column of X's can change to a column of O's is by reversing three boxes. The same three-box reversal method applies to the column of O's. This moving back and forth from one column to the next is what causes the chart pattern to form. This is where the Point and Figure chart drastically departs from the method of the bar chart. The Point and Figure chart leaves volatility out of the equation and gives you a clear picture of the battle between supply and demand. The bar chart on the other hand includes volatility totally in the equation because the chart must be updated every day no matter how inconsequential the move might be. This is why bar charts are subjective and difficult to read, and are rarely effective.

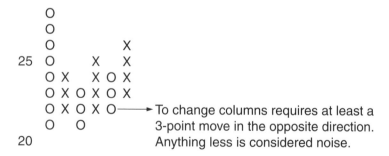

Figure 2.1   Basic Point and Figure chart.

Let's get into the mechanics of charting by looking at the values of the boxes we primarily use in constructing the chart. When I say box sizes, I mean the boxes on a simple sheet of chart paper. The box sizes change as the stock price moves through certain levels. This is why we call this method a *three-box* reversal method rather than a 3-point reversal method. It is important to think in terms of boxes rather than prices. Between 20 and 100, the box size is 1 point per box. If a stock is trading below 20 or above 100, we use other box sizes. Simply stated, when a stock is between 0 and 5, the box size on the chart is ¼ of a point. Between 5 and 20, the box size moves up to ½ point per box. Between 20 and 100, the box size is 1 point per box. Above 100, the box size rises to 2 points per box. Finally, above 200, the box size is 4 points per box. Keep the following table handy while you are learning to chart:

Price ($)	Box Size
0 to 5	¼ point per box
5 to 20	½ point per box
20 to 100	1 point per box
100 to 200	2 points per box
Above 200	4 points per box

The Internet age ushered in more higher priced stocks and, more importantly, more volatility. One of the best ways to adjust for that volatility is to increase the box size. Many stocks in the technology and Internet sectors are so volatile that we must increase the box size enough to compress the chart and obtain a normal picture of the supply-and-demand relationship of the stock. In fact, stocks like Yahoo in 1998 to 2000 often required 10 points per box to compress the chart to normal. And, these Net stocks and high-tech/high-wreck stocks have absolutely wiped out many investors in 2000. Think about this for a second. If we have to increase the box size from, let's say 1 to 5 to slow the chart down enough to get a good picture of supply and demand, this stock is too volatile for most investors. Many investors saw stocks drop 50 percent or more in a single second in 2000. Apple Computer, for example, reported less than expected earnings for the quarter. Wham! The stock was down 50 percent on the opening. This is important. As you embark on your investment endeavors, remember that stocks with 5-point box sizes are out of the realm of most investors' risk tolerance. If you find it compelling to invest in these stocks, buy 10 shares. This will help you slay that monster called volatility.

Let's go over these different box size values once again. I want this to be set firmly in your mind. If a stock were trading below 5, then each box would have a value of ¼ point. Between 5 and 20, the box size would be ½ point. If the stock were trading between 20 and 100 (where most stocks fall), the box size would be 1 point. If the stock were trading at 100 or higher, the box size would be 2 points; and above 200, the box size would be 4 points. Again, these are the standards or the "default" box sizes. On the DWA Internet site, however, we can tell the computer we want to increase that box size, such as for technology and Internet stocks, to adjust for volatility.

The key to making the chart relates to how the chart switches from one column to another. When a stock is rising and demand is in control, the chart will be in X's. Conversely, when a stock is declining and supply is in control, the chart will be in O's. It requires a three-box reversal or more to be significant enough to warrant changing columns. Therefore to change columns from X's to O's when the stock was between 20 and 100 would require 3 points. We established that between 20 and 100 the box size was 1, so three boxes equals 3. The same three-box reversal would only be 1½ points if the stock were between 5 and 20. If the stock were trading below 5, the same three-box reversal would only be ¾ of a point because the box size in a stock between 0 and 5 is ¼ of a point. Think in terms of box reversals.

Figure 2.1 illustrates how much the stock must rise or fall to create a reversal on the chart. In this chart, each column has at least three X's or three O's, maybe more, but never less. Although I am being redundant, that's okay—I intend to be redundant in this chapter to help you catch on to the basics of maintaining your own chart. The rest of the book will flow easily once you understand this concept. If you don't catch on after the first reading, go back and reread this chapter again and again until you are comfortable with the concepts. Believe me, it will be worth your time. When you become a craftsman at this easy method, you will join an elite group of investors and professionals who consistently make money and manage risk with this method.

Updating a Point and Figure Chart

When I lecture on this subject, I use the flowchart shown in Figure 2.2 to demonstrate how to update a chart. The basic concept is as follows. Whichever column the chart is in, you will remain in that column as long as the stock continues in that direction by one box or more. Let's stop and think about that statement for a second: "... as long as the stock continues in that direction by one box or more." So, if the chart was in a column of O's and declining, your first question of the flowchart at the close of the business day would be, "Did the stock decline one full box or more on the chart?" If the stock did decline one more box, let's say from 45 to 44, then record that move by making an O in the 44 box and stop—go no further that day. Keep in mind, all you are

IF THE CHART IS FALLING IN A COLUMN OF O'S

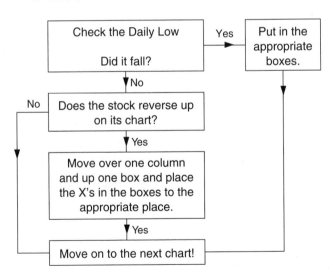

Figure 2.2   The flowchart for charting. When charting a stock, the updating process is essentially like one of the old flowcharts you have seen.

doing is recording what the stock does on each trading day, nothing more, nothing less. Don't think about the chart again until the close of business the following day. At the close of business the following day, you simply look at the high and low for the day (in the case we are now discussing, the low would be the most important) and ask the same question again. Since the stock is still in a column of O's, did it decline another box or more? Answer the question by looking at the low price for the day. If the stock in this case hit 43 or lower (declined one more box or lower), record the move by making an O in the box and stop. I don't care if the stock reversed later in the day and went to 100. You'll deal with that move tomorrow. You are only concerned with one direction per day. At this point, the stock is at 43 in a column of O's. Since the stock is still in a column of O's, the next day at the close of trading you ask the same question again. Did the stock decline one more box or lower? Today, the answer is no to flowchart question 1. The stock did not move lower by one more box or more today.

Because the stock did not decline enough to close one more box today, you go to the second and last flowchart question. Since the stock did not decline any further, or at least enough to close another box, the second and final question of the flowchart is, did the stock reverse up three boxes? Let's think about this for a second. Did the stock reverse up three boxes? In this example, we are discussing a stock that is trading between 20 and 100 so the box size is 1 point per box. So, a three-box reversal up would be 3 points higher than the last "O." Count up three boxes from 43, that would be 44, 45, 46. Okay, did the stock hit 46? Let's say it hit 45⅞. That's not good enough. That was only a 2⅞ reversal, not 3. What do you do? Nothing.

The next day, you go through the same process again. Since the stock is still in a column of O's, the first flowchart question that must be answered is, "Did the stock go down one box or more?" Get the picture? You go back to the first flowchart question and start again. At this point, there can only be two action points on the chart. The stock either does move one more box lower or it reverses up three boxes. The two action points that will cause me to make a mark on the chart are 42 or 46. Nothing else will cause a change on the chart. It either continues in its current column of "O's" or it reverses up into a column of "X's." That is about as difficult as it gets in maintaining a Point and Figure chart. Okay, back to the example, if over time, the stock does reverse up three boxes to 46 by following these two flowchart questions, you will find the chart now one column over to the right and that movement represented by three X's. The chart is now rising. The same process starts over again, only this time the first flowchart question is, "Did the stock move up one box or more?" That is really the whole ball of wax.

Once again, it takes three boxes to reverse from one direction to the other. For example, if a stock were trading in a column of X's with a top of 45, it would take a move to 42 to reverse this chart to a column of O's: 45 − 3 = 42. Anything less than three boxes would be considered market noise, not worthy of recording. Conversely, if the stock in question was trading in a column of O's with a current low at 45, it would need a rise to 48 before a reversal into a column of X's could be recorded; as before, anything less than three boxes would be considered market noise. Figure 2.3 shows some examples of reversals.

There is one exception to the preceding pattern. If a stock reversed from 21, for example, the required number of points would only be 2. This is because the stock will be moving through a *level*, where the box size changes. If a stock is moving up (in a column of X's) through the upper teens and has a high of 21, a reversal would take place at 19, a move of only 2 points. The three boxes in this case are at 20; then as the stock goes below 20, the box size changes to ½ point per box or 19½, 19, and so on. Once again, the box size between 20 and 5 is ½ point per box rather than the 1 point per box above 20. Keep break points in mind when you are charting at levels where the box size changes. If you

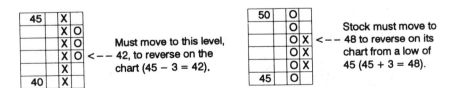

Figure 2.3 Examples of reversals.

just price the vertical axes properly, you need deal only with the boxes. Prices will take care of themselves. Keep it simple. Just assign the proper point value to the box, ½, 1, and so on and then count three boxes.

This brings you to the actual charting. The daily high and low quotations for a stock are all that you will need. In today's Internet world all you need do is go to our Web site and we do all the work for you. If you choose to do it by hand, most newspapers have a financial section. The only prices you are concerned with are those that cause changes in the chart. For example, a stock is in a column of X's and has a high of 28⅞. For charting purposes, we would read this as 28 because between 20 and 100 there are no fractions in the boxes. Each box is 1 point. In this case, ⅞ is not enough to close the box of 29. It's ⅛ point too low. To the Point and Figure chartist, ⅞ is simply market noise when the box size is 1 point. If a stock is in a column of O's, you are primarily interested in whether the stock declined on that day of trading and you would look at a stock's low first. Using the same example, a stock has a low of 28⅞. You read this as a low of 29. The stock must move to 28 to add another O to the chart. When you get a reversal of three or more boxes on a chart, you plot the reversal one column over and three boxes up or down depending on the direction of the reversal. The first change in direction would always be a three-box move because that is the minimum move required to shift columns. After the shift in columns, the moves could be as low as one box. If the stock reverses down, you will plot an O one column over and three boxes down. If the stock reverses to the upside, you will plot an X one column over and three boxes higher. When reversing up or down, your count does not begin at the last number. Up means begin counting up one box. For example, to begin counting a reversal up where the last box closed at say, 28 with an O, start counting up at 29, 30, 31. The first X of the three-box reversal up would begin at 29. A reversal down suggests you begin counting down one box below the highest X.

The only record of time in the Point and Figure chart is the replacing of the X or O with the number of the month when the chartist makes the first entry of that month. Placing the month in the chart has no significance except as a reference point. As the stock moves about, it alternates back and forth from one column to the next, X to O, O to X, and so on. At no time will you have an O in a column of X's nor an X in a column of O's. As previously mentioned, the first action point on the chart in any given month is represented by the number of the month. For example, if a stock rises one box, you would add another X to its chart, but if that X, or plot, is the first one for July, you would use a 7 instead of an X in that box. Seven signifies the seventh month of the year, or July. This also holds true on down moves. For example, if a stock declined one box, and that is the first action point in August, you would put an 8 in the box instead of an O.

Let's cover it again. If the chart is rising, first check the daily high, and add an X if the stock has risen enough to close the next open box or boxes. You would add as many X's as needed to represent the stock's move. If the stock rose 4 points during the trading session, and each box equaled 1, you would put four X's in the chart. If the same stock moved up 5 points, you would add five X's. Flowchart question 1 would have been satisfied and at that point you stop charting for that day. If, on the other hand, the stock did not move high enough to add another X, you go to flowchart question 2 and check the daily low to see if it has declined enough (3 boxes) to reverse on the chart. The reversal is the key feature of the Point and Figure chart. If it did reverse, move one column over and one box down, then add the three O's representing the reversal. If the stock did not decline enough to warrant a reversal, then there is no action on the chart for the day. Remember, the three-box reversal means all three boxes must be filled before you fill any of them (2⅞ points is not 3, and 3 is the requirement for a reversal if the point value of a box is 1). You cannot begin filling one box, then the next, until you get three. The chart will remain in its current column until it closes (hits) all three boxes on the reversal. I am being purposely redundant because it is incredibly important that you understand the concept of charting before we go on to the fun parts of the book.

By using a three-box reversal method, we eliminate the minor moves that often occur in the market and look for moves that are significant enough to warrant representation. If a stock is declining, use the same process in reverse. Look first to see if the stock has moved down enough to add another O. If it has, add the O or O's. If the stock did not decline enough to close another box, then

look at the daily high to see if the stock has rallied enough to reverse the chart up. If it has, move one column over and one box
up and add the three new X's. If it has not moved up enough to reverse, there is no action on that chart for the day. Some stocks
can sit for months without any change. In volatile markets, the
chart could continue in its present direction and then reverse. In
other words, the stock rose enough to close another box with an
X, but the last 20 minutes of trading that day, the stock declined
8 points on earnings news. You would simply stick to the flowchart, close the box with an X and forget the reversal at the end of
the day. You will deal with that reversal tomorrow. It is a good
idea to be aware of the stock's reversal at the end of the trading
session, even though you don't record it on the chart that day.
This can happen when earnings reports are released. The stock
rises one box on the day, but late in the session the earnings are
released. Let's say they are much less than Wall Street expected.
This could have the effect of immediately collapsing the stock
price thus producing what might seem like a reversal back down
the chart. A chart can only move in one direction a day. In this
case, you update the chart by moving it up in the column of X's. If
the stock has moved enough late in the day to reverse, you will
more than likely chart that reversal the following day, but not in
all cases.

If you have already gotten the hang of updating your chart,
you can move along to the next section; if not, let's recap for a
moment. If a stock is rising in a column of X's, you will record
any subsequent up-moves as long as that up-move equals or exceeds the next highest box. If the stock does not move up enough
to equal the next higher box, then you look to the low to see if the
stock reversed columns. To reverse into a column of O's from X's,
the underlying stock must reverse three boxes to be significant
enough to warrant a change in columns. Thus, the action points
in a stock that is rising and has the 50 box closed with an X will
be 51 for another X, or 47 to qualify for a reversal into a column of
O's. The opposite is true for a stock declining. The easiest way to
chart is to determine your two action points before you seek the
high and low for the day. In the preceding example, your action
points were 51 or 47. That's all you look for in the high and low
for the day. Did the stock hit 51? If the answer is no, then did it

hit 47? If one of those action points was hit, record the correct price and *stop*. Once you understand the concept of the reversal, you have mastered the nuts and bolts of this method. I urge you to keep studying this method. It will truly change your investment life. Sometimes we feel as if we are falling behind or failing when we try something new. Keep at it. I like to think about Thomas Edison, who failed many times before he found the right path.

Edison's life is a prime example of the American Dream. Without question, he was a giant among men. During his lifetime, he patented a record 1,093 inventions. Some of those inventions literally revolutionized the world. However, despite having one of the greatest minds in history, Edison, like all men, knew failure. In fact, he failed quite often. But like all great men, Edison accepted failure as a learning experience that would help him grow and develop. His son Charles Edison wrote about his father: "It is sometimes asked, Didn't he ever fail? The answer is yes." Thomas Edison knew failure frequently. His first patent, when he was all but penniless, was for an electric vote-recorder, but maneuver-minded legislators refused to buy it. Once he had his entire fortune tied up in machinery for a magnetic separation device for low-grade iron ore only to have it made obsolete and uneconomic by the opening of the rich Mesabi Range. But he never hesitated out of fear of failure. "Shucks," he told a discouraged coworker during one trying series of experiments. "We haven't failed. We now know a thousand things that won't work, so we're that much closer to finding what will." If you are reading this book, you are on your way to becoming a world-class investor by learning what works.

Now it's time to take what you have learned and construct a Point and Figure chart based on a series of highs and lows. As you plot this chart, remember that you are recording the supply-and-demand relationship of the stock in a logical, organized manner (see Figure 2.4 on pages 30 to 31).

Practice Chart: Technology One

We have used the price quotations shown in Figure 2.4 to construct the chart that appears in Figure 2.5. Take a look at that chart now. Notice how the last box closed in the chart in April is

DATE	HIGH		LOW		LAST	
20-APR	16	5-8	16		16	
21-APR	16	1-4	16		16	1-8
22-APR	16	7-8	16	3-8	16	5-8
25-APR	16	3-4	16	1-2	16	5-8
26-APR	17	3-8	16	1-2	17	3-8
27-APR	17	3-8	17	3-8	17	3-8
28-APR	18	1-8	17	1-2	17	3-4
29-APR	18	1-8	17	5-8	17	5-8
2-MAY	18	3-8	17	1-2	18	
3-MAY	18	1-4	17	7-8	18	
4-MAY	18	1-4	17	7-8	18	1-8
5-MAY	18	1-4	17	1-2	17	1-2
6-MAY	17	3-4	17	1-2	17	5-8
9-MAY	17	3-4	17	1-8	17	1-8
10-MAY	17	5-8	17	1-8	17	1-8
11-MAY	17	5-8	17	1-8	17	3-8
12-MAY	17	1-2	17	1-8	17	1-4
13-MAY	17	1-2	17	1-8	17	3-8
16-MAY	17	3-8	17	1-8	17	1-4
17-MAY	17	1-2	17	1-8	17	1-4
18-MAY	17	5-8	17	1-4	17	3-8
19-MAY	17	5-8	17	3-8	17	1-2
20-MAY	17	5-8	17	1-4	17	3-8
23-MAY	18		17	1-2	17	5-8
24-MAY	18	7-8	17	5-8	18	7-8
25-MAY	19	5-8	18	5-8	18	7-8
26-MAY	19	3-4	18	3-8	18	1-2
27-MAY	19	1-8	18	1-2	18	7-8
31-MAY	19	3-8	18	7-8	19	
1-JUN	22	1-4	19	5-8	21	3-4
2-JUN	20	1-2	19	1-2	19	3-4
3-JUN	21		19	7-8	20	1-2
6-JUN	21	3-4	20	7-8	21	
7-JUN	21	1-2	20	3-4	20	3-4
8-JUN	21	1-8	20	1-2	20	5-8
9-JUN	20	3-4	20	1-2	20	1-2
10-JUN	21	5-8	20	1-2	21	1-2
13-JUN	23	1-8	21	1-4	22	7-8
14-JUN	23	1-4	22	1-4	22	5-8
15-JUN	22	7-8	22	1-2	22	3-4
16-JUN	24	1-4	22	3-4	23	7-8
17-JUN	24	5-8	23	3-4	24	
20-JUN	23	1-4	22	1-4	23	
21-JUN	23	1-8	21	7-8	21	7-8

Figure 2.4 Technology One historical data.

30

DATE	HIGH		LOW		LAST	
22-JUN	22	1-4	21	1-8	21	5-8
23-JUN	21	5-8	20	3-4	20	3-4
24-JUN	21	3-4	20	1-2	21	3-8
27-JUN	21	1-2	21		21	1-2
28-JUN	23	5-8	21	1-4	23	5-8
29-JUN	24	1-8	23	1-4	23	7-8
30-JUN	23	7-8	22	1-8	22	3-8
1-JUL	23	1-4	22	1-2	22	7-8
5-JUL	23		22	1-2	22	3-4
6-JUL	22	5-8	22		22	
7-JUL	24		22		23	5-8
8-JUL	24	1-4	22	7-8	23	1-2
11-JUL	23	3-4	23		23	1-8
12-JUL	23	3-4	23	1-4	23	3-8
13-JUL	23	5-8	23	1-4	23	1-4
14-JUL	23	5-8	23	3-8	23	1-2
15-JUL	23	3-8	22	5-8	22	3-4

Figure 2.4 (Continued)

at the price of 16. We begin updating the chart from that point. Remember the easiest way to maintain a Point and Figure chart is to determine where your action points are. If the chart is in a column of O's, the first action point would be one box lower than the last one recorded. If the stock does not decline low enough to

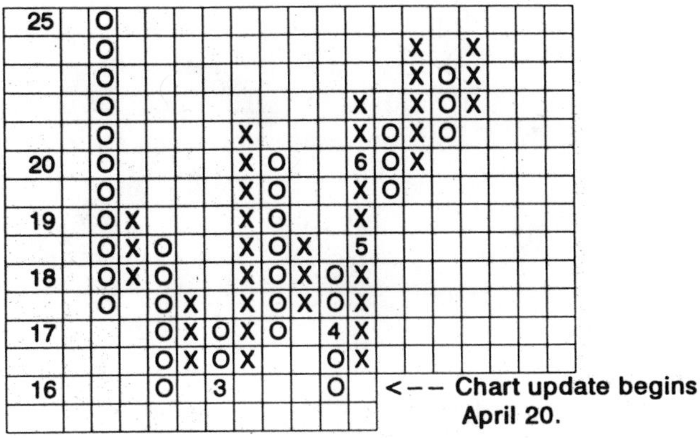

Figure 2.5 Technology One.

record the lower box, then your second and last action point would be a three-box reversal up. In the case of Technology One, the first action points from the bottom at 16 in April would be 15½ (one box lower) or 17½ (a three-box reversal up). From the 16 level, there are no other action points. Whichever action point is hit first, record it, then determine your next action point. That basically is all there is to updating a chart. Always think of your two action points.

Using Figures 2.4 and 2.5, let's update Technology One stock beginning at the 16 in April. As discussed earlier, there are numbers on the chart that correspond to the months of the year and provide a convenient reference point for the following steps:

1. On April 20, determine action points with the stock currently in a column of O's at 16. They are 15½ and 17½. Let's explain how we get these numbers one more time. Since we begin with the stock in a column of O's, the 15½ action point is simply one box lower than the last one recorded at 16. The 17½ action point corresponds to a three-box reversal up. Remember that each box below 20 and above 5 equals ½ point. Three boxes represents 1½ points, thus 16 + 1½ = 17½. In this case, 17½ is hit before 15½. Notice how, on April 28, 17½ is hit as well as 18. This action causes the reversal plus one box. Now go up to 18 in a column of X's.

2. On April 28, determine your action points. They will be 18½ for a one-box rise or 16½ for a three-box reversal. Record whichever comes first. It takes until May 24 for the stock to move enough to be considered significant enough to record. The stock rose to 18⅞ closing the 18½ box. This is a good example of why the Point and Figure chart is so important. The bar chartist would have been recording moves in the chart every day. The Point and Figure chartist would have done nothing from April 28 until May 24 because nothing significant happened between those dates. The Point and Figure chartist is not interested in noise.

3. On May 24, determine your action points. They are 19 on the upside and 17 for a three-box reversal. Now you wait to see which one is hit first, then establish your next action points. Easy huh? On May 25, the next day, Technology One hit a

high of 19⅝. This closed the action point box of 19 as well as the next box above it at 19½.

4. On May 26, determine your action points. They are 20 and 18. If the stock rises one more box and hits 20 make an X. If—instead of rising—it falls three boxes to 18 or lower, reverse into a column of O's and represent the move. On June 1, the stock hit 22¼. You can now move up in X's to the 22 box. Notice how the box size has changed. It was ½ dollar (point) per box below 20, now it is 1 dollar (point) per box above 20 up to 100.

5. On June 2, establish your action points. They are 23 and 19½. The 23 one is easy, the 19½ action point might confuse you a little. Remember the breakpoints in box size. Three boxes down from 22 would be 21, 20, 19½. Below 20 is ½ point per box. The very next day the stock declines to 19½, so you will reverse into a column of O's. Supply had taken control for the time being. Your action points will now begin with one box lower to continue in the same direction, or a three-box or more reversal into a column of X's.

6. On June 3, establish your action points. The chart is now in a column of O's at the 19½ level. Your action points are 19 and 22 for a three-box reversal. Once again, we cross the equator, the point where the box size changes from ½ to 1, so a three-box reversal up from 19½ is ½ point to 20 then 1 point to 21 and 1 point to 22. Note how the box size changes when you cross the 20 mark. Let's see which one is hit first. On June 13, the stock rises to 23, so the stock reverses up into a column of X's and the 23 box is closed.

7. On June 14, establish your action points. Since you are in a column of X's, your first action point is one box higher than the last one closed. That number is 24. A three-box reversal would be 20. So we are looking for 24 and 20. On June 16, 24¼ is hit closing the 24 box.

8. On June 17, establish your action points. We are looking for 25 or 21. A one-box rise is represented by 25 and 21 the three-box reversal. On June 23, the stock declines to 20¾. This reverses it back down the chart and into a column of O's. The 21 box is now closed with an O.

9. On June 24, establish your action points. We are looking for 20 and 24. On June 29, the stock hits a high of 24⅛. The stock

now reverses back up into a column of X's. The reversal forms a double top (we cover these patterns in Chapter 3).

10. On June 30, establish your action points. They are 25 and 21 for a three-box reversal.

This has been an interesting exercise because the stock crossed the equator a couple of times demonstrating three-box reversals using ½-point and 1-point box sizes.

One of the reasons Point and Figure charts are so practical is that the chart formations stand out because we move over and down a box when making a reversal. This is easily seen by looking at a chart that has just broken out. By moving down a box when the stock reverses down, the tops, or resistance areas, stand out. By moving up a box when the stock reverses up, the lows or support areas stand out. Figure 2.6 provides examples of such movements.

Trend Lines

Trend lines are one of the most important guides you have in Point and Figure charting. In fact, we have created a new trend line indicator "The Percent of Stocks Trading above Their Trend Lines," which is discussed in Chapter 6. I am always amazed how a stock will hold a trend line on the way up or down. Trend lines are very easily drawn using the Point and Figure method, whereas bar chart methods involve a lot of subjectivity. Two basic trend lines are used in Point and Figure charting: the Bullish Support Line and the Bearish Resistance line. We will discuss each of these separately as well as two other trend lines, the Bullish Resistance Line and the Bearish Support line. For long-term investors, a stock's main trend

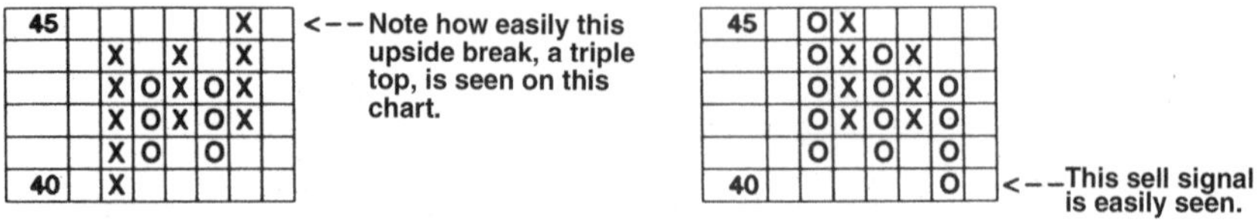

Figure 2.6   Buy and sell signals.

is always bullish if it is trading above the Bullish Support Line. I call this line Interstate 95 North. On the East Coast, I-95 is the main artery moving north and south. Conversely, a stock's main trend is said to be bearish if it trades below the Bearish Resistance line. I call this line Interstate 95 South. These trend lines are typically used for long-term investors. Traders are much more flexible and find the truth lies somewhere in between most of the time.

The Bullish Support Line

The Bullish Support Line is a major component of a stock's chart pattern. It serves as a guide to the underlying securities trend. Typically, these lines are like brick walls. It is uncanny how so many stocks will hold the trend line as they rise in price. In general, investors should not buy stocks that are not trading above their Bullish Support Lines. Drawing the line is very simple and has not changed since the inception of the Point and Figure method. Once a stock has formed a base of accumulation below the Bearish Resistance Line and gives the first buy signal off the bottom, we go to the lowest column of O's in the chart pattern and begin drawing a trend line starting with the box directly under that column of O's. You then connect each box diagonally upward in a 45-degree angle. Unlike bar charts, which connect prices, the Point and Figure chart never connects prices. The angle for a Bullish Support Line will always be a 45-degree angle. The Bearish Resistance Line will always be the reciprocal of the 45-degree angle or a 135-degree angle.

We typically give a stock the benefit of the doubt if it gives a sell signal while it is trading close to the Bullish Support Line. Once a stock rises significantly above this trend line and gives a sell signal, followed by another buy signal, a shorter term trend line can be drawn. Simply go to a level that is one box below the bottom O in the column that gave the sell signal and connect the boxes up diagonally. This will serve to be your new trend line, although I would still leave the first trend line intact because it will give you some longer term perspective. The first Bullish Support Line will always serve to be the long-term trend line and may very well come into play years later. These shorter term trend lines serve as visual guides. The short-term trend lines can also be valuable in identifying the short-term direction of stocks. Traders often initiate a long trade when the stock has declined near the Bullish Support Line because the stock is then close to the stop-loss point. The most important characteristic of the Point and Figure method is its clear guidelines for whether a stock is on a buy signal or a sell signal and whether it is in an uptrend. But above all, remember this is an art not a science. H_2O does not necessarily equal water in the investment world. You are an integral part of the equation; never forget that. Many investors are looking for the black box that can make them instantly wealthy without becoming personally involved. It ain't happening. You will find that this method is equally effective in helping you avoid the big hit as it is in helping you to buy the right stock at the right time. Often in investing, it's what you did not buy that is responsible for your success.

When the stock violates the Bullish Support Line and simultaneously gives a sell signal, it is a critical event and a strong sign to sell the stock, or at a minimum, recheck the fundamentals. Something is generally wrong when this happens. Not until some days down the road will light be shed on the reason for the trend line break. When a stock gives a strong sell signal such as previously mentioned, I will begin to scale out of the position instead of selling all the stock. A stock frequently will give such a signal, then regroup, and begin moving up again giving you a better out with respect to the rest of your position but that bounce only results in a lower top. Things take time in the market. It often is not an overnight thing. I like to take my time in investing. Often the truth is not black or white, it's gray. To qualify as a violation of the trend line, the stock must move through it by one box or more, not just touch it. There is no such thing as the line being a little violated. It is or it isn't. In Figure 2.7, the stock maintained the trend line all the way up from 15 to 25. Soon after, supply took control of the stock. When the stock hit 21, it not only gave a double bottom sell signal but also violated the Bullish Support Line. The violated support line was the key sign there was a high probability that the trend had changed. This is what I would take to be a wake-up call. You can hit the snooze button if you wish but situations like this generally require that you take some action.

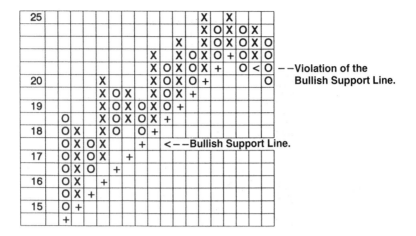

Figure 2.7 The Bullish Support Line.

The Bullish Resistance Line

I must preface my comments with the fact that we rarely use the Bullish Resistance or Bearish Support lines. The more lines you begin drawing, the more complicated it becomes. The next thing you see is a screen that looks like the old game of pick-up sticks. Keep it simple. That being said, the Bullish Resistance Line is drawn by moving to the left of the last buy signal (at the point the signal was given, where the X exceeds the previous column of X's) and going to the first wall of O's to the left. Remember, it is not the first column of O's but the first wall of O's. A wall of O's is usually that last down-move in the stock from which it begins to bottom out. This is the point where demand begins to take the upper hand. Figure 2.8 on page 38 best demonstrates this. Then go to the column of X's right next to the wall of O's and begin drawing your trend line, beginning with the empty box above that top X. This line will be a 45-degree angle, as is the Bullish Support Line. Typically, a stock will encounter resistance as it moves to the Bullish Resistance Line though this line may have to be drawn a number of times. The boundaries of the Bullish Support Line and the Bullish Resistance Line form a trading

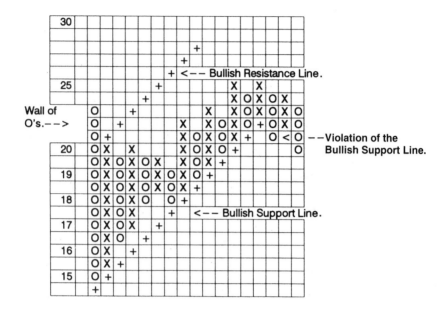

Figure 2.8   The Bullish Resistance Line.

channel. In Figure 2.8, the Bullish Resistance Line is drawn from the wall of O's beginning at the 21 level. In reality, we do not use these lines much at Dorsey, Wright. We tend to be much more concerned with the Bullish Support Line when a stock is rising.

The Bearish Resistance Line

The Bearish Resistance Line, which is the exact opposite of the Bullish Support Line previously discussed, is shown in Figure 2.9. When a stock forms an area of distribution above the Bullish Support Line and gives the first sell signal, you can go to the top X and begin drawing the trend line in the box directly above that last column of X's. Next connect the boxes diagonally down in a 135-degree angle, the reciprocal of the 45-degree angle of the Bullish Support Line. Actually, all you need to do is connect the boxes and the angle will be 135 degrees. The same principles and trading tactics apply in reverse to the Bearish Resistance Line. We typically prefer not to go long when below the Bearish Resistance

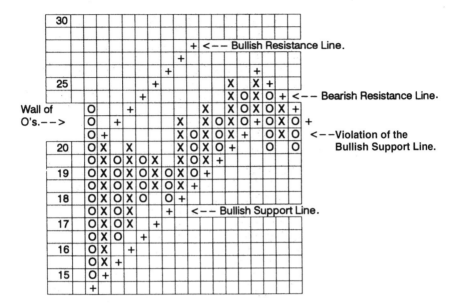

Figure 2.9 The Bearish Resistance Line.

Line. This line, like the Bullish Support Line, can be as strong as a brick wall. We say a stock is bearish when it is on a sell signal and below the Bearish Resistance Line. Or, as I often say on CNBC, the stock is on I-95 South. Be wary of buy signals that come from just below this resistance line as they tend to be false or best suited to traders. Stocks that are moving up to this line typically find formidable resistance there. Also, a stock must be on a buy signal to penetrate the Bearish Resistance Line. Short sales can be initiated in weak stocks when the underlying stock rallies up to the resistance line but is still below it. This is the optimum point to sell short on any of the bearish chart patterns.

The Bearish Support Line

As shown in Figure 2.10, the Bearish Support Line is the reciprocal of the Bullish Resistance Line and is drawn by moving to the left of the Bearish Resistance Line to the first *wall* of X's. Again, not to the next column of X's but to the first wall of X's. Then

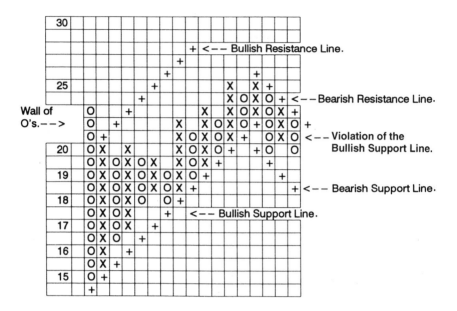

Figure 2.10   The Bearish Support Line.

move to the first column of O's next to it and begin drawing your support line down from the empty box below the last O. The line, which will automatically be a 135-degree angle by connecting the diagonal boxes, can be used as a guide to identify where any decline might be contained. The Bearish Resistance Line and the Bearish Support Line in combination form a channel that the stock can be expected to trade in. Movement down to the Bearish Support Line is likely to cause bottom fishing as investors create demand supporting the stock at that level. As the stock rises to the resistance level, investors who have been stuck holding the declining stock will elect to sell on rallies.

Price Objectives

Price objectives in Point and Figure technical analysis are derived through two methods called the horizontal count and the vertical count. Our charts on our Web site automatically calculate the vertical price objective for you. But again, while the computer saves us a lot of time in doing some of these calculations, you need to understand where they come from. The methods of determining price objectives come from the science of ballistics and have been used in Point and Figure analysis for many decades. The distance a bullet will travel can be calculated if the following factors are known—the size of the powder keg that will propel the projectile, the length of the barrel, the resistance the projectile will experience traveling through the barrel, the air temperature, and the attitude of the rifle. The best definition describing this science was written in an *Encyclopaedia Britannica* article in the 1920s. The following passage is from the book *The Point and Figure method— Advanced Theory and Practice* (distributed by Morgan, Rogers, & Robertson, Inc., New York, copyright 1934):

> Exterior ballistics is that part of the science of ballistics in which the motion of the projectile is considered after it has received its initial impulse. The factors involved are the pressure of the powder or gas in the chamber of the gun from which the projectile secures its initial velocity, resistance of the bore before the projectile leaves the barrel, the resistance of the air, and the influence of gravity, all must be calculated in order to determine the probable objective of the projectile.

These same principles have been applied to stock and commodity trading to arrive at a rough estimate of the price objective following a breakout of a consolidation area. The vertical count is the most reliable and should be used whenever possible. At Dorsey, Wright, we use the price objective as an ingredient for helping us determine our risk-reward ratio. Whenever we initiate a position, as an investor or trader, we want to have 2 points on the upside for every point on the downside, and the price objective is one of the tools we use in determining the risk-reward ratio. Other factors that we look at include trading bands and other resistance on the chart. We cover both of these concepts later on. But there is one statement I must make about price objectives here. Just because a stock hits its bullish price objective does not mean we will automatically sell that position. If relative strength and trend are still strong, we very well may elect to sell a partial position and hold on to the core position.

The Vertical Count

When a stock finally bottoms out and begins to move up, it will give a simple buy signal at some point. A buy signal comes when a column of X's exceeds a previous column of X's. Once a buy signal is given, the stock will rise to a certain level where supply again takes over. When the stock reverses into a column of O's, the first column of X's off the bottom is finished. No more X's can be placed in that column. At this point, count the number of boxes in the column of X's, and multiply times 3 (if you are using the three-box reversal method). Then multiply that figure by the value per box. Add the result to the bottom of the line of X's (where that column began). This will give you a rough estimate of the stock's price objective on that move. Remember, the price objective is a guide, not a guarantee. It is not set in concrete, because many stocks meet their first price objective and continue on up, so keep the chart formation, trend line, and relative strength in mind when deciding whether to sell the stock. Just because a stock has met its expected price move, it does not mean you must sell. It does, however, suggest you reevaluate its potential from that level.

Notice that in the example of the vertical count shown in Figure 2.11, box sizes change. You must first count the boxes below 5 as each box represents $\frac{1}{4}$ point. Then count the boxes above 5 as they represent $\frac{1}{2}$ point per box. There are four boxes representing $\frac{1}{4}$ point. Multiply them times 3 and then multiply that number by $\frac{1}{4}$ ($4 \times 3 = 12 \times \frac{1}{4} = 3$). Now count the boxes above 5 and ending at

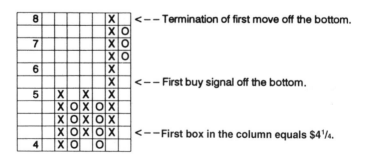

Figure 2.11   The vertical count.

8. There are six boxes at ½ point per box (6 × 3 = 18 × ½ = 9). Now add the two counts together, and you get (3 + 9) = 12. Okay, here's the last step. Add the 12 to the dollar value at the first box in that column. The potential move is 4¼ + 12 = 16¼. This example helps you understand how to use the count at breakpoints.

Vertical Count for Short Sale

Calculating the vertical count for a short sale is similar to that of a long position with one exception. Instead of multiplying the move by 3, you multiply by 2. In Figure 2.12, we count the number of boxes in the first down move off the top, which creates the first sell signal. There are seven boxes in that column. Multiply 7 times 2 and that comes to 14. Now multiply 14 times the box size, which is 1. That comes to 14. The last step is to subtract 14 from the level of the first O in the column, which is 30. The price objective is 30 − 14 = 16.

The Horizontal Count

A horizontal count is taken by counting across the base a stock has built, multiplying by 3 and then multiplying again by the value per box. This is similar to the vertical count except you count horizontally across the formation as opposed to the vertical move off the bottom. I look at the horizontal count as an exercise in counting the size of the powder keg that will propel the projectile. In ballistics, the powder keg is the amount of gunpowder in

			X		X		X			
30		O	X	O	X	O	X	O		
		O	X	O	X	O	X	O		
		O	X	O	X	O		O		
		O		O				O		
								O		
25								O		
								O		

Figure 2.12   The vertical count for a short sale.

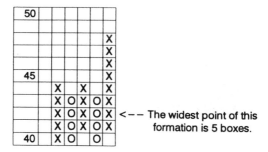

Figure 2.13   The horizontal count.

the shell casing, and the projectile is the bullet that will fly when the charge is detonated. I associate the vertical count with the distance the projectile travels before gravity takes control and pulls the bullet back to earth. This analogy always helped me understand the concept of the count when I was learning this method many years ago. Try to keep this as simple as possible because the count is only a guide. It is far more important to consider the market, sector, relative strength, and chart pattern when initiating a long or short position. This book places more emphasis on these variables than on the count.

In Figure 2.13, you would simply count the number of boxes horizontally at the widest point of the formation. That number is multiplied by 3 and the product of that multiplication is again multiplied by the box size. Looking at Figure 2.13 and counting across the widest part of the formation, both X's and O's, you get 5 columns. We then multiply this by 3. Finally, in this example, the box size is 1 ($5 \times 3 = 15 \times 1 = 15$). Then add the product of this multiplication to the lowest point of the formation, which is 40. The expected move is thus $15 + 40 = 55$. Again, where the count really comes into play is in determining your risk-reward relationship. You should have at least two points of potential profit for each point potential loss before initiating a trade. Keep in mind that there are thousands and thousands of stocks to trade. Don't get hung up on one stock for any reason. There is always another train coming down the track. All you have to do is watch for it.

Chapter 3

CHART PATTERNS

Recording the Battle Between Supply and Demand

ECON 101

The backbone of the Point and Figure analysis is the chart pattern. The beauty of this method is its ability to form simple chart patterns that record the battle between supply and demand. The reason this method is so credible is that it is founded on the irrefutable law of supply and demand, which affects our life on a daily basis. Although just about everything we come in contact with has some association with supply and demand, it wasn't until my first course in college-level economics that I really thought about and came to understand this basic law. Heck, for the previous 22 years, I had simply taken price change at face value—prices changed and that was it. It was that ECON 101 class in college that taught me to appreciate the laws of supply and demand. You know what? Most people never gain a full understanding of it. This is why I strongly feel that as a requirement for high school graduation every student should take an economics course using the textbook *Economics in One Lesson* by Hazlett (Random House, 1981). Since it seems unlikely I'll be elected to any office where I will be able to institute this course of instruction, it will have to remain in the pages of this book.

Take it to heart and have your kids learn these basic concepts. They will be well rewarded later in life with a clarity of vision others will never have. While many of the concepts I learned in ECON 101 are outmoded now, one remains unchanged—supply and demand. It is the driving force behind all price changes. If there are more buyers than sellers willing to sell, then the price will rise. If there are more sellers than buyers willing to buy, then the price will decline. This is as true for the price of tomatoes as it is for the price of stocks. It is as simple as knowing why we have lemonade stands in the summer and hot chocolate stands in the winter. Although these price changes affect our lives on a daily basis, we rarely think much about the law that governs these changes.

In the stock markets, prices change daily. Buyer and seller battle it out for control of the stock. Eventually one side wins the battle, and the stock begins to take on a trend. I have taught this method of stock analysis to children in grade schools by using the analogy of a tennis match described in Chapter 1. Virtually the same pattern occurs with stocks. Over the near term, stocks seem to move back and forth randomly the same way players may win alternate sets of a tennis match. Eventually, however, either demand or supply will win out and establish a trend. In the Point and Figure method, a particular pattern will form signaling that either demand or supply has taken control of the stock. We are not interested in making commitments in the stock market on the evidence of the sets. We are only interested in making commitments on the evidence of a completed match.

History Repeats Itself

The usefulness of the Point and Figure chart patterns lie in their repetition. The patterns of a Point and Figure chart tend to repeat themselves and thus provide a high degree of predictability about the future move of the underlying stock. When teaching the importance of chart patterns in the Point and Figure Institutes held in Richmond, Virginia, I use this example. To begin the session, I will throw a ball to someone in the audience without the participants knowing I am going to do it. The person's reflex is to reach up and catch the ball. Then I throw another ball into the audience, and then another. Even though the participants know what is coming, the natural reflex is the same—they hold up their hands to catch the ball. This is just like a Point and Figure chart, the pattern is repeated. Every time the market throws a triple top, or a bearish signal reversed pattern, or a bearish triangle pattern at me, I know the action that I must take. More often than not, the action taken was the right one. All too often, investors buy stocks that are clearly being controlled by supply simply because they never venture past the fundamentals of the company. What we try to accomplish is to stack as many odds as possible in our favor before we make a stock commitment. That includes fundamentals and technicals.

While the chart pattern is very important in the decision-making process, other factors should go into any decision. This method is an art not a science. So many investors think they can simply look at a particular chart pattern with no additional evaluation and experience instant success. It just doesn't work like that. You are an integral part of this process. Other things we evaluate along with the chart pattern are overall market, sector, trend, and Relative Strength. Before we get to those concepts, however, it is essential that you understand the chart patterns of individual stocks. This is of utmost importance because the markets are made up of individual stocks. The market is like the aggregate of all the fish in the sea. These fish can be broken down into schools of fish, and then to individual fish. It is imperative to understand the basics of looking at a stock's Point and Figure chart before graduating to market indicators, sector indicators, and Relative Strength.

Increasing Your Odds of Success

A good friend of mine, the late Jim Yates, used the following analogy when explaining profits and probabilities. Consider a basketball game in which one player is dribbling the basketball down the court. Along the way, he receives a personal foul from an opposing team player. A personal foul simply means the player can go to the foul line and take two shots (free throws) at the basket, unencumbered by the opposing team. Each shot he attempts is independent of the other. Prior to his shooting, the television commentator says that this player is a 70 percent free-throw shooter. This means that he will make 7 out of 10 baskets when he attempts a free throw. Keep in mind that he has two opportunities to make a basket, each one independent of the other. What is the probability that he makes both shots? When I present this problem at seminars, most people will answer 70 percent, whereas the actual probability of making both shots is 49 percent (0.70 × 0.70 = 0.49%). What this suggests is this basketball player, over time, will be successful less than half the time at completing two free-throw shots.

You, as an investor, have the same problem. You must perform two tasks correctly, each one independent of the other. You must buy the stock right and you must sell the stock right. Have you ever bought a stock, had it go up, and—before you sold it—watched it go right back down again? If you haven't, I have. I have also had the distinct displeasure of buying a stock and having it go right down without the benefit of a rise first. In the latter case, I never even made the first basket. This whole book is designed to help you increase your odds of success and have the greatest probability of making both shots. We outline the whole game plan as we go along.

Right now, let's deal with chart patterns. Chart patterns are like road maps. They are really not any different from a map you might study to find the best interstate for a vacation trip to New York from Richmond, Virginia. If you were to choose I-95 South instead of I-95 North, it would take you to Key West, Florida, first. Selecting the wrong route is a common mistake most investors make. They set out on a trip to New York from Virginia and choose I-95 South to get them there. They select a fundamentally sound stock that is clearly controlled by supply and likely to go down, not up. As a broker, I did this many times simply because I didn't know any better. My approach was like starting out on a road trip and taking the first road I hit as the direction to my destination. What we did back then was simply buy the stocks that research recommended we buy without any other input. We tended to emphasize the "What" question and never considered "When."

Many stockbrokers and investors buy a stock on the fundamentals because it is usually the only form of analysis they understand, and there is plenty of this type of research around. It's the story that catches the investors' interest, and it is pleasant to talk about at cocktail parties and the like. I'm in no way suggesting fundamental analysis isn't important. It is essential in answering the question *what* stock to buy; it is the first line of defense. It is our preferred method of analysis to create our inventories. Fundamentals, however, provide only half the equation. Once the stock has been selected and is determined to be fundamentally sound, the next task is to determine whether it has a high probability of going up or down. This is the point where technical analysis comes into play. When I was a stockbroker, technical analysis was never used. It was considered black magic even though it had been around in the United States for over 100 years. We sold the sizzle on the steak. That's what customers wanted to hear, and that is what we sold. Had my firm included technical analysis along with fundamental analysis and trained us to understand and use it, what a difference that would have made. It would have been like the Fourth of July for both brokers and customers. Even to this day, most broker dealers operate the same way they did in 1970. I must also add there are many who now make technical analysis part of their research. Over the past 14 years, we have had a major impact in the way technical analysis is used on Wall Street.

The best results in investing are achieved by using fundamental and technical analysis together. At Dorsey, Wright & Associates, we look at several sources of fundamental recommendations to answer the *what* question. There are many excellent sources of fundamental information. Value Line and Standard & Poor's both produce fantastic rating systems that are easy to use. And for 50 cents a day you can get some great earnings numbers right out of *Investors Business Daily* newspaper. These numbers coupled with Point and Figure analysis are very powerful. Most of the traditional brokerage houses also publish reports now available to all investors with their fundamental stock picks. The Internet has fundamental information everywhere you turn. It's virtually everywhere and free on the Net. In fact, on our Web site I keep several portfolios of fundamentally sound stocks that I work from. What I then do with those fundamentally sound portfolios is bring the technical side into the equation. Technical analysis is more difficult to find than fundamental but most of the time this step in the investment process truly determines whether an investment is successful. You are reading this book so that you can take control of the technical research yourself. There is no one who will watch over your own investments more diligently than you.

The reason technical research is so important is that it answers the question *when* to buy. All too often, investors and stockbrokers buy a stock because it is a great company, but great companies don't always make great stocks. In fact, I just got a call from a broker client of ours asking what my opinion was on a stock named Integrated Devices. He related to me how the company just had an extended news release talking about how their earnings were going up 50 percent and how things were just wonderful. His question to me concerned how the stock could move down on that news by $5. I looked at the chart and 30 points higher the stock was screaming at anyone who would listen, to "get out." The supply-and-demand relationship was already suggesting supply was in control. This broker never went past the fundamental roses and was totally perplexed that he had lost his clients $5 in one day (and I surmise he would lose more in the days and weeks to come). If I created a balance sheet of technical indicators for that stock, it would be extremely heavy on the debit side. You need to know when a great company is also a great stock. That is where this broker went wrong. He should have listened to the fundamentals and then put the stock name in a drawer of "things to do later." Once the technicals came around to positive and the fundamentals were still positive, it would be a "go."

The power of the computer has made this process much easier than it was even six years ago. In those days, we would literally page through chart books looking up the symbols of fundamentally sound companies that had strong chart patterns. Today, we enter those fundamentally sound portfolios into our Web site (www.dorseywright.com) and then use the Search/Sort function to filter out those stocks that meet our technical requirements for a stock we expect to rise in price. It is this combination of fundamental and technical analysis that is so powerful. The computer reduces to a matter of seconds the time-consuming task of looking at hundreds of stocks to come up with a small basket of actionable stocks. The computer can never replace the analysis of a specific issue, but it can help narrow down the list of evaluees to a reasonable number based on some basic technical attributes we feel are important. One of those technical attributes is the chart pattern of the stock.

Chart Patterns

If you wait for the right chart pattern to form before making a stock commitment, you dramatically increase your probabilities of success. In our day-to-day operation evaluating and trading the markets, we have found that when the market is supporting higher prices (we cover these indicators in later chapters), sticking to the bullish chart patterns when going long stock usually produces superior results. Conversely, we have found that when the market is not supporting higher prices, sticking to the bearish chart patterns when shorting a stock usually produces superior results. If the market is not supporting higher prices, the odds of success in trying to buy a stock with a bullish chart pattern is like trying to swim against the current. You may make some headway but not nearly as much as if you just wait for the tide to change so you can swim with the current.

While I cover chart patterns as one of the first concepts in this method of stock market analysis, other indicators must be added to the equation before you can decide what to buy. The tendency of those new to the Point and Figure process is to focus only on patterns when evaluating an individual equity. This is a very important step in the process, but not the whole process. That having been said, let's delve right into covering the Point and Figure chart patterns.

Had I known about this during my broker years, I would have been able to save a lot of heartache for both my clients and me. We always tried to recommend stocks that were fundamentally sound, but we never knew if we were on I-95 North or South. It is such a simple concept, yet most brokers and investors never get a handle on it. I remember a time I put on a trade for a client without paying much attention to the underlying stock. This good client of mine called to discuss some possible trades in the market. I had just learned about an option strategy called "covered writing" that involves buying a stock and simultaneously selling a call option against the position. The client and I talked at length about the stock. We discussed how Burlington Industries was a great company (the leader in the textile business at the time). He liked the covered-writing concept, so we did the trade, bought the stock, and sold the call option against the position. I sold it as a conservative strategy. I was really thrilled that I had been able to explain the concept of a covered write on the phone.

After the close of business, I went with my broker buddies to the Bull and Bear club, as we did every evening, to have a beer and discuss the day's business. I mentioned to them that I had done a covered-write trade that day and the underlying stock was Burlington Northern. One of the fellows responded, "oh, the railroad." I broke out in a cold sweat. I said no, I had bought the textile company, not the railroad.

As it turned out, I had in fact bought the client Burlington Northern, the railroad, despite discussing the merits of Burlington Industries, the textile company. The names Burlington Northern and Burlington Industries are close, right? Well, the names might be close but their businesses are like the North and South Poles. The trade turned out fine, and I was probably better off with the railroad than I would have been with the sock company. In fact, Burlington Industries didn't even have listed options at that time. Talk about stacking the odds in your favor—I shut my eyes and took a shot in the dark. I wasn't sure what coast the stock was on, much less what interstate and what direction. This happens more often than you can imagine.

Many investors simply feel they can't grasp the nuances of the investment process to become better investors. They believe Wall Street is somehow over their heads. But, I've seen it time and again: Brokers and investors who take that first "toe dip" into learning this material are quickly hooked and eventually become true craftsmen at the investment process. It's like the first time you learned to employ a little strategy in a game of chess or backgammon. Before you know it, you are hooked.

The Chart Patterns

Double Top

In Chapter 2, you learned how to maintain your charts. The most basic chart patterns are the Double Top and Double Bottom. The Double Top requires 3 columns: two columns of X's and one column of O's. The key to interpreting the chart patterns is to determine where the stock exceeds a point of resistance or support. A feature of Charles Dow's charts that caught the eye of some astute turn-of-the-century investors was the charts' accurate identification of levels of distribution and accumulation. Distribution corresponds to a top (resistance) and accumulation corresponds to a bottom (support). Resistance is the point at which a stock reaches a particular price and encounters selling pressure. Back to the supply-and-demand scenario. This is the point where supply exceeds demand. For example, let's say that CSCO rises to 60 and meets selling pressure. This selling pressure exceeds the demand at that price, and the stock retreats back a few points. Remember, it requires a three-box reversal to change columns. If the selling pressure was enough to force CSCO back to 57 or lower, the chart would revert to O's from X's. In the tennis match analogy, supply would have won one set. The match continues. Let's say over the next few weeks, demand once again creeps back into the stock at 57 and causes the price to rise to 60 per share. This is another three-box reversal back up into a column of X's, and CSCO now sits at the same price level that previously found supply.

The question now is whether the sellers that forced the stock back before are still there. I have seen stocks hit resistance numerous times over many months until the selling pressure was finally exhausted. The only way to find out if the sellers are still operating at that price is to see how CSCO negotiates that level. If it is again repelled, then the sellers are still there. If it instead is able to move to 61, then we can say that demand has prevailed at this price by exceeding the level where supply was previously in control. By exceeding this level of resistance, the Point and Figure chart gives its most basic buy signal, the Double Top. Naturally, you must consider other things before purchasing the stock but in this most simple pattern, we can say demand is in control. If you could give me no other information on CSCO, my decision would be to buy the stock. By CSCO exceeding that point of resistance, we can say that demand won the match. The chart pattern would look like the one shown in Figure 3.1.

Let's cover the Double Bottom. In this pattern, supply wins the match. Let's say instead of CSCO exceeding the previous point of resistance, it instead reversed and exceeded the previous

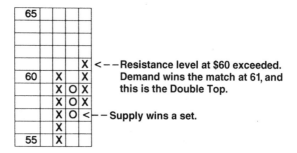

Figure 3.1   The Double Top.

level of support. You can see in Figure 3.2 that the stock declined to 56, at which point demand overtook supply and the stock reversed back up into a column of X's. At 59, the stock encounters selling pressure that drives CSCO back down the chart to the 56 level where demand previously took the upper hand providing support. This time, however, the buyers are not there as before, and the selling pressure persists until the stock exceeds that level of support. The match is over. Supply wins and the probability is lower prices. The reason supply overtook demand is not important. How the stock reacts to the supply and demand is all that matters, for in the end, supply and demand cause stocks to move up and down and nothing else.

You can now see why we call this pattern Double Top and Double Bottom. The stock rises or declines to the same level twice. You can probably already guess what we might call the pattern if it rose or declined to the same level three times.

In Figure 3.3, you can see that when the stock rose back to 60, it was repelled for the second time. This clue suggests to us that there is formidable resistance at that level and the sell signal

60	O			
	O	X		
	O	X	O	
	O	X	O	
	O		O	**Double Bottom Sell**
55			O	<--Signal given at 55.

Figure 3.2   The Double Bottom.

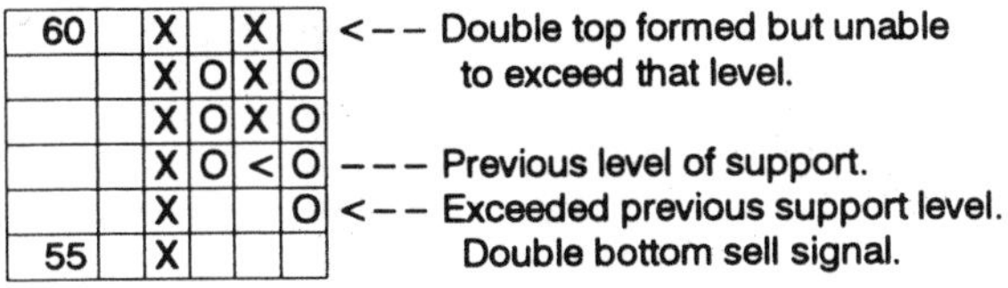

60	X		X		<-- Double top formed but unable
	X	O	X	O	to exceed that level.
	X	O	X	O	
	X	O	<	O	--- Previous level of support.
	X			O	<-- Exceeded previous support level.
55	X				Double bottom sell signal.

Figure 3.3   Double Bottom with resistance.

is that much more important. Looking at this chart, we can tell that the upside potential is only 60. Naturally, things can and do change, but this is all we have to go with for the time being. Short sellers always want to know points of resistance because a penetration of these levels might signal a reversal in trend.

Figure 3.4 shows us that there is good support at 55 simply because that is the price where the stock stopped going down on two separate occasions. For some reason, there are buyers at that level. We consider this a level of accumulation or support. This Double Top buy signal is more important than the previous one because there is more information available with which to make a decision. The stock found support twice at the 55 level suggesting that the stock will hold there in the event it experiences further weakness—just a little clue the chart in Figure 3.1 did not have.

The Bullish Signal

We add one more dimension, an added clue, to the pattern this time. In Figure 3.5, notice how the last column of O's does not extend down as low as the previous column of O's. We call that a rising bottom. It signifies that supply is becoming less a factor in

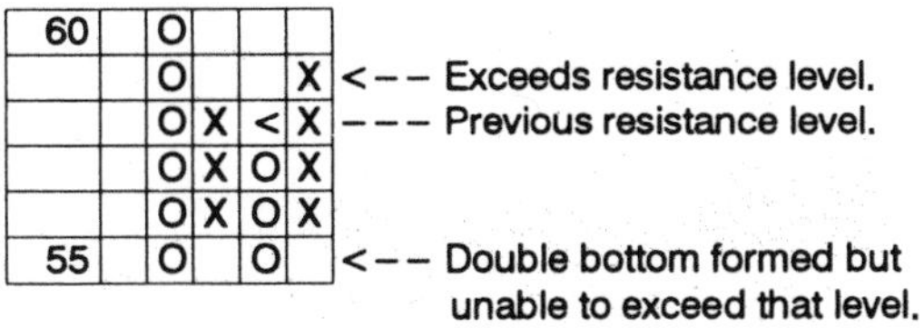

60	O				
	O			X	<-- Exceeds resistance level.
	O	X	<	X	--- Previous resistance level.
	O	X	O	X	
	O	X	O	X	
55	O		O		<-- Double bottom formed but
					unable to exceed that level.

Figure 3.4   Double Top with support.

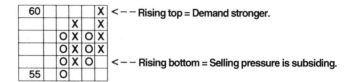

Figure 3.5 Double Top with a rising bottom.

driving the stock. On the other side of the coin, demand is getting stronger as the last column of X's exceeds the previous column of X's. The rising bottom provides added guidance when evaluating the supply-demand relationship of the underlying stock. Of the three double tops discussed thus far, this one is the strongest and would warrant the largest commitment.

The best way to understand these patterns is to take a legal pad and pencil and simply write down in 50 words or less exactly what you see (no different from the composition 7-year-olds sometimes have to write for homework, describing their room). This is what I observe in Figure 3.5:

1. I see a tennis match that only took four sets (columns) to complete.
2. I see two sets where McEnroe won (columns of O's) and two sets where Connors won (columns of X's).
3. The last column of X's exceeded the previous column, giving a Double Top buy signal at 60.
4. The second column of O's did not decline as low as the previous column of O's suggesting McEnroe is losing strength.
5. The last column of X's exceeds a previous column of X's suggesting Connors is gaining strength.

Breaking the pattern down to its lowest common denominator, simplifies analysis.

The Bearish Signal

The Bearish Signal is the opposite of the Bullish Signal. Figure 3.6 shows that demand in this case is becoming less strong as the last

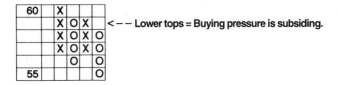

Figure 3.6 Double Bottom with a lower top.

column of X's fails to reach the previous level. Selling pressure however is increasing as evidenced by the lower column of O's. These clues simply suggest demand is losing strength and supply is gaining strength. All too often, investors buy stocks in this condition only to see them erode further.

So far, we have discussed the Double Bottom and Double Top. All other patterns that we cover are expansions of this basic form. By now, you can see how simple this method is to grasp. Let's go on to the Triple Top buy signal.

Triple Top

The Triple Top is exactly what the name suggests—a chart pattern that rises to a certain price level three times. The first two times the stock visits that level, it is repelled by sellers. The third time the stock rises to that level, it forms the Triple Top. The buy signal is given when the stock exceeds the level that previously caused the stock to reverse down. This pattern is shown in Figure 3.7.

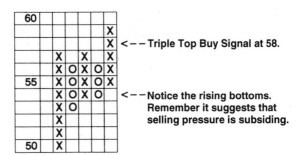

Figure 3.7 The Triple Top.

There are many reasons a stock will encounter supply at certain levels. Think back to a time when you bought stock thinking it was the bottom, or at least an opportune price level to buy, and instead of rising the stock immediately declined. We have all had one or two experiences like that. The thought that probably crossed your mind as you saw the stock lose value was to get out if the stock got back to even. This is a perfectly normal human reaction. When you place that order to get you out at your break-even point, you are in essence creating supply at that level.

If more sellers are willing to sell their stock at that level than buyers are willing to buy, the stock will decline. The only way we know whether the selling pressure has been exhausted at a particular level is by the stock exceeding that price. If the stock is repelled again, the sellers are still there. I have seen stocks bounce off certain prices for as long as 18 months. There have been numerous examples of this over the years. Coca-Cola (KO) from 1992 to 1994 was a trading range with neither supply nor demand winning until finally in September 1994 demand won and the stock took off. Another memorable example was Intuit (INTU). This stock spent 11 months trading between 23 and 35. Finally, when the stock broke out, it took off like a rocket rallying to 90 in a matter of two months. When a stock trades up to an area of resistance numerous times and then finally breaks out, we refer to that as a "big base breakout" in the office. You know, it sounds a lot like a country song. Yet another big base breakout that comes to mind is Oracle (ORCL). In 1999, this stock traded up to 39 six times. Finally the stock hit 40 breaking a spread sextuple top and there was nothing but grease between here and the trees for that stock for the next year.

Expansions on the triple top are merely patterns that take longer to complete. Patterns like the Quadruple Top or Quintuple Top are rare. The more tops a pattern has, the more bullish; and the faster the pattern develops, the more bullish. The more times a stock bounces off a resistance level, the stronger the breakout will be when it comes. It was said years ago that the degree to which a stock will rise is in exact proportion to the time the stock took in preparation for that move. In other words, the wider the base from which a stock breaks out, the higher the stock will rise. Over the past 12 years or so, we have found that a good strategy to use with the Triple Top or greater breakout is to buy partial positions on the breakout and then average in on a pullback. Half of the time, a stock will pull back after the Triple Top breakout.

Triple Bottom Sell Signal

The Triple Bottom sell signal, like the Triple Top, has a high degree of reliability. When I teach seminars on this subject, I use Figure 3.8 as an example of how dangerous it can be for investors to exclude technical analysis when buying a stock. Consider an investor who buys this stock at 31 per share and then leaves on vacation for one month. He checks the Internet frequently and notices that his stock is still around the price he paid for it, only down a point. Not bad for a market that had been volatile for the past month he thinks, and he continues to feel comfortable with the stock. The fundamentals are all in place. What is he missing in this puzzle? What he is missing is that a whole tennis match between supply and demand has been completed with supply winning the match.

The probability of lower prices is very high. The Triple Bottom does not mean that the stock will cave in immediately, it suggests that the risk in that position has increased tremendously. Whether this investor chooses to do anything about the signal or not, he should at least be aware of it. If the investor does nothing other than increase his awareness of a potential decline, he is far ahead of the investor who holds the same position without any warning. Other considerations, such as Relative Strength,

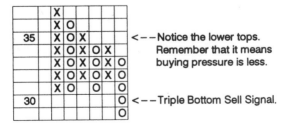

Figure 3.8 The Triple Bottom.

sector Bullish Percent, overall market condition, and trend lines, are discussed in later chapters.

In analyzing the Triple Bottom pattern, keep a close watch for declining tops. Think back to the Double Top formations. When the stock declined but was unable to decline as far as it previously did, it implied that selling pressure was drying up. Conversely, if the tops or columns of X's are making lower tops, it suggests that demand is drying up. These two clues make the chart more bullish or bearish respectively. This will hold true with any chart pattern.

Keep in mind that other factors must be taken into consideration when evaluating a chart. We put it all together in the chapters ahead.

The Bullish and Bearish Catapult Formation

The Catapult (Figure 3.9) is simply a combination of the Triple Top and the Double Top. This pattern is a confidence builder. The Catapult comprises a Triple Top buy signal followed by a pullback producing a rising bottom. Following the pullback, the stock resumes the trend giving a Double Top buy signal. Take a look at the pattern in Figure 3.9. Notice the Triple Top buy signal followed by the pullback into a column of O's. Notice how the column produces a higher bottom. The resumption of trend completes the Catapult by giving a Double Top buy signal.

Let's look at the Catapult in pieces to better understand what it is saying to us. The Triple Top is saying that the stock has a

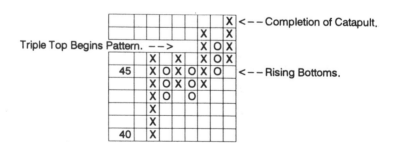

Figure 3.9 The Bullish Catapult formation.

very high probability of rising in price, assuming the market is in a bullish mode. In fact, this type of pattern has a success probability of 87.5 percent in bull markets. The subsequent reversal producing a higher bottom suggests that supply is beginning to dry up or becoming a less significant factor. The resumption of trend and subsequent Double Top buy signal simply confirms the Triple Top. The Catapult is a confidence builder. This is the pattern that you should be most aggressive with when the overall markets are in a bullish mode, the underlying sector is in a bullish mode, and the fundamentals are superior in the stock.

The steps involved in stock selection resemble the steps involved in taking the trip from Virginia to New York City. Before you begin the trip, you need to gas the car up, check the oil, and check the water in the radiator. Then you must select the most direct route to New York (I-95 North). Gassing the car, checking the oil, and so on are similar to checking the fundamentals of the underlying stock. Selecting the proper interstate to embark on is similar to evaluating the technical (supply and demand) picture of the underlying stock. Many investors are diligent in doing the fundamental work on a stock they want to buy but ignore evaluating the probability of it rising in price. Buying a fundamentally sound stock that has just completed a chart pattern that suggests lower—not higher—prices is like making all the preparations for a trip to New York, then embarking south on Interstate 95 toward Florida. The idea is to stack as many odds in your favor before you begin the journey. There still isn't any guarantee. As much as people try to make investing a science, it remains an art.

In teaching this subject to grade school children, I have observed it takes only 30 minutes of instruction for them to make the right selection when evaluating a bearish and bullish chart together. The beauty about teaching children is that you don't have to deprogram them. Adults have preconceived ideas about how the market is supposed to work, mostly derived from watching TV programs about finance. All we are trying to ascertain with these chart patterns is whether supply or demand is in control of the underlying stock. If you go any farther than that, you've gone too far. Keep it simple. The law of supply and demand causes prices to change whether it's in the supermarket or the stock market.

Trading Tactics Using the Catapult

The Catapult is a confirmation pattern—the final double top that completes the Catapult simply confirms the previous Triple Top. It's a confirmation that demand is in control at this point in the stock's trend. The first part of the pattern is the basic Triple Top. In the last 10 years buying on the pullback, or reaction from breakouts, offers a higher probability of success in the trade. Once a Triple Top has exceeded the previous column of X's and then pulls back, the potential for a Catapult exists. Investors might consider buying half their position on the three-box reversal from the Triple Top. This gives them a good entry point for the first portion of the position and gets them in close to their stop point. Let's talk about the stop for a second. At what point will investors have to stop out of the position if they are wrong in their assumption that the stock will rise? In this case, with the only information being the chart pattern, the only logical stop would be the Triple Bottom. At that level, the pattern would suggest that supply was in control. If the stock is selected using strong fundamentals, has strong Relative Strength, and is trading above the Bullish Support Line, the probability of a failure in this pattern is low. Still, investors must consider what to do when things go wrong. There needs to be a plan of action if the trade begins to go sour. Remember, this is not an exact science, it's an art.

Once half the position is bought on the three-box reversal and the mental stop is in place, investors can begin to execute the plan to buy the other half of the position on the completion of the Catapult. Traders can then raise their stop to the new Double Bottom sell signal that is formed when the stock reverses back up to complete the Catapult. Long-term investors will keep their stop on the violation of the Bullish Support Line, otherwise known as the trend line. In Figure 3.10, we would have to assume that supply had taken control if the stock violated the trend line and simultaneously gave a Double Bottom sell signal. The stop-loss point would come at the 42 level once the Catapult formation was complete. Just keep in mind that as long as a stock trades above the Bullish Support Line, we consider it bullish. Long-term investors will only stop out on violations of the trend line. Traders will be more apt than investors to take the sell signals above the trend line.

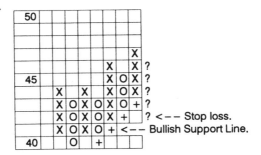

Figure 3.10 Knowing where to set the stop.

So far on our order entry using the Catapult, we have bought one half the intended position on the pullback to 43 and entered a mental stop-loss point at 40. Now, for the second half of our intended position, we enter an order called a "Good until Cancel" (GTC) order. The GTC order simply allows you to select a price you are willing to pay for your stock, and your order remains on the specialist's books until the stock reaches that price. In this case, you would place an order to buy the remainder of your position at 47, the level where the bullish Catapult formation will be completed.

You can now see where you bought the second half of your intended position. Notice how the stop has risen now to the new Double Bottom sell signal that has formed at 42. This new stop allows us to protect profits should supply suddenly take control of the stock. It is important that long-term investors only use the trend line to stop out of a position. Traders are much shorter term in nature and may select a percentage of the entry price as their stop. A.W. Cohen, one of the pioneers in this method of analysis, always suggested that investors risk no more than 10 percent in a stock. In today's more volatile markets, a 10 percent decline can happen fast. We find it more useful to carefully select our entry point and then give the stock some room to perform.

By looking at the Catapult formation, you can see many other combinations of entry points that you can use (see Figure 3.11). The key is you have an organized and logical guide to assist you in finding entry and exit points when investing. No other charts that I am aware of can do this. The Point and Figure charts are,

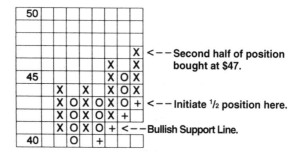

Figure 3.11   Trading with the Bullish Catapult formation.

without a doubt, the best and most accurate guides an investor can use.

Bearish Catapult Formation

The Bearish Catapult formation can be interpreted exactly opposite the Bullish Catapult formation and is particularly useful in timing short sales. Entry and exit points would be selected the same way we did with the Bullish Catapult. Stop points are particularly important in selling short. The risks in short selling are theoretically unlimited. In reality, that is not probable, but I have seen situations where stocks received buyout offers that significantly increased their price. The problem with being short in these unusual situations is that the stock stops trading and opens at a higher price without anyone being able to get out. These situations, however, are few and far between. It is very important to plan your entry point so you have a palatable stop price. A short seller might plan to sell half his intended position short on the first reversal back up in the chart pattern following the Triple Bottom sell signal. This will allow him to initiate the short relatively close to his stop point. Trend lines are even more important in short selling. The second half of his intended short position can be initiated when the stock reverses back down and completes the Bearish Catapult formation. Let's look at Figure 3.12.

You can see that this pattern is the exact opposite from the Bullish Catapult. Watch carefully for this pattern as it clearly

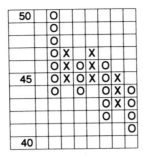

Figure 3.12   The Bearish Catapult formation.

suggests lower prices in the underlying stock. Whether you understood Point and Figure charting or not, if you looked at two
fundamentally sound stocks, both in the same group, one with a
Bearish Catapult formation and one with a Bullish Catapult formation, it wouldn't take long for you to determine which stock
you wanted to buy.

These same patterns are used to assist the investor in using the
options market. I have always looked at puts or calls as being sur-
rogates for the underlying stock. We only use in-the-money calls or
puts because the delta (the amount the option will move in relation to a 1-point move in the underlying stock) is much closer to 1
for 1. If an in-the-money long call is used as a substitute for buying
the underlying stock, then use the same entry and exit points that
you would use if you were buying the underlying stock. The same
goes for put purchases as substitutes for outright short selling. Another school of thought in options buying is to let the premium be
your stop. If you use this strategy, never buy more options than you
would otherwise have an appetite for round lots of the underlying
stock, either long or short. If you were normally a 300-share buyer,
then only buy three options. If you allow the premium to be your
stop, then you have the staying power to hang in the position until
expiration. I have seen numerous times where a stock declines sub-
stantially early in the trade only to come back strong a few months
later. We could devote a whole book to this subject, but let it suf-
fice for now that Point and Figure chart patterns can be very useful
in assisting the investor with entry and exit points for options trading as well as stock trading (options are discussed in Chapter 8).

The Triangle Formation

The Triangle formation is a combination of patterns we have seen before. The key to understanding chart patterns is being able to sit down with a pencil and paper and write down exactly what you see. Don't look at the whole pattern and try to decipher it. Evaluate the parts making up the pattern, and you will then understand the pattern in total. In Figure 3.13, you can readily see the rising bottoms and lower tops in the pattern. To qualify as a Triangle, the pattern must have five vertical columns. The rising bottoms suggest that supply is drying up. You will also see the series of lower tops. The lower tops suggest that demand is becoming less of a factor in driving the stock. In our tennis analogy, the two players are getting more tired after each set, and the players have equal ability. Eventually, something will have to give. One player or the other will get a second wind or begin to take the upper hand. It is at this point that we want to make a commitment in the underlying stock. There is nothing to do but wait and watch the match. If the pattern resolves itself on the upside, it will give a Double Top buy signal. The Double Top buy signal simply suggests that demand has won the match and the probability is higher prices in the stock. Now look at the Bearish Triangle in Figure 3.13. Notice how the match is won by supply. The Double Bottom sell signal suggests that the probability is lower

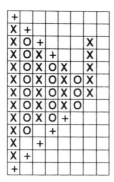 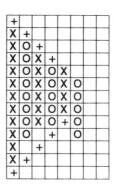

Figure 3.13   The Triangle formations.

prices in the stock. These patterns are simply road maps. They are not crystal balls.

There are a couple of other things that we want to point out about the Triangle pattern. First, usually a stock in an uptrend will resolve the triangle on the upside (i.e., a Bullish Triangle). Similarly, a stock in a downtrend will usually resolve the triangle on the downside (i.e., a Bearish Triangle). Second, it is usually feast or famine with the Triangle pattern. We will either see very few triangles forming, or we will see a whole host of them developing. Most of the time when we see quite a few triangles forming, it is during a choppy or sideways market and supply and demand are battling it out for control. Third, breakouts from the Triangle pattern typically result in quick, explosive moves so it behooves you to be ready to act when the signal is given. Look at the chart pattern in Figure 3.14. The stock in this graphic is forming a Triangle pattern right at the Bullish Support Line. A move to 55 would break a Double Top and complete the Bullish Triangle pattern and long positions could be taken. On the other hand, if the stock hits 49 it would not only complete a Bearish Triangle but also violate the Bullish Support Line. The stock could be shorted at 49. On our Internet site, we have premade reports that allow you to see the charts of all stocks breaking out of a Bullish Triangle, Bearish Triangle, and all the other different patterns.

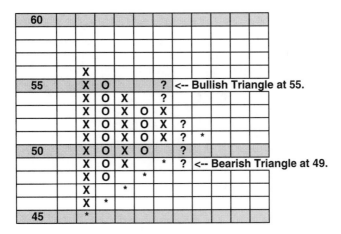

Figure 3.14 Planning the trade with a Triangle pattern.

Variations of the Triple Top

I usually call this pattern the Diagonal Triple Top, but I hesitate to use the name because it sounds too difficult. Possibly a better name would be a Bullish Signal. I have said many times if investing gets too difficult for a seventh grader to understand, the system is needlessly complex. It is important to keep it simple especially in technical analysis. We don't usually use this pattern as a Triple Top, but older publications classify it as one. This variation is simply two Double Top buy signals, one right after the other. This is the sign of a good strong uptrend. A stock in a strong uptrend will produce rising bottoms and rising tops, and that is exactly what this pattern demonstrates. Notice in Figure 3.15 that you simply have two consecutive Double Tops with rising bottoms.

Variations on the Triple Bottom

This pattern is simply the reverse of the Diagonal Triple Top or Bullish Signal. We can simply call this the Bearish Signal. It has a series of lower tops followed by lower bottoms. Just looking at Figure 3.16 suggests that supply is in control. This is all you want your chart pattern to alert you to. Another way to look at it is two consecutive Double Bottom sell signals. We almost never evaluate this pattern as a Triple Bottom although A.W. Cohen clearly classifies it as such.

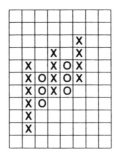

Figure 3.15   The Diagonalized Triple Top.

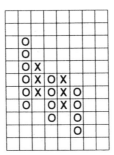

Figure 3.16 The Diagonalized Triple Bottom.

The Spread Triple Top and Bottom

This pattern is simply a Triple Top that takes a little more space on the chart to complete. Notice the gaps between the tops in Figure 3.17. This is where the spread comes in. The normal Triple Top has no gaps between the tops. The same philosophy applies in this pattern as in the Triple Top. In each case, the stock rises to a certain price level and is repelled two times. The third attempt at that price is successful by the stock moving through the level shown by a column of X's exceeding the point of resistance. Since the stock was repelled twice at that same level, there are apparently sell orders there. The reason is not important. What is important is that

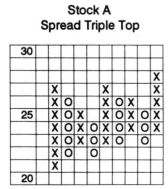

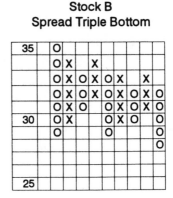

Figure 3.17 The Spread Triple Top and Bottom formation.

there are sellers at that particular level. The only way to know if demand can overtake the selling pressure is to see how the stock negotiates the level again. Simply stated, if the stock is repelled again at this level of resistance, the sellers are still there. You need not know any more. If the stock exceeds that level, then demand has overcome the supply that previously caused it to reverse. This is why we always wait for a particular level to be exceeded before we make a long or short commitment in the stock. In the 1980s, we typically just bought or sold the breakouts. Starting in the 1990s, we found out that it was best to buy on the pullbacks. For most of the 1980s, stocks went up. From the 1990s forward to 2000, stocks continued their rise. Then in March 2000 something major happened. The technical balance sheet on the Nasdaq turned decidedly negative while the technical balance sheet on the NYSE turned positive—one door of opportunity closes while another one opens. For the rest of 2000 into the first quarter of 2001, tech stocks were virtually decimated. It's been a stock picker's environment and likely to remain so for the foreseeable future. Figure 3.17 shows what the pattern looks like for both the Spread Triple Top and the Spread Triple Bottom.

Notice that in these two patterns, the stocks are trading at the same price. Consider that both stocks are fundamentally sound and each is being recommended by a major firm on Wall Street. Both stocks are in the same industry group and pay about the same dividend. You have studied the fundamentals of the two stocks and are now trying to determine which stock to buy. It's the moment of truth. Which stock do you select?

Without the chart patterns shown here, you would be in a quandary. Looking at the fundamental data alone, both stocks are equal, therefore both stocks should do about as well in the future. Not so. If you had the benefit of evaluating the Point and Figure charts in Figure 3.17, the selection process would become much easier. With the information I have just given you, which stock do you select? It doesn't take an in-depth understanding of this method to determine stock A is in an uptrend with the probability of higher prices and stock B is in a downtrend with lower prices likely.

This simple exercise shows why charts are so important and why you can achieve the best results in the market when you use both fundamental and technical analysis. The fundamental work answers the question *what*, and the technical side of the equation answers the question *when*. Both are equally important. The first question, *what*, is easily answered because fundamental research is everywhere on Wall Street and the Internet. Anyone doing business with a broker of a major firm on Wall Street, either through their Internet online system or direct through a broker, has access to all the fundamental ideas that the firm produces along with its related research. Technical analysis is much harder to come by, but with the information in this book, you will be perfectly capable of performing that task yourself.

The market and sector represent 75 percent of the risk in any particular stock. The problem most investors have is that they concentrate 75 percent of their effort on evaluating the fundamentals. It is extremely important to buy stocks when you are in possession of the ball (the market is in a bullish mode). We cover the market indicators in later chapters. We start this book with the discussion on individual chart patterns because these patterns make up the market indicators.

Once again, stack as many odds in your favor as possible before you make a commitment in the stock market. I don't know how many times acquaintances have come up to me and asked what I think about a stock tip they just got from a friend. They usually say it's a very reliable source. My answer is always the same: If it's inside information, you won't have it. The second you have it, it's outside information and those who are really in the know have already acted on it. In almost every case, you can look back on the Point and Figure chart and see clearly where the insiders were operating. Once you get the handle on this method, which has remained true to form for over 100 years, you will see why the Point and Figure chart is as good as inside information. We have a four-step game plan that we follow, and this is the sequence of events you should follow before you make a stock commitment. Step 1 is to evaluate the overall market; Step 2 is to evaluate the sector you are investing in; Step 3 is to answer the question of "what to buy" (the fundamentals); and finally Step 4 encompasses stock selection, which answers the question of "when to buy."

Bullish Shakeout Formation

This is one of my favorite patterns. We keep a strong eye out for this pattern because it has a high degree of reliability. The Shakeout is a relatively new pattern; we've only been watching this one for the past 20 years or so, but we have found it very useful in real-life application. It is called the Shakeout because the pattern easily deceives investors when the sell signal is given.

There is a big difference between the chartist and the technician: Many chartists operate on chart patterns alone without any other input, whereas technicians use other indicators to assist them in evaluating stocks. Don't forget there are other considerations besides just the chart pattern when making a stock selection. The chart patterns should be used to determine whether supply or demand is in control of the underlying investment vehicle. Because so much risk is associated with the market and sector, it is imperative to thoroughly evaluate both factors before considering the underlying stock. If you are buying stocks in a down market, you will surely lose money. If you are selling stocks short in an up market, you will surely lose money. We want to drive home this point, because the Shakeout pattern works best in strong bull markets. We have not had much success, as you might imagine, using this pattern in a bearish market.

With that caveat, let's look at the six attributes of a Shakeout formation:

1. The stock and market should be in a strong uptrend.
2. The stock should be trading above the Bullish Support Line.
3. The stock must rise to a level where it forms two tops at the same price. Note this says "forms" two tops, not breaking the double top.
4. The subsequent reversal of the stock from these two tops must give a Double Bottom sell signal.
5. This sell signal should be the first in this uptrend.
6. The Relative Strength chart must be on a buy signal or at least in a column of X's.

Sounds like a lot doesn't it? It's not really. In our day-to-day operations, we fudge these parameters a little, but in general the

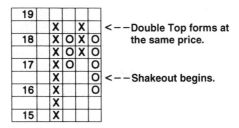

Figure 3.18 The Shakeout formation.

Shakeout has these characteristics. Remember, the whole idea in using chart patterns is to determine whether supply or demand is in control. Don't forget that, and don't read too much into it because you will usually overthink the position, which in turn results in losses. The best machine is the one with the fewest moving parts.

The Shakeout pattern shown in Figure 3.18 is also great for trading. Since the stock must be in a strong uptrend to qualify for the Shakeout pattern, you very well may already have an existing position in the stock. The Shakeout can provide you with an opportunity to add to that strong position or if you aren't already long, it can provide an opportunity to get in a dip.

The Shakeout begins by giving the Double Bottom sell signal. We never know what level the sell signal will carry the stock down to so our action point for entry into this stock is on the first three-box reversal back up the chart (see Figure 3.19). This is the only point where we know demand is back in control. Once

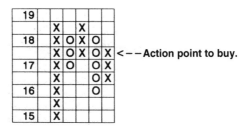

Figure 3.19 Action point on the Shakeout.

the stock reverses back up into a column of X's, the position can be taken.

The next consideration is, what to do if things go wrong? Where is the stop-loss point? We always use the Double Bottom that is formed when the stock reverses back up as our exit point. Normally, this is 4 points' risk. Remember that the reliability of this pattern, and any other bullish pattern, diminishes when the overall market is in a bearish mode and your stop-loss point has a higher probability of being hit. Look at Figure 3.20 to see how entry and exit points are established. If the trade was established at the action point, and the stock immediately reversed, the stop point would be the first sell signal the stock gives. The stop is at 15½.

The Long Tail Down

This is one of our favorite bottom-fishing patterns. To qualify for a Long Tail Down, the stock must have declined 20 or more boxes without a reversal. After such a decline, the first reversal up usually provides a good trading opportunity. We use to see the 20-box-down movement only in stocks that were already in strong downtrends and that move was the final capitulation. However, with increased volatility in stocks, especially in technology, we have now seen stocks in uptrends pull back 20 boxes—just above strong support areas. Of course, this begs the question, "Do you really have the risk tolerance to buy a stock that can move 20 points in one day?" Nonetheless, this pattern can be a good trading pattern.

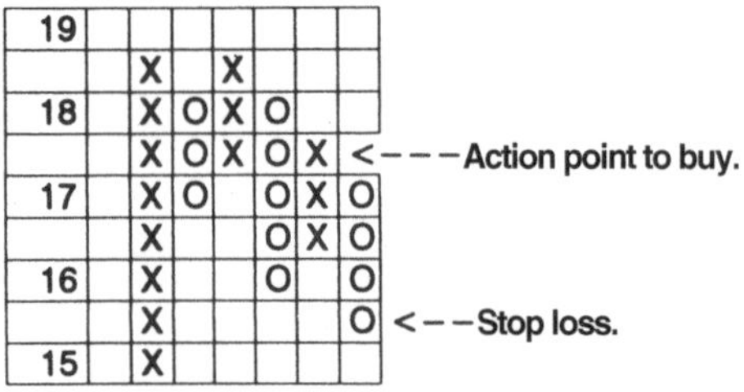

19							
	X		X				
18	X	O	X	O			
	X	O	X	O	X		<---Action point to buy.
17	X	O		O	X	O	
	X			O	X	O	
16	X			O		O	
	X					O	<---Stop loss.
15	X						

Figure 3.20   Stop loss on the Shakeout.

I remember a time we thought the pattern was infallible. It had worked for a string of trades, so we decided to pound the table on the next one we came across. It seems that Murphy is always hanging around when you alert the world to a particularly lucrative situation (you know Murphy's Law: If anything can go wrong it will). One day we came across a Long Tail Down in Apple Computer. Apple is a great trading stock as the volatility is high and it seems everyone has played it at sometime or another. Apple had just gone through one of these 20-box down patterns. We knew we had a winner. This time we pounded the table with the recommendation to buy on the first three-box reversal back up the chart. I mean we pounded the table. When the reversal came, I think most of our customers took the trade and many of our customers are large institutions. You guessed it, the stock struggled up a point or so and then caved in. It was the first one in many moons that didn't work. It always seems to work out like that. The one you get everyone to buy, fakes you out. Apple did it again in 2000. The stock came with less than expected earnings and "bang" down 50 percent and over 20 boxes. The stock reversed up a few days, only to reverse down again. It did that two more times.

On balance, this is a good trading pattern. The idea is simple. When a stock has declined 20 boxes or more, you take the first three-box reversal back up the chart as your action point. The stop-loss point is the Double Bottom sell signal that is set up when the stock reverses up into a column of X's. The longer it takes for the stock to decline 20 boxes, the less reliable the pattern is. This is for trading purposes only and not for investors. A stock that has declined 20 boxes or more usually has something wrong with the fundamentals. One of the better ways to play the trade is through the call market. This will give you staying power to expiration, and you need not worry about your stop point being hit. If the stock rises from your entry point, you can raise your stop to each subsequent sell signal that forms. This will allow you to get the full ride if no sell signals are given. It also prevents you from taking a profit too quickly. Always allow your profits to run as much as possible and take as much subjectivity out of the equation as possible. Figure 3.21 shows the Long Tail Down pattern.

The same philosophy can be applied to a long run of X's up but with a much smaller degree of success. As a stock rises, the

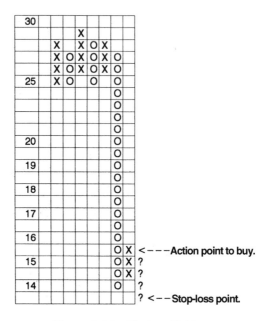

Figure 3.21   The Long Tail Down.

fundamentals are coming to fruition and there are no dissatisfied investors. For this reason, we just don't see enough selling pressure to warrant a trading commitment in a stock that rises 20 boxes without a reversal. Pullbacks in strong stocks like these appear as opportunities to buy not to sell and can easily generate demand. Remember, there are no dissatisfied investors at tops. Still the very nimble can take advantage of it. I usually don't. I am much more apt to attempt a trade on a 20-box down move. However, the three-box reversal down from a run up of 20 boxes or more can be very useful in providing a stop-loss point for traders to take profits or a place for an investor to take partial positions off the table.

The High Pole Warning Formation

This pattern was pioneered by the late Earl Blumenthal. We have seldom taken action on this pattern; however, we have always used it as a warning. This pattern is most reliable in bear-configured markets. To qualify for a High Pole, the Point and Figure chart must have exceeded a previous column of X's by at least three boxes. Following the rise in X's, the stock must pull back more than 50 percent of that last up-thrust on the chart. The thought behind the formation is that there must be something wrong with the supply-demand relationship if the stock subsequently gave up 50 percent of the last move up. It's a warning that supply might be taking control of the stock. I will usually give the stock some room and place more emphasis on the trend line as my guide for a potential stop for stocks. The High Pole does, however, increase my awareness of a potential change in the supply-demand relationship of the underlying stock especially in bear-configured markets. Figure 3.22 is an example of a High Pole Warning formation.

The Low Pole Formation

I find this pattern more useful than the High Pole simply because investors are more apt to make a commitment in a stock that appears to be a bargain than to sell a stock that has done well for them. The Low Pole simply means the selling pressure that had been driving the stock down is probably over to a great degree. This does not mean that you jump on the stock with unbridled enthusiasm. The company probably still has problems. Remember, you want to buy stocks that are fundamentally sound. That is your first line of defense. Traders, on the other hand, can attempt to make money on a bottom-fishing expedition. The trader's best play is to wait for a pullback following the Low Pole and enter the

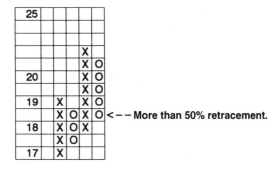

Figure 3.22 The High Pole Warning.

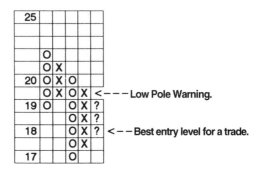

Figure 3.23 The Low Pole Warning.

stock there (see Figure 3.23). Buying on the pullback will establish the entry point closer to the stop level. It also sets up the potential for a nice Double Top buy signal on the next reversal back up the chart. It is usually best to allow the stock to come to you if possible.

We use the High Pole and Low Pole Warnings with two indicators, the Dow Jones 20 Bond Average and the Advance-Decline indexes. Therefore it will be important to understand the pattern when we discuss these two indicators later in the book. In everyday practice, we rarely use the two patterns with individual stocks.

The Broadening Top Formation

The Broadening Top formation is simply a variation on the Shakeout formation. The primary difference between the two is that the Broadening Top gives a buy signal prior to the sell signal being given. Let's look back for a moment. If you don't have the Shakeout firmly in mind go back and look at the pattern (Exhibits 3.18–3.20). You will see that the underlying stock has risen up to a certain level two times but was unable to exceed that level the second time. The stock in essence formed a Double Top. Subsequently, it reversed and gave that first sell signal in the uptrend. In the case of the Broadening Top formation, the stock exceeds that previous top the stock made. In other words, it gives a Double Top buy signal. The subsequent reversal gives the sell signal. The combination of the higher top and lower bottom has the appearance of broadening the pattern. To complete the pattern, the stock then reverses back up the chart to give another Double Top buy signal (see Figure 3.24). If you look at those two consecutive Double Tops, you will see the same pattern as the Diagonal Triple Top described in the section Variations on the Triple Top; the only difference is the sell signal in the pattern. I always think in terms of economics when I evaluate a Point and Figure chart. What is it telling me in economic terms? The forces that cause price changes in anything are supply and demand. Since these patterns are nothing more than a logical, organized method of recording supply and demand, the answer must lie in basic economic principles.

The Broadening Top formation usually takes place after a stock has run up nicely. What the formation is basically saying is that supply and demand had equal power at the point the pattern was broadening out. The Double Top buy signal was suggesting that demand was still in control. The Double Bottom was suggesting that supply had taken the helm and the uptrend was in question. The subsequent buy signal clearly showed that demand was still in control and that the stock had found enough sponsorship to move higher. When that Double Bottom sell signal is given, it alerts us to take a closer look at Relative Strength and the broad market and sector indicators before taking action. If all those things are positive, we will likely give the stock a little latitude.

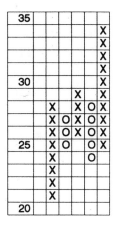

Figure 3.24 The Broadening Top formation.

The Bearish Signal Reversed

We almost always play this pattern. It is seldom seen, but when it is, you should pay close attention. Investors can detect the pattern while it forms, which allows them to plan their trade. Often, we will show the pattern and discuss the underlying stock in our report days before the pattern is complete. In this great chess game, it helps tremendously to be able to plan your moves. To qualify for the Bearish Signal Reversed, the pattern must have seven columns in it. Each column of X's must be lower than the one before and each column of O's must carry lower than the one prior to it. In the tennis match analogy, the player symbolized by X is underperforming the player symbolized by O. You can easily see this. Remember keep it simple. Look at the pattern in the context of a tennis match where each column in the pattern represents a set within the match. You can see that when a column of O's takes control of a set it carries lower than the previous column. Action like this demonstrates supply is getting stronger. When the column of X's takes control, it is unable to carry up as high as it previously did. By evaluating a pattern in this context, you can easily see supply is stronger than demand and the probability is lower prices. This action is what we characterize as the "Bearish Signal." Now let's look at the "Reversed" part of the pattern. The reversal up into a column of X's with the subsequent Double Top buy signal shows a change in this supply-demand relationship. Something has happened to cause demand not only to win a set by reversing up but to win the match by exceeding a previous top and thus giving a buy signal. What makes this buy signal more important is that it exceeds a series of lower tops. In essence, it breaks the spell. Figure 3.25 shows this pattern.

The reversal is often caused by some sort of news that is not widely disseminated or understood by Wall Street. Insiders are usually operating at this point. Ask yourself a question. Why would such a negative pattern that is being controlled by supply change abruptly midstream? Is it possible that an upcoming earnings report is likely to be better than Wall Street expects? Usually there is some fundamental change in the stock that is not widely known. Like the Triangle pattern, the results from this pattern usually happen in a quick, explosive move.

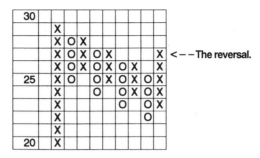

Figure 3.25 The Bearish Signal Reversed.

The Bullish Signal Reversed

This pattern is the reverse of the Bearish Signal Reversed. This pattern shows seven columns of rising bottoms and rising tops—the exact opposite of the Bearish cousin (see Figure 3.26). When the last top is made in the seventh column, the stock reverses and without a period of distribution declines to give a Double Bottom sell signal as well as break the series of rising bottoms. We have seen this happen in drug companies where FDA approval of a particular drug was not forthcoming. Someone usually knows of this before Wall Street does. There are many other reasons for the quick reversal. It is usually brought on by insiders selling. When I say insiders, I don't necessarily mean the management of the company. What I mean is simply any investor who has information that is not widely known on Wall Street. I can truly say that

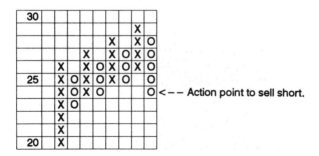

Figure 3.26 The Bullish Signal Reversed.

I have never made money on so-called inside information. When anyone calls you with a tip or posts one on an Internet chat board, the whole street usually knows it. Whenever someone gives you a tip, ask yourself what the person had to gain from telling you. In the final analysis, you will find that frequently the reason for clueing you in was that the tipster had stock to sell. This type of action runs rampant on the Internet. So be very careful what chat room you participate in. Most investors are providing free information that serves their investment objectives, not yours. Remember, there are no disinterested parties when it comes to investing. Everyone has an ax to grind some way or another. I get e-mails all the time from professional or individual clients who point out the positive fundamentals and technicals of a particular stock. Of course, they are just giving me this information to be nice, right? Wrong! In most cases, they are hoping I will recommend it in our report in the hopes we will run the stock up for them. I've had people ask me to mention a particular stock on my next CNBC appearance. I would never do that, but it shows you there are no disinterested parties on Wall Street.

In *Barron's* recently, I saw an interview with a well-known money manager. The interviewer asked him for some of his best picks, and he generously named some stocks that he thought were great values at current prices. I looked in the back section of the paper for the list of stocks that the mutual funds were buying and selling and, "low and behold," his fund was selling a stock he had just recommended for purchase. If this analyst was buying the stock, why would he publish it? So investors could compete with him in the market and possibly drive the price up? Not likely. What is likely is that he had bought the stock earlier at much better prices and was more interested in selling it. Be wary of tips, especially at cocktail parties and Internet chat rooms. Those giving the tips usually have a vested interest.

Before we leave the Bullish Signal Reversed, let's look at Figure 3.26 and discuss the pattern using the tennis match analogy. The rising tops show that demand is in control of the match. Each time the X wins a set (rises in a column), it does it more convincingly by exceeding the level it previously hit. Each time the O wins a set (declines in a column), it does so less convincingly as it is unable to decline as low as it previously did. Then, without the stock moving back and forth at the top (distribution), it declines in a straight column to give the sell signal and break the series of rising bottoms. In terms of economics, supply has taken control of the stock at 24. This is the point where you could enter a short position, especially if the stock was also violating the Bullish Support Line. It would also be a point at which if you were long, you should begin to examine that stock closer to determine what types of defensive strategies you should take. We could go through all kinds of examples of stops, but in the real world of investing it just isn't cut and dried. Many factors come into the equation, not the least of which is the investor's temperament. In most cases, long-term investors will only use the trend lines as stops. Traders have different problems that generally surround trading capital preservation. Watch for this pattern. It won't show up often but when it does, take action.

You know, one of the most asked questions I get is, "Have you got any back testing done on this method of analysis?" My answer is, yes. If you look in the first edition of this book, you will see a study done by Purdue University on the probabilities associated with the chart patterns we use. However, I have chosen not to use them in this book because it suggests this method is a science not an art. You are the most important part of the method. Yes, you! Without you—the well-educated and experienced captain of this ship—it will drift aimlessly. Like anything else in life, the more you practice and use the method, the better you will become with it. The following article explains exactly what it takes to become world class at something.

Flash of Genius*

On Becoming a Craftsman

I was cleaning up my desk to start out the new year with a clean desk and I came across this article from *Forbes* along with some of my commentary. What caught my eye was the sentence "We need to pay much more explicit attention to teaching pattern

---

Forbes, November 16, 1998.

recognition." This comment was made by Professor Herbert Simon. The article went on to say, "Simon won a Nobel Prize in Economics in 1978 for theories of decision making that turn on the nature of human expertise. His central finding was that pattern recognition is critical. The more relevant patterns at your disposal, the better your decisions will be." I found it quite interesting when he discussed chess mastery. Most would think that mastering the game of chess relates to analysis but Dr. Simon suggests that isn't the case. Success in chess relates to pattern recognition. I can picture Bobby Fischer playing Kasparov of Russia in a chess match. Each is seeing patterns on the chessboard just as we would see patterns on a stock chart or a Bullish Percent chart. On Intel's chart, it was clear to the trained eye that the stock was making higher long-term bottoms as the broad averages made lower bottoms in 1998. The untrained eye would not have picked up on this subtlety, but this pattern spoke volumes about the probable direction of Intel. It's like a color-blindness test. Have you ever taken one in a doctor's office? Most people have. The patient looks at a card with colored spots on it. The person who is not color-blind can, without difficulty, see the number within the dots. Those who are color-blind cannot. The craftsmen in Point and Figures can see patterns that the uninitiated will never see, and this ability shifts them up to a much higher plane compared with other professionals in the business. By understanding these patterns whether on a chessboard or the big board, the initiated have the confidence to act rather than react.

"What makes a good doctor, lawyer or stock picker?" Simon asks. It all relates to pattern recognition. It relates to experience as well. "Mozart composed for 14 years before he wrote any music you'd regard as world class, . . . you can tell juvenile Mozart from 18 year old Mozart." He suggests it's the same in all fields. "Bobby Fischer got to grand master title in chess in just under ten years, and so did the Polgar girl. Brain power matters but so does experience." He goes on to suggest that even your doctor has probably diagnosed your problem before you finish telling him all the symptoms. We at DWA often know the answer to portfolio questions asked by our broker clients before they finish illuminating the problem.

What Does It Take to Do World-Class Work?

No matter what profession you are in, there are those who are world class and those who are other than world class. Professor Simon says: "It takes at least ten years of hard work—say, 40 hours a week for 50 weeks a year—to begin to do world class work. We found it takes eight seconds to learn a pattern for a day, and quite a lot longer to learn it permanently. That takes you to the million pattern estimate, if you allow for certain inefficiencies in learning and also for forgetting." This is why there are relatively few professionals in the investment business who could be called world class. The term we use for it is *craftsman.* How long do you think it took a cobbler in the seventeenth century to learn his craft? How about a cooper? I surmise that it would have taken about 10 years. Those who have reached world-class level have seen approximately 1 million patterns. This is exactly why it takes so long to become world class in the investment business. So many professionals jump from one thing to the next—they never take the time to do one thing well. To be world class, you must choose something to become a craftsman in. One of our analysts, Susan Morrison, calculated that over the past 10 years, in charting about 400 stocks per day for 50 weeks a year, she has seen about 1 million stock charts. This is why she has such insight into the Point and Figure Chart patterns of stocks, sectors, and the market. The rest of the analysts at DWA have similar experience. I get asked frequently, "What will happen when everyone is doing Point and Figure analysis." My response has always been that to become truly good at it one must take years of study,and most people do not have the time or the inclination to become a craftsman at this method of analysis. Only a select few will go the distance. A method becomes self-fulfilling when investors follow a "guru" (e.g., Joe Granville in years past) and simply do what he tells them to do until the inevitable happens. These investors are not interested in becoming well versed in the investment process. They simply want someone to tell them what to do.

Here is what normally happens. A broker reads our report and gravitates to the breakout page. He looks at one symbol that says Double Top Buy Signal, buys that stock with no other analysis, and gets whacked. He then says this doesn't work and moves on to the next strategy. Every now and then, a broker will pick up my book *Point and Figure Charting* and read it. He will then begin to implement the strategy. Somewhere down the road, he will keep a few charts by hand himself. His feel for the subject then increases tremendously. He loves the new confidence he has. He continues to learn and apply the method; years later he looks back and can see a distinct difference between his abilities then and now. His journey has still much further to go to reach world class, but he is on the way. His client retention is now high as is his confidence. He now maintains 200 stocks a day and looks at many more through our Internet system. When he nears the tenth year, he is approaching world class and the number of chart patterns he has viewed is approaching 1 million. He no longer needs to read the financial newspapers, or watch the financial TV shows. Major statements made by Wall Street pundits have no effect on his thought process. He (or she) instinctively knows what to do in various market conditions. He is like a child who has totally memorized the multiplication tables, and now instinctively knows 9 times 9 equals 81.

How many of you have been doing this for longer than five years and are now feeling comfortable with this investment process? You're on the road to world class. There's nothing like being world class at something. To get there takes determination, patience, and hard work. There are many other methods of analyzing the market that you might choose, from astrology to Gann angles. Whatever you choose, go the distance, become a world-class investor. You only have one life to live.

Chapter 4

THE IMPORTANCE OF RELATIVE STRENGTH

Relative Strength (RS) is one of the primary tools we use to evaluate stocks and sectors. Over the past 10 years, we have enhanced our use of Relative Strength and now have more RS tools at our disposal to help in the stock selection process. Relative Strength, as the name implies, measures how one security is doing compared with another. You can do an RS reading on anything to determine overall strength, or outperformance, versus a market or sector index.

Since the basic objective of most investors is to outperform the averages, Relative Strength is the best way to measure outperformance or underperformance. In a practical application, Relative Strength generally allows you to let your winners run and to cut your losses short. This has been very evident in our Broker Institutes. During these Institutes, we conduct a case study that tests the attendees' understanding of what they have learned. It is a team event, whose goal is to make the most money for the imaginary client. Over the years that we have administered the case study, one of the main criteria cited for success of the winning team(s) has been paying attention to Relative Strength—focusing buying on the strong RS names, and avoiding or selling the weak RS names. We recommend that you place similar importance on Relative Strength in the management of your investments.

Different Types of Relative Strength

We use three types of Relative Strength charts. Two of the measurements pertain to the individual stock, while the third evaluates how a particular sector is faring versus the broad market. Let's take a detailed look at each of these measurements:

1. *RS versus Dow.* This is the more common and most widely used of our Relative Strength calculations. It measures how a stock is performing compared with the market in general. For this comparison, we use the Dow Jones Industrial Average. We often refer to this as the stock's *Market RS.* The Relative Strength calculation is simply done by dividing the price of the stock by the price of the Dow Jones, then multiplying by 1,000. We move the decimal point merely to have an easier number to work with. This number can then be plotted on a Point and Figure chart, using the same charting principles discussed in earlier chapters. We use the Dow Jones Industrial Average as the divisor for a stock's Market RS, but you can choose to use another market index, such as the S&P 500 or Value Line; just be consistent and always use the same index when you update your RS chart. Using the Dow Jones makes sense to us, though, since it is a price-weighted index rather than a capitalization-weighted index like the S&P 500. A price-weighted index more closely approximates how investors weight their portfolios, and more closely matches up with the one-stock, one-vote mentality of the Point and Figure research.

2. *RS versus DWA Sector Index.* This is also known as Peer Relative Strength. It measures how a stock is performing compared with its sector peers, as measured by the Dorsey, Wright Sector Indexes. For example, the Peer RS reading would measure how Microsoft (MSFT) is doing relative to other software stocks. This RS chart allows you to determine the strongest stocks within a particular sector, or what we like to call "the best in class." The Peer RS calculation is equally simple, and is done by dividing the price of the stock by the appropriate DWA Sector Index chart, then multiplying by 100 to come up with a plottable number. The DWA Sector Indexes were created for each broad industry group we follow. These DWA Sector Indexes are equal-weighted and include a nice mix of stocks with varying

capitalization, unlike the exchange sector indexes, which tend to be more narrow and capitalization-weighted.

3. *Sector Relative Strength.* This RS reading measures how a particular sector is performing compared with the market in general. For example, Sector RS would measure how the Retail sector is performing versus the market in general. This allows you to determine which sectors are outperforming the market. Because sector risk is the greatest contributor to price fluctuation in a stock, it is extremely important to determine Sector Relative Strength. The Sector RS calculation is similar to those previously discussed. Once a week, each DWA Sector Index and each Exchange index, such as the Retail Index (RLX), is divided by the S&P 500 (SPX), then multiplied by 100. Those resulting readings are then plotted on their respective RS charts.

How to Calculate Relative Strength

Now that you understand the three basic Relative Strength charts we use, let's look at an actual example of each type of RS calculation.

Stock Relative Strength versus the Market

$$\frac{\text{Stock price}}{\text{DJIA}} \times 1,000 = \text{Stock RS versus Market}$$

- Say, for example, XYZ was at 85 and the Dow was at 11,500.
- If we divided 85 by 11,500 and moved the decimal (0.00739 × 1,000), we would get 7.39.
- We would plot this number on the RS chart of XYZ.
- Let's say the following week the stock fell to 80 and the Dow dropped to 10,000. (We do our Relative Strength calculations once a week using Tuesday's closing data.)
- We now divide 80 by 10,000 and get 8 (0.008 × 1,000).

In this case, the stock dropped in price, the Dow dropped, but the Relative Strength reading went up. This tells us that the stock is performing better than the Dow, and it is possible that the only reason it has fallen in price is that the overall market has dragged it down. These positive RS stocks will likely be the first ones to snap back once the overall market does. As a general rule, stocks with positive Relative Strength versus the market will typically outperform the market during a bullish market condition, and will be more likely to hold up and weather the storm in a bearish market condition.

Stock Relative Strength versus DWA Sector Index (Peer RS)

$$\frac{\text{Stock price}}{\text{DWA sector index price}} \times 100 = \text{Peer RS reading}$$

- Let's say Microsoft (MSFT) was at 87.31 and the DWA Software Index was 190.50.
- If we divided 87.31 by 190.50 and moved the decimal (0.4583 × 100), we would get 45.83.
- We would plot this number on the Peer RS chart of MSFT.
- Let's say the following week MSFT rises to 89.62 and the DWA Software Index moves up to 200.55. (We do the calculations once a week using Tuesday's closing data.)
- We now divide 89.62 by 200.55 and get 44.68 (0.4468 × 100).

In this case, MSFT rose in price, the DWA Software Sector Index moved higher, but the Peer Relative Strength reading for MSFT went down. Now, let's substitute Oracle (ORCL) for Microsoft in the previous example:

- Let's say, Oracle Systems (ORCL) was at 16.06 and the DWA Software Index was 190.50.
- If we divided 16.06 by 190.50 and moved the decimal (0.0843 × 100), we would get 8.43.
- We would plot this number on the Peer RS chart of ORCL.
- Let's say the following week ORCL rises to 18.38 and the DWA Software Index moves up to 200.55. (We do the calculations once a week using Tuesday's closing data.)
- We now divide 18.38 by 200.55 and get 9.16 (0.0916 × 100).

In this case, ORCL rose in price, the DWA Software Sector Index moved higher, and the Peer RS reading for ORCL moved up.

This comparative example demonstrates how ORCL is outperforming its Software sector peers, while MSFT is underperforming its peers. ORCL's Peer RS reading moved up from 8.43 to 9.16, while MSFT's Peer RS reading fell from 45.83 to 44.68. This particular type of Relative Strength reading allows you to identify the stocks that are the strongest of the group—the best in class—and these are the stocks that will likely perform the best within that group.

Sector Relative Strength

$$\frac{\text{Sector index}}{\text{SPX}} \times 100 = \text{Sector RS reading}$$

We will calculate the Sector RS reading for three indexes, the DWA Retail Index, the S&P Retail Index (RLX), and the DWA Drug Index:

- Say, for example, the DWA Retail Index was at 218, the RLX was at 774, and the DWA Drug Index was at 276, while the S&P 500 (SPX) was at 1,340.
- If you do the appropriate division, the Sector RS readings would be:
    DWA Retail Index = 16.27
  S&P Retail Index (RLX) = 57.76
    DWA Drug Index = 20.59
- These Sector RS readings would then be plotted on the respective Sector RS chart.
- Let's say the following Tuesday, the DWA Retail Index rose to 231, the RLX moved up to 801, and the DWA Drug Index rose to 278, while the SPX rallied to 1355.
- We now divide each of these numbers by the SPX and get:
    DWA Retail Index = 17.04
  S&P Retail Index (RLX) = 59.11
    DWA Drug Index = 20.51

In this comparative example, all three of these sector indexes moved higher in price along with the market, but only the retail indexes improved on a Relative Strength basis. Said another way, the DWA Retail Index and S&P Retail Index (RLX) outperformed the market, while the DWA Drug Index slightly underperformed the market. Groups that are exhibiting positive Sector Relative Strength versus the market are the ones to gravitate to when deciding which sectors to buy.

How to Interpret the RS Chart

In evaluating the RS chart, buy signals are given when a column of X's exceeds a previous column of X's (also referred to as *positive RS*). Conversely, sell signals are given when a column of O's exceeds a previous column of O's (also referred to as *negative RS*). The pattern doesn't matter with the RS chart (e.g., whether it is a double top or triple top buy signal), just whether the most recent signal is a buy signal or a sell signal. As well, the RS "reading" doesn't matter. In fact, the only reason I need a number is to plot the RS chart. Once the chart is plotted, that is where I look for guidance. Is the RS chart in X's or O's? Is it on a buy signal or a sell signal? Unlike other Relative Strength methods, the number is unimportant. Positive Relative Strength suggests the stock will outperform the market, while negative Relative Strength suggests the stock will underperform the market. But just because a stock has positive RS doesn't mean that it can't fall in price; it merely means that it should not fall as much as the market averages. It is also important to watch for RS reversals, or changes in columns, for shorter term guidance. If the most recent column on the RS chart is X's, it suggests the stock (or sector) is outperforming in the near term; conversely when the most recent column on the RS chart is O's, it demonstrates underperformance by the stock (or sector) in the near term. The best combination for the RS chart is to be on a buy signal and in a column of X's; the worst is for it to be on an RS sell signal and in O's.

The beauty of Relative Strength is that it can keep you invested in strong stocks for a long time, allowing you to participate in the gains. Think about it for a second. If a stock continues to have positive RS for years on end, all while the market averages continue to record notable gains, what does that say for the particular stock? Well, the only way a stock can continue to have positive RS versus a market that is moving higher, is for it to move higher in price, too. Relative Strength allows you to let your profits run. This statement fits with the fact that a stock's (market) RS signal will typically last about two years; and generally speaking, it tells us the overall expected trend of the stock. Let's look at General Electric (GE) and Cisco Systems (CSCO). GE's Relative Strength chart has been positive since April 1993. CSCO has been on a Relative Strength buy signal since October 1992. During these respective time frames, GE has risen approximately 580 percent, while CSCO is up roughly 6500 percent!

Now, another beneficial aspect of Relative Strength is it allows you to get off a horse not running the race and to move to one that is. This is where it's imperative to keep up with weekly changes in Relative Strength. From week to week, changes in Relative Strength will occur—some stocks will move from an RS buy signal to an RS sell signal and vice versa, and some will show changes in column on their Relative Strength chart. The point is, you must constantly monitor the Relative Strength chart for changes. If you own a stock that has just given a Relative Strength sell signal, it is time to evaluate whether that stock should be sold. Also, by knowing when a stock has given a new RS buy signal, or reversed up into a column of X's, it will alert you to a potential turnaround situation. A great example of this is Wal-Mart (WMT).

Wal-Mart (WMT) had been one of the darling stocks of the late 1980s and early 1990s, an institutional favorite, if you will. The stock had rewarded investors justly for years, evidenced by looking at Wal-Mart's Relative Strength chart, which was on a buy signal for over a decade. But the tide changed in August 1993. The RS chart for Wal-Mart gave a sell signal, suggesting this stock would underperform the market for some time. This is exactly what happened, as shown in Figure 4.1. WMT treaded water, at best, for the next several years, while the market averages recorded phenomenal gains. This Relative Strength change was right on the money. From August 1993 to early 1997, you would have been better off putting your dollars in passbook

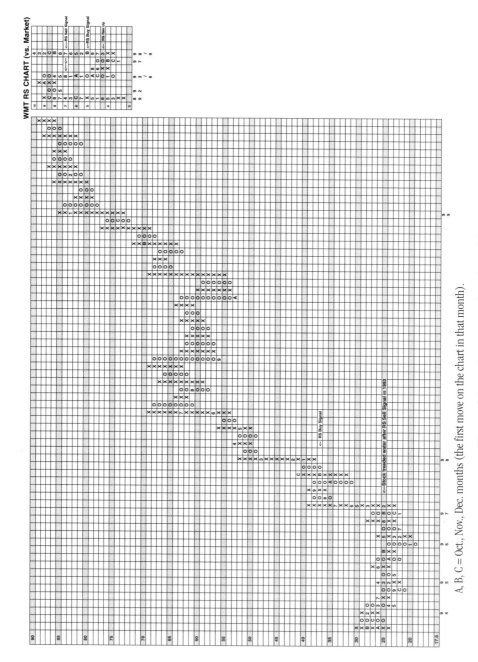

A, B, C = Oct., Nov., Dec. months (the first move on the chart in that month).

Figure 4.1 Wal-Mart Stores (WMT) trend chart.

savings than investing in Wal-Mart. Better yet, imagine if you had swapped your Wal-Mart for GE in 1993!

But just as things turned gloomy for WMT in 1993, they brightened back up in 1997. In March 1997, Wal-Mart reversed back up into a column of X's on its Relative Strength chart, coinciding with a big-base breakout on its trend chart. This reversal in RS for WMT occurred at the same time the Retail Sector Relative Strength was improving. This Relative Strength change made us refocus our attention on WMT. The RS continued to improve for WMT as the year progressed, and by November 1997, Wal-Mart moved high enough to break a previous top on its RS chart, thereby giving a Relative Strength buy signal. This Relative Strength buy signal demonstrated that WMT was outperforming the market, and would likely continue to do so. All this was occurring during the onset of the Asian flu—the markets were in turmoil, yet WMT was holding its ground. The stock merely went through a Shakeout pattern, then completed a Bullish Catapult formation. This was a stock screaming to be bought. WMT promptly gained 100 percent within a year.

This leads us to a discussion on market divergence. It behooves you to pay attention to Relative Strength changes as they occur. It is also important to use Relative Strength to determine market divergence during times of weakness in the overall market. As discussed in later chapters, our market indicators will help dictate whether you should be playing offense or defense against the market. When defense is recommended, it becomes necessary to evaluate your portfolio positions closely. This is a great time to get rid of your underperforming stocks. If those stocks haven't kept up while the market has headed higher, they are not likely to hold up well if the market moves lower. Relative Strength becomes a valuable tool to help determine which stocks get sold and which stocks are kept. Given that the market goes up two thirds of the time, and down one third of the time, going to 100 percent cash by selling all your positions is a huge bet. A more sensible approach is to weed out the poor RS performers and sell those stocks to raise the cash level in your portfolio. Keep the strong, positive RS stocks since they will be more resistant to decline, and will likely snap back once the market gets back on solid footing.

Wal-Mart proved its ability to snap back in 1998. By then the Asian flu was in full swing, Russia was defaulting on its debt, and its currency was collapsing—all serving to push the equity markets into a tailspin. After topping at 69 in July, WMT begrudgingly fell to an October low of 53, right above its Bullish Support Line. We had experienced a meltdown in the stock market, but WMT managed to move higher on its Relative Strength chart. By definition, this meant that WMT had held up better than the market during the correction; market divergence is very easy to pick out during a market decline—just look at the RS chart (Figure 4.1). Therefore, it was not surprising to see Wal-Mart snap right back once the market bottomed in October 1998. The stock rocketed from 53 to 106 in six months—another 100 percent gain.

There is another aspect, or way to visualize market divergence and Relative Strength. During market corrections, it is important to observe whether a stock (or group of stocks in the same sector) is showing higher bottoms on its trend chart, while the market averages are making lower bottoms. Often there is a change in leadership after a market correction. In many cases, subtle signs will occur even before the market as a whole has bottomed out. Intel (INTC) was a good example of this in 1998. The semiconductor sector had been out of favor, so to speak, compared to other technology sectors, with the group topping out early in the year; Intel put in its high in February 1998, well before the market topped out. By June, INTC and other semiconductor stocks had fallen precipitously while the market flew to new all-time highs. Then all of a sudden, we began to notice subtle changes in the chart of Intel. The trend chart of Intel, which is shown in Figure 4.2, says it all. Each time the market sold off further, to make a new bottom or test its old lows, Intel was showing higher bottoms. It was showing a "positive" divergence from the market. The trend chart itself was speaking volumes about the future prospects of Intel. It was displaying improvement in Relative Strength. This phenomenon was not relegated just to Intel, other semiconductor stocks showed a similar pattern; a change in sector sponsorship was underway. Intel, the anointed benchmark stock of the group, vaulted 86 percent within the next few months, carrying its sector brethren along with it.

This Intel example displays how, as Yogi Berra used to say, "You can observe a lot just by watching." Changes in sector

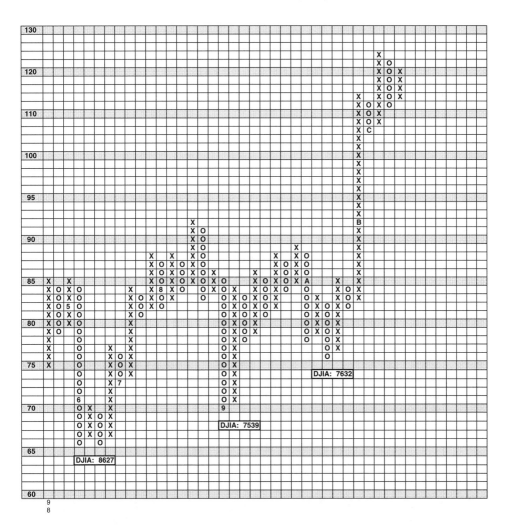

Figure 4.2   Intel Corp. (INTC) trend chart.

sponsorship often present themselves in the form of an RS change, noticeable right on the trend chart as was the case with Intel; or you may see a cluster of stocks in the same group give Relative Strength buy signals all around the same time. In October 1990, we noticed the Relative Strength charts of Dominion Resources, Houston Industries, Scana Corporation, and Texas Utilities turned positive for the first time in four or more years. This positive RS change was prescient not only for the utility sector, but boded well for the economy and market as a whole. One month later, our market indicators gave major buy signals. A similar case happened in November 1991. In one week, we saw Hercules, Briggs & Stratton, and Cummins Engine turn positive on their Relative Strength charts after being negative for years. The message was clear—the cyclical stocks were ready to take the lead.

It can be equally important to pay attention to Relative Strength changes in columns. When a stock reverses back up into a column of X's on its RS chart, it is displaying positive near-term outperformance. This can be helpful in two ways. Let's say you have a stock, such as EMC Corporation (EMC), that is on a longer term Relative Strength buy signal. The RS chart reversed to O's in April 1999, suggesting this stock would take a breather. The stock did mark time for a few months, but in September EMC recorded a reversal back up into X's on its Relative Strength chart (see Figure 4.3). The RS chart was on a buy signal and now back in a column of X's, the best RS combination. This implied that EMC was ready to take the baton again, and boy did it. In the next 11 months, EMC was up 149 percent, the Dow Jones was up 5.5 percent, and the Nasdaq Composite gained 36.5 percent.

An RS change in column (to X's) can also be helpful in identifying a turnaround situation. This can be especially true if the Relative Strength chart had previously been in a long column of O's down, either because the stock itself has been shunned or because the sector as a whole has been out of favor. Such instances can result in that long tail of O's on the RS chart. As a result, to technically get a buy signal on the RS chart, the column of X's back up would have to travel a long way to break the previous column of X's. For this to occur, the stock will have likely already experienced a huge move to the upside. Therefore, after a Long Tail Down, it is acceptable to consider an RS reversal to X's as a buy signal. This particular situation happened with Ascend Communications (ASND). We jokingly had renamed the stock "Descend Communications" as a consequence of its fallen angel status. But after declining to the low 20s by the end of 1997, ASND started to base out. By late January 1998, the stock started edging higher, its trend chart improved, and the Relative Strength chart reversed up into X's from a Long Tail Down. That suggested the winds of change were blowing. ASND never looked back,

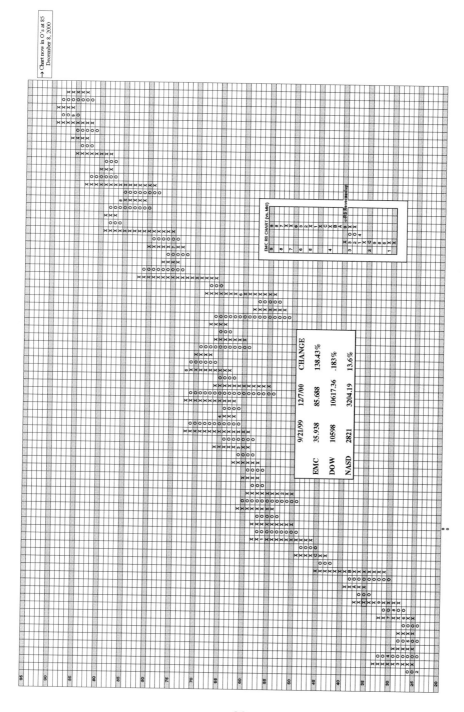

Figure 4.3 EMC Corporation (EMC) trend chart.

moving from the low 20s to over 100 by June 1999, when it was taken over by Lucent (LU). We also noticed a similar occurrence in 2000. Stocks such as FMC Corporation (FMC), Emerson Electric (EMR), and Duke Energy (DUK) all reversed up (in X's) on their RS charts in late 1999 or early 2000, hinting that the NYSE type names were ready to move after having been forsaken vis-à-vis technology stocks. These three stocks were up 40 to 50 percent each at the end of 2000. Not bad, considering what a tough year 2000 was.

With respect to RS changes in column to O's, you want to look at it exactly opposite as laid out in the preceding paragraph. Strong RS stocks that reverse to O's portend lower prices or possibly a period of consolidation for the stock, a breather if you will. At such time, positions in that stock could be lightened up, or possibly hedged by selling calls against the stock. Overall weak RS stocks that reverse back to O's are dangerous, and in most cases should be avoided, or potentially shorted. A case in point is WorldCom (WCOM). This telecom stock gave a Relative Strength sell signal in May 2000 (see Figure 4.4). In June and July, WCOM managed to rally along with the Nasdaq enough so that its RS chart showed a reversal up into X's in July (yet longer term, the RS chart was still on a sell signal). This upside RS reversal was short-lived for WorldCom. The RS chart reversed right back down into O's in August. A hasty retreat ensued, and by November WCOM had been cut in half—falling from 36 to 14½.

Peer RS Interpretation

The evaluation and interpretation of the Peer Relative Strength chart is the same as the stock's RS chart versus the market. Similarly, we are interested in the most recent signal on the Peer RS chart, and current column the chart is in, be it X's or O's. Here, as well, the best combination for a Peer RS chart is to be on a buy signal and in a column of X's. Since Peer RS measures how a stock is doing relative to its sector compatriots, a positive Peer RS (buy signal) reading implies the stock is outperforming an index of its related peers. The purpose of Peer RS is to steer you to the stock(s) that will likely perform the best within any given sector.

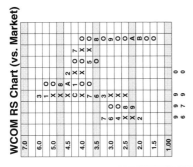

WCOM RS Chart (vs. Market)

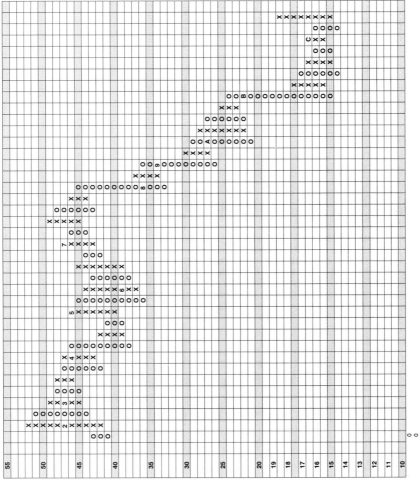

Figure 4.4 WorldCom Inc. (WCOM) trend chart.

A good illustration of this is the Software sector. In early April 2000, Adobe Systems (ADBE) gave a Peer RS buy signal while Microsoft (MSFT) was already on a Peer RS sell signal. A subsequent evaluation of their performance in December 2000 showed ADBE was up 45 percent since April, while MSFT was down 34 percent during that time frame. This is a simple example of how you can potentially choose the right sector to play, but not necessarily the right stock. Peer RS endeavors to guide you to the best in class, in this case to ADBE rather than MSFT. A good general rule, then, is to focus your buying on those stocks that have positive Relative Strength versus both the market and their peers. This will greatly help in narrowing the list of potential buy candidates down to a reasonable number.

Peer Relative Strength becomes extremely beneficial when a sector rotates back into favor. We all know that sectors rotate in and out of season just as vegetables and fruits do in the grocery store. Therefore, to achieve consistent returns over time, it is crucial to maneuver in and out of sectors as the indicators dictate. (We have numerous sector evaluation tools at our disposal to help guide us to the right sector(s) at the right time; we discuss these in more detail later.) The Peer RS chart is quite valuable in this maneuvering process, specifically when it comes down to actually selecting the stock(s) you want to play within that sector. When you have a group move back into favor after reaching an oversold, washed-out condition, there typically are very few stocks that have been outperforming the market averages (exhibiting positive market RS). Therefore, you must turn to Peer RS to guide you to the best stocks within the group. By identifying the stocks within the sector that are outperforming their peers, you are able to find the strongest of the group—they are the ones most likely to perform the best as the sector strengthens. The Search/Sort function on our online database is extremely effective in handling this task. We have a favorite search that we conduct when trying to find the best stocks in a sector that have rotated back into favor. Let's assume that the Telecom sector have just moved back into favor from oversold territory; the search criteria would go as follows:

- All stocks that are on an RS buy signal versus the market, but allow for the most recent column to be either X's or O's.

- All stocks whose Peer RS chart is on a buy signal and in a column of X's.
- All stocks that are members of the Telecom sector that have given a buy signal.

The results of the query would give us a list of Telecom stocks that have been outperforming the market over the longer term (denoted by the RS buy signal versus the market). Because we allowed the columns in the query to be either in X's or O's, however, the stocks might not be outperforming in the short run. With respect to the sector, we chose to have the stocks displayed to be on RS buy signals and in X's suggesting outperformance within their sector on both a short-term and long-term basis (denoted by Peer RS buy signal in X's reading). This list of candidates could be narrowed down further by requiring the stocks to be fundamentally sound. With a couple of clicks of the mouse, this query would allow us to reduce the number of potential buy candidates down to a very reasonable number. A further technical review could then be administered to decide which stock(s) should be bought from this list. This process would pinpoint those stocks within the sector with the best Relative Strength, and as you have learned, it is these stocks that will likely lead the sector up as it strengthens. Sounds like a lot of work doesn't it? I recently heard Justice Thomas of the Supreme Court talking to some high school students. He said his father told him, "Hard work doesn't guarantee success. However, success cannot be achieved without hard work." It's the same in investing. Remember your hard-earned money is at stake here.

Another application of Peer RS involves sector divergence. As stated earlier, the importance of paying attention to Relative Strength changes, and this also applies to Peer RS. If you have representation in a particular sector, there may be times you should swap out of one name and into another because of a Peer RS change. For example, let's say you currently own Talbot's (TLB) in the Retail sector, and this sector continues to be an area where you want exposure. TLB then gives a sell signal on its Peer RS chart, and the technical picture in general has deteriorated. One strategy would be to swap out of the Talbot's into a stock with positive Peer Relative Strength, such as Safeway (SWY). This allows you to have sector representation in Retail, but realigns the token position to one with better Peer RS, which by definition has a better likelihood of outperforming the discarded Talbot's.

Sector Relative Strength Interpretation

When interpreting the Sector Relative Strength chart, the process is basically the same as outlined previously. In like fashion, we are concerned with the most recent signal on the RS chart, and the most recent column the RS chart is in. Given that Sector RS measures how a particular sector is performing compared with the overall market and that "sector" is the greatest contributor to price fluctuation in a stock, it is imperative to evaluate this on an ongoing basis. (We can't emphasize this point enough!) Those sectors exhibiting positive Relative Strength versus the market are the ones to focus on for new buying. Sector RS buy signals are given when a column of X's exceeds a previous column of X's. But of equal importance for Sector RS is what the most recent column is on the RS chart. This is the one slight difference in RS evaluation (compared with a stock's Market RS or Peer RS). When a sector index reverses up into a column of X's on its RS chart, we consider that to be a buy signal. Utmost attention is paid to column changes for Sector RS, because such a reversal will often be the beginning signs of a significant switch in sponsorship for the particular sector. We still regard the best reading for the Sector RS chart as being on a buy signal and in a column of X's.

Probably the most valuable aspect of Sector Relative Strength is that it not only steers you to the sector(s) moving into favor, but keeps you invested in sectors that are market leaders, even if the sector(s) is considered overbought by other measures. This really is why we first started charting Sector Relative Strength. Back in 1996 to 1997, the best performing sector was the Bank/Financial group. This sector had performed very well in 1995, after bottoming out in fairly oversold territory. The group raced to an extremely overbought condition, as measured by the sector Bullish Percent chart, by October 1995. Member stocks, such as Citigroup (C) and Chase Manhattan (CMB), recorded phenomenal gains during this time. Citigroup posted a 70 percent gain, while Chase Manhattan gained a remarkable 100 percent. But the upmove didn't stop there. Both Chase and Citigroup doubled in price during the 1996 to 1997 time frame. This is where Sector Relative Strength came into the equation (see Figure 4.5).

We became less enthused with the Bank sector in late 1995 because, as stated, the group was overbought. Our cautious approach

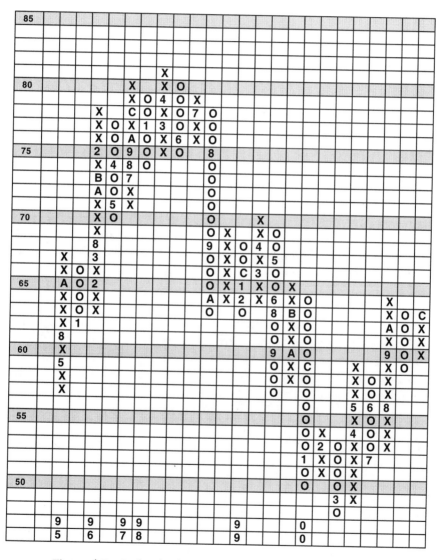

Figure 4.5 Bank Index (BKX) versus S&P 500 Relative Strength chart.

to new recommendations in the group was, in hindsight, a mistake. But as we always endeavor to do, we learned from our mistake and developed our Sector Relative Strength charts. In assessing the Sector RS for the Bank sector, we realized that the group had been outperforming the market, hands down! The Bank group sneakily ascended to top dog status despite being in the believed shadow of technology stocks. The lesson here, don't judge a sector by its cover. Be willing to delve below the surface and evaluate the group's Relative Strength chart. In application, move to those sectors rotating into favor, stay with those sectors that continue to exhibit positive RS, and eschew those groups that turn negative on their Sector RS charts (reverse to O's or break a previous bottom). Bottom line, if you hope to outperform the market, you had better be invested in those sectors with the best Relative Strength.

As shown, Sector RS enables you to pinpoint those groups that deserve your investment dollars. The obvious course of action is to buy the stock(s) in a strong RS sector, which possess positive RS versus the market and their peers. An alternative is to use options or exchange-traded funds to take advantage of a Sector Relative Strength change. (In Chapter 8, we discuss, in detail, both of these products.) Let's assume the DWA Semiconductor Index and the PHLX Semiconductor Index (SOX) have both just given a Relative Strength buy signal. Rather than select a particular stock or two to buy in that group, an alternative would be to buy index calls on the SOX, or to buy the Semiconductor Holders (SMH). This avenue gives you leverage and/or diversification all in one simple transaction. A caveat to this strategy is the "weighting" issue.

As mentioned early on, our DWA sector indexes are equal weighted, whereas the majority of the exchange-traded indexes, such as the SOX, are capitalization-weighted. Therefore, a couple of stocks can be responsible for the bulk of the move in an index. For example, three stocks—Intel (INTC), Applied Materials (AMAT), and Texas Instruments (TXN)—are responsible for 50 percent of the move in the SMH. Similarly, 50 percent of the move in the S&P Retail Index (RLX) is attributable to Wal-Mart (WMT) and Home Depot (HD). All we are trying to say here is be aware of what makes an index or Holder (Exchange Traded Fund) move. If you buy the SMH when the Semiconductor Index RS gives a buy signal, realize you are placing a big bet on the prospects of INTC, AMAT, and TXN.

Along those same lines, let's say the RLX gives a Relative Strength buy signal, but we do not see the DWA Retail Index follow suit. The advisable strategy here, if you want to take advantage of the RS change, would be to buy either WMT or HD versus a small cap retailer. The good news is the DWA sector index Relative Strength charts will typically move in tandem with the exchange indexes, but not always, so act accordingly. By and large though, to ascertain a truer measure of a sector's Relative Strength, focus on the DWA sector index RS charts since they are equal-weighted and have a good mix of small, mid-, and large cap representation.

Tying It All Together

Over the course of this chapter we have tried to impress on you the importance of Relative Strength. As presented, we use three different RS calculations in our research. You have learned the definition and how to calculate and interpret each RS chart. The significance of each RS measurement by itself is notable, but the power lies in bringing all three together. Individual pictures or frames may tell a short story, but strung together they can make a movie. Therefore, to tie the pieces together, let's look at examples of using all three RS calculations concurrently.

You have learned that Relative Strength will help you navigate the uncertain waters of the stock market. RS can guide you to new opportunities, while also steering you away from danger. In April 2000, this was never more evident.

The month of April heralded in lasting changes for the year 2000. Technology stocks were so hot they made the Chicago Fire look like dinner by candlelight. All the market pundits were tossing around a new word, bifurcation, referencing the disjointing of the NYSE and OTC market. The NYSE stocks were considered the forsaken stepchildren of the equity market, while the OTC market, heavy-laden with tech issues, assumed the spoiled brat, only child role. We all know this bifurcation didn't last; instead a role reversal occurred. The NYSE, which has a large proportion of financial-related stocks as members, stole the baton from the OTC. Heck, it didn't just steal the baton, it kicked butt. The proper course of action was to refocus attention on such sectors as Banks, Insurance, Utilities, and Finance, among others, at the expense of technology-related sectors, such as Telecom. Unfortunately, many investors didn't make the required shift. Yet, all they needed to do was consult the Relative Strength charts. Once investors bought into the media's portrayal of tech stocks being the be-all and end-all of the investment arena, they had a hard time thinking out of the box. Virtually every article in the periodicals proclaimed that technology was the place to have your serious money invested. Well, it all blew up like a "Black Cat" firecracker on the Fourth of July.

In Figure 4.6, Bank of New York (BK) and its related RS charts are shown. In this instance, it is easy to see the positive RS shift by this stock and the Bank sector. BK reversed up into X's on its Market RS chart in April, while the Bank Index (BKX) reversed up and gave a Relative Strength buy signal versus the market. BK's Peer RS chart was already in X's, and it continued to get stronger. This was telling us a change was at hand. More evidence existed. The Insurance sector similarly reversed up on its Relative Strength charts (IUX and DWA Insurance Index) in April. American International Group (AIG), a premier insurance stock, chalked up a gain of roughly 45 percent from April 2000 to the end of the year, and Bank of New York's move wasn't paltry, gaining 23 percent during that time frame.

The real darkhorse of 2000, though, was Electric Utilities. This sector rotated back into favor (on its sector Bullish Percent chart), reversing up from very oversold levels. Again, the Sector Relative Strength chart spoke volumes. In Figure 4.7, the PHLX Utility Sector index (UTY) is shown reversing up into a column of X's in April, displaying outperformance versus the market. The RS reading continued to move higher as the year progressed, logging in one X after another. Around the same time, we noticed member stocks, such as Duke Energy (DUK) and Dominion Resources (D), were reversing up on their RS charts versus the market, too. Again, you can observe a lot just by watching. Our money managers, Mike Moody and Harold Parker, did exactly that. They noticed the significant change in Electric Utilities and took action by purchasing

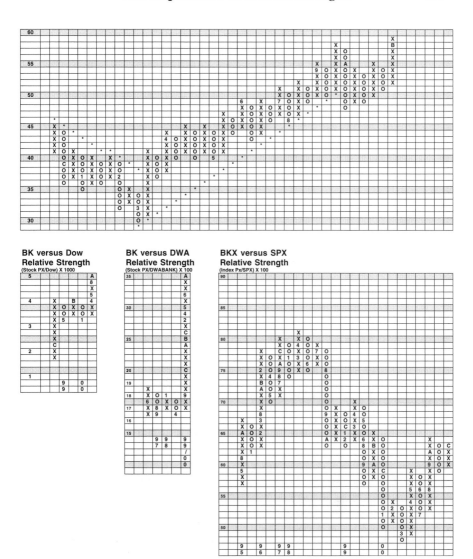

Figure 4.6 Bank of New York (BK) trend chart.

PECO (PE), which later changed its name to Exelon (EXC). EXC was also exhibiting positive RS, having reversed up into X's on its RS chart in February 2000. Who would have ever guessed that EXC would turn out to be one of their best performers for the year? EXC was up roughly 60 percent for the year, and the Electric

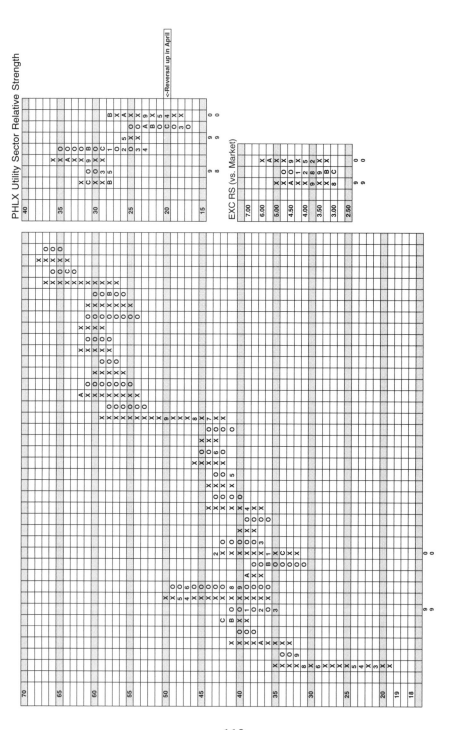

Figure 4.7 Exelon Corp. (EXC) trend chart.

Utilities sector was the best performing group for the year! Amazing. Can you imagine an investor who had bought into the Internet/technology scenario, even considering the purchase of a utility? Why—Utilities don't go up 50 percent a week. Utilities are for old people who need dividends. Not for investors looking to build wealth. Well, wrong again. Technology turned into the wealth destruction sector while Utilities were the wealth generation sector. That is why I have said time and again: Everything that is written in the general stock market media publications is designed to make you do the wrong thing.

Just as the Banks, Insurance, and Utility Relative Strength charts were shouting "buy," the Telecom Sector Relative Strength was crying "sell." In April 2000, the DWA Telephone Index and the Amex Telecom Index (XTC) both reversed down into a column of O's on their respective Relative Strength charts versus the market. What a killer this was. This negative reversal came after months and months of outperformance by the group and was an accurate forecast of bad things to come. At the same time that the RS was faltering, the sector had given a sell signal after reaching overbought territory (on its sector Bullish Percent chart). Figure 4.8 shows these two sector RS reversals. The wavering RS condition of the group was none too evident in Qualcomm (QCOM). This stock alone foretold the impending train wreck that was ahead. QCOM had been the homecoming queen of tech land. But its crown started to show tarnish early in 2000. The stock topped out in January at 200, despite the stratospheric price target of 1,000 bestowed on it by a Wall Street analyst. A series of lower tops were formed on its trend chart and numerous sell signals were given. Then in April, QCOM's crown was knocked off its head when it gave a Relative Strength sell signal (see Figure 4.9). Sound familiar? Remember, the Telecom Sector RS charts also gave sell signals in April. In a matter of a few months, QCOM had fallen to a low of 51½, a far cry from 1,000!

The moral of the story? Beauty is in the eye of the beholder. Imagine what pain could have been avoided by numerous investors if they had sold the homecoming queen, Qualcomm, and bought the homely Exelon (EXC). Relative Strength has no bias, it tells you like it is. By making Relative Strength a key component to your sector and stock evaluation, you will increase your odds of success. It's as simple as that.

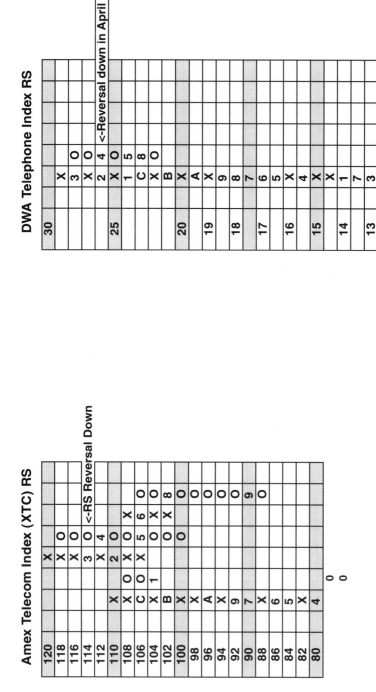

Figure 4.8 RS versus S&P 500.

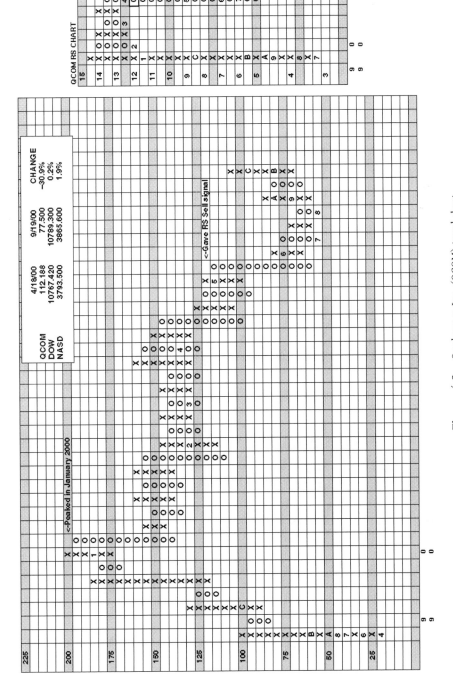

Figure 4.9 Qualcomm Inc. (QCOM) trend chart.

113

Chapter 5

THE NEW YORK STOCK EXCHANGE AND OTC BULLISH PERCENT CONCEPT

The Most Important Market Indicators

Introducing the NYSE Bullish Percent Index

This chapter on the New York Stock Exchange (NYSE) Bullish Percent covers a critical area of investment strategy (see Figure 5.1A). It is of paramount importance that you grasp this concept thoroughly. This index is our main coach and dictates our general market posture. Since my first book was published, our experience with this concept has strengthened my conviction that this is the absolute best market indicator. This index, in combination with the Nasdaq Bullish Percent, has guided our decisions through the murky markets of 1999 and 2000 with flying colors.

It wasn't until January 1987 that I began to fully understood what the Bullish Percent Index was all about. That was the month my partner and I started Dorsey, Wright & Associates. Before that, I was Director of Options Strategy at a large regional brokerage firm. Although my department was self-contained, in that we did our own research and never piggybacked off the firm's recommendations, we did use another outside service for our intermediate-term

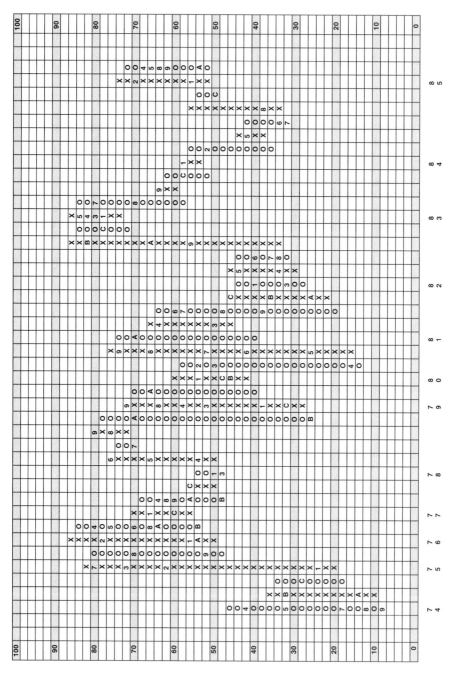

Figure 5.1A NYSE Bullish Percent, 1974–1985.

116

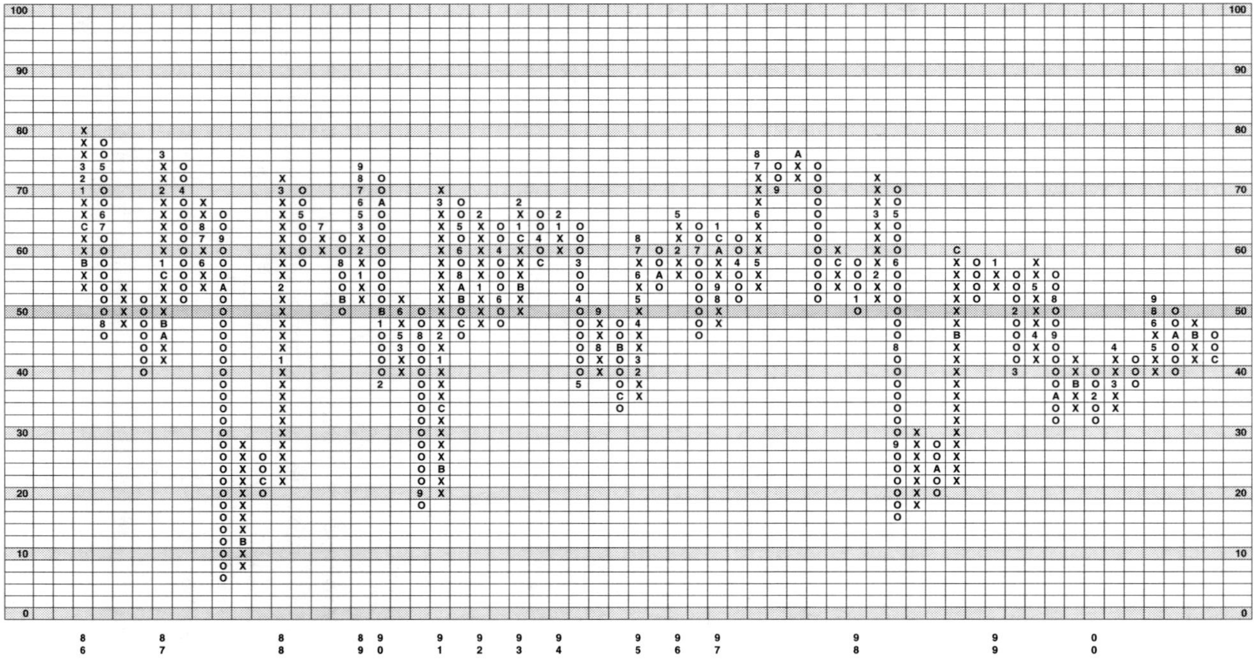

Figure 5.1B NYSE Bullish Percent, 1986–2000.

market outlook in addition to the Bullish Percent Index. I am an adamant believer in the KISS principle ("keep it simple stupid"), from investing to running a company. When we started our own company, I wanted to keep the game plan simple by sticking with the basics, and this continued to draw me back to the Bullish Percent concept I had used as Director of Options Strategy. What we found is that when the market in general had an upward bias the call recommendations generally worked. When the general market was losing ground, the call recommendations did not work as well, but the put recommendations worked really well. In other words, we found that the first step in our game plan for investing was to determine the general direction of the market. Was the market supporting higher prices or not?

This concept has been numerically quantified by several studies including one by the University of Chicago and another described in the book *The Latant Statistical Structure of Securities Price Changes* by Benjamin F. King. What these studies quantified is that 75 percent to 80 percent of the risk in any individual stock is in the market and the sector. Only 20 percent of the risk in any individual stock is related directly to that issue. Therefore, as we began building our business, we put tremendous credence in the Bullish Percent concept to tell us whether the tide was rising or falling in the market, and this guided our recommended strategies in the market. I have used this Bullish Percent concept now through every kind of market you can imagine including the 1999 and 2000 market mentioned earlier. We have successfully negotiated the crash and subsequent recovery of 1987, the recession and war in the Middle East during 1990 to 1991, the stealth bear market of 1994 and subsequent phenomenal bull market for the next several years, the bear market/Asian crisis of 1998, the bull market in indexes and bear market in stocks from 1998 to 2000, and the OTC meltdown of 2000. As the different types of markets have come and gone, I am even more impressed with how the Bullish Percent concept saw us through each market in fine form. Some markets are more volatile than others and require more vigilance, but they don't differ much from a football game. Some games are marked by many turnovers while others are marked by long periods of possession of the ball. Still other games are defined by how a certain team played defense. The stock market is the same way.

Every game is different, but the process and rules of playing the game never change. It is imperative that you learn this concept well, and keep it in the forefront of all your market decisions. The Point and Figure method of analysis is not a science as most would like it to be. It is, however, an art. H_2O in the stock market does not necessarily equal water. The more you use this Bullish Percent concept, the better you will be at interpreting it and thus better at the investment process. Remember, you are an integral part of this whole program; nothing works without your involvement.

Do You Have an Operating System?

During the 1980s, the market pretty much went up. This decade made the reputations of many investment advisers, who then slipped back into obscurity in the 1990s. We primarily focused on the option stock universe in the beginning, and to a lesser degree on the general market of stocks that did not have options attached to them. As mentioned, stocks generally rose during this period, so the focus was on catching the next rising star. The 1980s were wild indeed. Things were popping, and the listed derivatives market was only about 7 years old, having debuted in April 1973. By the time the 1980s rolled around, options derivatives were the fastest game in town. If I were asked to define that period with one word, it would be *overleverage*. It seemed everyone had a stake in the game. By 1987, the game had gotten easy and everyone, it seemed, had become comfortable with the state of the market. Rising prices translated into easy money in options. Until October 1987, that is.

Misuse of put options had a dampening effect on the options market. Put options can be viewed as insurance products. Buyers of puts are typically seeking insurance to hedge some market risk they are unable or unwilling to accept. The seller of puts on the other hand is contracting to provide the insurance the buyer is seeking. A put seller stands ready to purchase stock at a certain price for the life of the contract, no matter how far below that price the stock declines. This is similar to an insurance company insuring your car for the stipulated duration of the contract. The insurance company will make you whole if you have an accident.

If no cars ever had any accidents, the insurance business would be the greatest business of all, good premiums and no risk. Because stocks rarely had accidents during the early 1980s, investors decided to enter the underwriting business. You know what happens when everyone thinks some investment is too good to be true—it generally is. Well, in October 1987, every automobile in the country (every stock on the stock exchanges) had an accident the same day. The casualty companies of the stock market (put sellers) all went bankrupt. I am referring to the investors who sold those puts that, up until October, usually expired worthless. This expiration month, they didn't. From that day on, the options market changed.

You know something though? This isn't anything new. It's been going on since the tulip craze in the 1600s. It happened again with Internet stocks in the late 1990s and early 2000. You would think investors would learn from their mistakes or at least learn from history, but the conventional wisdom always seems to suggest that "this time is different." Most investors make the same mistakes year in and year out. Their biggest mistake is operating in the markets without a logical organized method of analysis. I see it day in and day out. So much information is available today that investors are more confused than ever on how to manage their money. Most investors and brokers don't operate in the markets with a defining process, an operating system if you will. However, a select group of brokers have taken it upon themselves to see that they are well educated in this methodology. They have attended our Point and Figure/Stockbroker Institute in Richmond, Virginia. These craftsmen brokers have a solid game plan for their customers that incorporates the strategies of wealth preservation and wealth accumulation based on the Bullish Percent concept and associated Point and Figure discipline.

If I could impress on you one fact, it would be that at least 75 percent of the risk in any stock is associated with the market and sector. If the overall market is not supporting higher prices, very few stocks you own, if any, will do well. In the past, I spoke at the Yale Club's annual Wall Street Night with Merrill Lynch's Director of Investment Strategy, PaineWebber's Director of Investment Strategy, Jim Rogers, Abbey Cohen, and some of Wall Street's top economists. In all, some of Wall Street's brightest people. The second year I was invited to speak I brought a chart I always use when I explain the Bullish Percent concept. This chart is a schematic of a football play we often see on TV during football games. This chart is my way of demonstrating how we view the market as a football game where the play shifts from offense to defense throughout the game. Once the other panelists had finished discussing the market's outlook, it was my turn. The first chart I put up was a football schematic like the one John Madden writes on the TV screen with his grease pencil showing what just happened on the last play. This chart (see Figure 5.2) drove home the point I was trying to make that evening: The first thing an investor must know before investing any money is whether the offensive team or defensive team is on the field.

In a football game, two forces operate on the field at any one time, offense and defense. The same forces act in the marketplace. There are times when the market is supporting higher prices, and times when the market is not supporting higher prices. When the market is supporting higher prices, you have possession of the ball. You have the offensive team on the field. When you have the ball, your job is to take as much money away from the market as possible; this is when you must try to score. During times when the market is not supporting higher prices, you have in essence lost the ball and must put the defensive team on the field. During such periods, the market's job is to take as much money away from you as

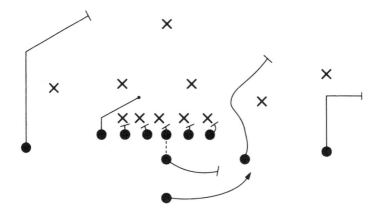

Figure 5.2   Bootleg option right.

possible. Think for a moment about your favorite football team. How well would they do this season if they operated with only the offensive team on the field in every game? They might do well when they had possession of the ball, but when the opposing team had the ball, your team would be scored on at will. The net result is your season would be lackluster at best. This is the problem most investors have. They don't know where the game is being played, much less which team is on the field. Let's face it, most American investors only buy stocks, they never sell short. The market is fair. It has something for everyone. It goes up and it goes down. The NYSE Bullish Percent signals when the environment is ripe for offense or defense. I want to stress that *there is a time to play offense and a time to play defense.* You must know which is which.

How the Bullish Percent Concept Developed over Time

The need for a soulless barometer started with Earnest Staby in the mid-1940s. He was thinking about the market indicators in existence and determined there was a problem that needed to be addressed. He reckoned, that if one were to look at any chart of the broad averages, whether it was a Point and Figure chart, bar chart, line graph, candle chart, they all looked bullish when the market was at its absolute top, and conversely, they all looked bearish when the market was at its absolute bottom. He determined that we needed a soulless barometer that would guide us to become more defensive at market tops and more offensive at market bottoms. A contrary indicator if you will. Well, Earnest was not able to come up with this soulless barometer, but A.W. Cohen did in 1955.

What Cohen was trying to create was a market indicator that was bullish at the bottom and bearish at the top. Something that was totally contrary to how most investors operate in the market. Normal trend charts of indexes like the Dow Jones and the S&P 500 are always bullish at the top and bearish at the bottom. Thus trend charts of market indexes invariably lead investors to buy at the top and sell at the bottom. Here's how the Bullish Percent concept works. It is contrary and goes against the prevailing wisdom. Most market pundits think the Point and Figure method is a trend-following system. It is not that at all in the initial stages of investment. What this method endeavors to do through the Bullish Percent indexes is to buy stocks when they are washed out and virtually everyone has denied them. Kind of like a "Value Investor" might operate, not the other way around. Although once a stock does make a move off the bottom and starts a long term uptrend, it can be bought along the way. But, the method tries to initiate the buying of stocks when they might be considered value stocks whose momentum has recently turned up for the better. If a stock is moving up off the bottom, as it gains sponsorship at the price of, let's say, 40, it will likely be good at 45, 50, 60, or even higher. Remember stocks that are the first to double in a bull market are typically the first to double again. So this method of analysis that is really a contrary investment style, turns into a trend-following style once the vast majority of stocks have moved off the bottom. Just because you did not catch a stock at the bottom doesn't mean you are out of the ball game.

The NYSE Bullish Percent is simply a compilation of the percentages of stocks on the NYSE on Point and Figure buy signals. Think back for a moment to Chapter 3. A bullish chart is one where the last signal is a column of X's that exceeds a previous column of X's. If you simply thumbed through all the Point and Figure chart patterns of the stocks on the NYSE and counted the ones that were on buy signals, then divided by the total number of stocks evaluated, you would have the NYSE Bullish Percent reading for that day. A sixth grader could do it. We have computers that do the counting for us. Let's say there were 2,000 stocks on the NYSE and 1,000 of them were on Point and Figure buy signals. The Bullish Percent would be at 50 percent (1,000 / 2,000 = 50%). Each box constitutes 2 percent, and the vertical axes runs from 0 to 100 percent. That is the football field we are playing on. When the index is rising in a column of X's, more stocks are going on buy signals suggesting sponsorship is increasing in the market.

Think about what actually takes place if the index is in X's at 50 percent this week and over the next week rises to 52 percent. Changes in the index can only come from *first* signals that are given, not subsequent signals. What do I mean by first signal?

Let's say XYZ stock is on a sell signal, bottoms out after declining, and then gives that first buy signal off the bottom. That signal turns the stock from bearish to bullish (see Figure 5.3). It is this first buy signal that is recorded. All subsequent buy signals are not counted—one stock, one vote.

To be sure you understand how this index can move from 50 percent to 52 percent, let's theoretically cut the number of stocks trading on the NYSE down to 100. Over the next week, 12 stocks experience a new buy signal like the one shown in Figure 5.3, and 10 stocks experience new sell signals. The net result of the action for the week is two net new buy signals (e.g., 2% more stocks went on buy signals than went on sell signals). Remember that each box on the chart represents 2 percent, so a 2 percent net change in new buy signals allows the chart to rise one box. Think about the importance of what I just said. I get questions all the time about how this index correlates to the Dow Jones or the Nasdaq or the S&P 500. It doesn't correlate at all. These indexes are either price weighted or capitalization weighted. In the case of the Dow Jones, the highest price stock has the most votes. In the Nasdaq and S&P 500, the stocks with the largest capitalization have all the weight. It can take only a handful of stocks to move these indexes. Let's say IBM was bought out tomorrow 100 points higher than it is at today's close. Do you think it would have an effect on whether the Dow Jones rose or not that day? It sure would. The Dow Jones Average would rise today, but it would be only one stock that is causing all the action. If the top 20 highest capitalization stocks in the S&P 500 went up sharply one day, the

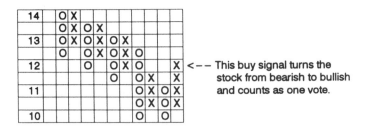

Figure 5.3   Bearish to Bullish.

S&P 500 would rise as well. Now, what does this type of action do to a basic chart of these indexes? It obfuscates reality, that's what it does. If IBM was bought out tomorrow 100 points higher than its close today, it would only count as one positive stock on the NYSE Bullish Percent Index. It would have virtually no effect on moving the index. It is important to keep the Bullish Percent separate in your mind versus indexes that are a measure of performance of a handful of stocks. The Bullish Percent is an assessor of risk in the market not performance. This is the main difference.

Why Use the Bullish Percent versus a Chart of an Index

One of our clients sent us an interesting article by James Surowiecki entitled "The Financial Page Markets Always Outsmart Mavens" (from the *New Yorker,* October 9, 2000). That article had an interesting take on the markets and Long-Term Capital Management. That firm had bond trader John Meriwether and some of the smartest minds on Wall Street, yet the fund managed to blow up. The author compares the TV show *Who Wants to Be a Millionaire?* with Long-Term Capital. The premise of *Who Wants to Be a Millionaire?* is simple. Contestants pick one of four answers to a trivia question, with the value of each question getting greater until they reach the final million-dollar question. A contestant who answers a question wrong is out. The show gives contestants three "lifelines." If they are stumped on a question, they can use the lifelines to help them out. One lifeline is a 50-50, which takes away two of the wrong answers and leaves one correct and one wrong answer for the contestant to select from. Another lifeline is to call a friend to see if he or she knows the answer, and finally a contestant can poll the audience. To do this, each member of the audience keys in his or her choice for the right answer; then the computer displays what percentage of the audience voted for each answer. What the show's producers have found is that when the participant phones a friend for an answer, the person is right two thirds of the time. When the contestant polls the audience, however, they are right nine times out of ten. So what gives here?

Your supersmart friend is right less often than an audience of people who come from all walks of life and have diverse educational backgrounds.

In short, you are more likely to find right answers from a diverse group of people than from one person you deem to be extremely bright and well rounded. As Surowiecki says in the article, "Long-Term specialized in esoteric trading strategies, which meant that most of the time there were relatively few people it could trade with. If you want to buy stock in Cisco Systems, there are lots of folks out there who will sell it to you at a reasonable price. But if you want to buy, say equity volatility (don't ask), as Long-Term did, there are really only four or five dealers in the entire world who buy and sell this stuff. And they all know one another. These people may have been financial wizards, but, as 'Millionaire' demonstrates, if you want to find the answer to a question—like 'What's the right price for equity volatility?' you're better off asking a big, diverse group, rather than one or two experts." Keep in mind that two of the principals of Comprehensive Capital are Nobel Prize Laureates.

You can test this phenomenon pretty simply with an old trivia game, "How many jelly beans are in the jar?" Surowiecki asserts in his article that a college professor does this with his classes and invariably the collective guess is within 3 percent of the actual number. At our last Broker Institute, we tried this experiment. We had an intern count out peanut M&M's into a large jar and write down the number. Then, the eight people in the office guessed how many M&M's were in the jar. The average guess of eight people who were teaching the seminar was 840. At the seminar, in which there were 80 attendees and all voted, the average guess was 1,398. Now, get this—the number of M&M's was 1,396! We found it absolutely amazing that the group came so close. We took all the guesses and applied the statistical concept of a bell curve to it. What we saw was a perfect bell curve. There were some outlying guesses but the collective guess was right on the money. Again, the larger the sample, the better the average guess.

Norman Johnson, a physicist at Los Alamos National Laboratory, quantified this hypothesis. He built a computer-simulated maze in which a person could navigate in numerous ways and tested people's ability to get through it. Johnson took the sample group and found what he called the "collective solution." In other words, he took the turn in the maze that the greatest percentage of people picked. This "collective solution" was just 9 steps long compared to an average of 34.3 steps the first time a person worked through the maze. Furthermore, he found the bigger and more diverse the group, the smarter the collective solution was. As Surowiecki points out in his article, "The miracle of markets is that a hundred million ordinary people, just by going about their daily business, end up allocating resources much more efficiently than would five guys talking on the phone, no matter how smart those five guys are." Or as Michael Mauboussin, the chief investment strategist at Credit Suisse First Boston, puts it, "The market is smart even when the people within it are dumb." Does this speak in any way about the wisdom of the politicians we elect? Maybe the best way to solve world problems is through a collective vote of all Americans on the Internet. Hey, don't laugh, it might solve the hanging chad and dimple problems in Florida.

Our Bullish Percent concept relies on the same approach as the jelly bean, M&M, or maze tests. The larger and more diverse the sampling, the better or more accurate picture we get of risk in the marketplace. We view the Bullish Percent as "polling the audience" in the "Millionaire" show, while the most often quoted market indexes take the "phone a friend" solution. The audience members get it right more often than the phone a friend, and that is what we see with the Bullish Percent—it is better at assessing risk in the market than the indexes. Remember, it is the risk in the market we are assessing, not the market's performance. Each week when we calculate the Bullish Percent reading, we are in essence polling our audience, which happens to be the NYSE (or OTC) stocks. This audience of about 3,000 for each market is better at assessing risk than the top 20 capitalized stocks in the S&P 500 or Nasdaq 100. Remember, the bigger the sample size, the more accurate a picture you get. Each week, we ask the stocks comprising the NYSE (and OTC) what is the correct level of the Bullish Percent. Should it be 50 percent, 70 percent, 30 percent, or somewhere else? It is then up to us to interpret the reading and decide what type of strategies we want to integrate.

Mechanics of the Bullish Percent

Let's go back to the mechanics of charting the index. We use the same three-box reversal to shift columns in this index as we do in the normal Point and Figure chart; however, we do not look for chart patterns in this index. Field position and what column you are in are the two most important considerations. Remember the only way to switch from one column to the next is through a three-box reversal. Since each box in the NYSE Bullish Percent is worth 2 percent, it would take a sum total of 6 percent net buy or sell signals to cause a reversal. Reversing from one column to the next is tantamount to losing or gaining possession of the ball.

The chart is made up of columns of X's and O's with the vertical axes running from 0 to 100 percent. We think of this as a football field consisting of 100 yards. There are two things we try to ascertain with this chart: (1) Who has the ball (offense/defense)? (2) What is the field position (current level from 0 to 100 percent)? If you colored the area above the 70 percent level in red and the area below 30 percent level in green, these would represent the two extremes much like the end zones of a football field. The higher the index climbs, the more overbought it becomes because more and more investors become fully invested and those investors who are inclined to sell tend to hold off. The lower it drops, the more oversold it gets because more and more people who have an inclination to sell, do and those who have an inclination to buy, hold off. When the index is rising in a column of X's, we say you have possession of the football. When you have possession of the ball, you must run offensive plays. This is your time to attempt to score against your opponent, the stock market. When the index is declining in a column of O's, the market has the ball and your job is to try to keep it from scoring against you. The numbers in the boxes on the chart represent months of the year, so you can see the time spent in a column of X's or O's is generally a number of months, not weeks.

It is important to fully understand this index, so let's go back to our discussion about how the index rises and falls. It takes a net change in buy or sell signals to move the index. The minimum percentage move in the index is 2 percent to advance a box or decline a box. It requires a 6 percent net change between new buy and new sell signals to change columns. This 6 percent change is the critical part of how this index moves from column to column. Typically, I look at the index as a gauge of how many players are on the field. In July 1990, the Dow Jones was making all-time highs with the NYSE Bullish Percent Index at 52 percent. This showed that the Dow might have been at a new high but only 52 percent of the NYSE players were on the field. In other words, the NYSE Bullish Percent was at 52 percent and in a column of X's. One would have expected to see more than 52 percent of the stocks participating in the rally when the Dow was at new highs. This goes back to our discussion on how it only takes a few strong stocks to push and pull the index. A few weeks later, Iraq invaded Kuwait, and the same day the NYSE Bullish Percent reversed over into a column of O's signaling investors had lost the ball once again. Those who heeded the signal avoided a major crunch in the market. The net result was the index declined to the 18 percent level in October 1990, which was the bottom. The first week in November the index reversed into a column of X's signaling investors had once again taken possession of the ball. Those who were willing to listen bought stocks right at the bottom. Those who preferred to listen to the news media were expecting a depression or worse. I am continually amazed with the accuracy of this index. It helps the investor understand the most important question in investing, "Who's got the ball?"

NYSE Bullish Percent Risk Levels

There are six degrees of risk in the index similar to the different signals a traffic light can give. A.W. Cohen felt if the index was rising in a column of X's and above the 50 percent level, the market was bullish. Conversely, if the index was declining in a column of O's and below the 50 percent level, the market was bearish. Earl Blumenthal fine-tuned the NYSE Bullish Percent to include 6 degrees of risk. Although I have found that field position and whether the index is in X's or O's is about as sophisticated as you need to get with this concept, Blumenthal nonetheless did some great work on the concept and I want to present it. The six different risk levels he developed are followed by an explanation of each:

1. Bull Confirmed
2. Bull Alert
3. Bull Correction
4. Bear Confirmed
5. Bear Alert
6. Bear Correction

Bull Confirmed Market

This is typically the strongest of markets and should be aggressively played on the upside. You have possession of the football, so you must run plays and attempt to score against your opponent. This type of market occurs when the Bullish Percent gives a buy signal by exceeding a previous column of X's, as illustrated in Figure 5.4. It is equally important to evaluate the relative field position of the index. Bull Confirmed at the 70 percent level is very different from Bull Confirmed at the 30 percent level. Bull Confirmed at 70 percent puts the index in overbought territory where you must use hedge strategies for any commitment in which you buy stock. Bull Confirmed at 30 percent has the index in oversold territory. With this field position, you would want to simply buy stock outright. One of the problems with this risk level is, many investors get confused with the strongly bullish title. "Bull Confirmed" has a very bullish connotation but at the upper levels of the index grid, it becomes much less bullish and above 70 percent it becomes downright cautious.

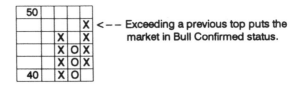

Figure 5.4   Bull Confirmed status.

Bull Alert Market

This market occurs when the Bullish Percent reverses up into a column of X's from below 30 percent and the previous Risk level was Bear Confirmed or Bear Alert. If the previous Risk level was Bull Correction, then the Reversal up would be Bull Confirmed. The index does not have to exceed the 30 percent level, simply reverse up (see Figure 5.5). At the 30 percent or lower level, many stocks are making their lows. The actual reversal to the upside suggests most lows have been made and the probability is up from there. A long trading posture can be established here. Many times when the Bullish Percent gets down to very washed-out levels, near 20 percent or lower, you will see an initial reversal up and rally in the Bullish Percent and then a retest of the lows, with stocks making higher bottoms. The good thing about initiating new positions in this status is that the market is already washed out. As with any other status, you want to follow your game and set stops, raising those as the chart allows. One thing to focus on in this risk level is relative strength. The stocks that held up best during the decline are most likely to be the ones that lead the next bull market. This risk level change is tantamount to a red light changing to green. Keep one thing in mind, however. Like Bull Confirmed, Bull Alert near the 70 percent level is much less bullish than when it happens below 30 percent. It is not often that the NYSE Bullish Percent will rise from below 30 percent to above 70 percent without a reversal, but it has happened. This action would have the effect of keeping Bull Alert status in effect all the way up. Just keep that in your mind if this situation does arise. When we look at sector Bullish Percents, we routinely see this happen.

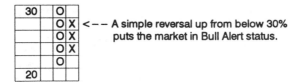

Figure 5.5 Bull Alert status.

Bull Correction Market

The bull market is getting a little extended at these levels, and the market is currently digesting its excesses. The bull trend is likely to resume shortly. It is characterized by a 6 percent reversal down from a Bull Confirmed status that takes place below the 70 percent level. It is telling us that the market leaders will likely drop in price due to profit taking. Defensive option strategies can be taken at this point. Selling call options or purchasing puts as insurance against a potential decline in the broad averages might be a desired strategy here. The bull market is still intact; it's just taking a breather. The traffic light would have changed from green to yellow in Bull Correction status. You will want to note the field position in which Bull Correction takes place. Bull Correction at 60 percent is a more serious reversal than Bull Correction at 34 percent. The next reversal back up into a column of X's reverts the risk level back to Bull Confirmed, as shown in Figure 5.6 by the column of question marks (?).

Bear Confirmed Market

This market is characterized by the Bullish Percent Index penetrating a previous bottom, as shown in Figure 5.7. We never second-guess this market. Traders can establish short positions in the indexes or in common stocks. All other long stock positions should be hedged in some way. Field position is important to

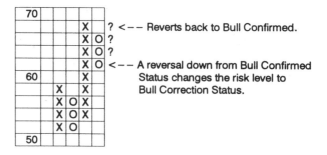

Figure 5.6   Bull Correction status.

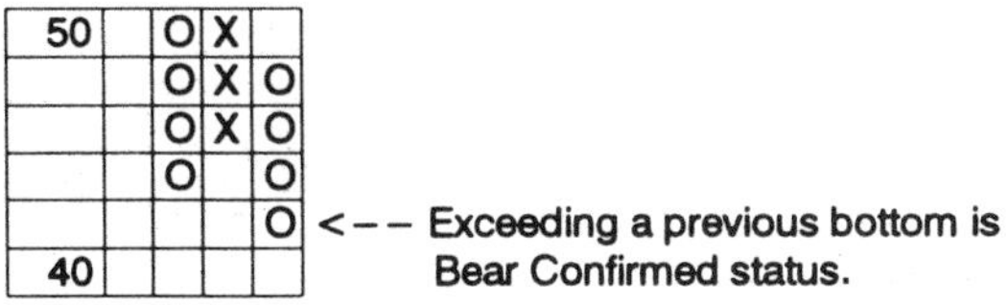

```
50  | O | X |   |
    | O | X | O |
    | O | X | O |
    | O |   | O |
    |   |   | O |  < – – Exceeding a previous bottom is
40  |   |   |   |        Bear Confirmed status.
```

Figure 5.7   Bear Confirmed status.

consider in this risk level. Bear Confirmed at 30 percent is not as dangerous as Bear Confirmed at 70 percent. Always keep the field position in mind. The traffic light is red in this risk level.

Bear Alert Market

When the Bullish Percent goes above 70 percent and then drops below 70 percent without penetrating a previous bottom, a Bear Alert occurs suggesting you bring the defensive team on the field (see Figure 5.8). These corrections usually bring the Bullish Percent down to the 50 percent level at a minimum. A 6 percent reversal back up in the columns of X's will put the market back in a Bull Confirmed status. In the Bear Alert market, defensive action should be taken using the options market for hedging purposes. Short positions can be established in the S&P or common stocks. This status can slip to Bear Confirmed if a previous bottom is exceeded, or it can revert back to Bull Confirmed on the next three-box reversal up. The traffic light in this risk level changes from green to red, and this particular status is especially worrisome as

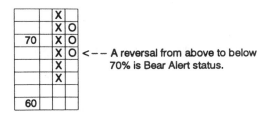

Figure 5.8   Bear Alert status.

the defensive posture can only be achieved by going into the "red zone" and then reversing down.

Bear Correction Market

This indicates a pause in a bear market in which stocks will retrace some of their decline. This phase is characterized by a 6 percent reversal into a column of X's from above the 30 percent level from a Bear Confirmed status. Let's think about field position for a moment. If the NYSE Bullish Percent Index was at 32 percent and reversed up, the risk level would change to Bear Correction. If the index instead was at 30 percent and reversed up, the risk level would change to Bull Alert. Note the importance of the 30 percent level. Remember that reversals from 30 percent or below change the risk level to Bull Alert. The same thing would happen on the upside. A reversal at 68 percent from Bull Confirmed status would change the risk level to Bull Correction. A reversal from Bull Confirmed status at the 70 percent level would be Bear Alert status. The Bear Correction risk level is like a red light changing to flashing red. It may be okay to proceed through the intersection, but be sure to stop, look both ways for Mack trucks, and be fully aware that the opposing traffic have the right of way. Good stop-loss points must be established on any new long stock commitments here. Again here, we pay close attention to the field position. A reversal back down into a column of O's reverts the risk level back to Bear Confirmed. In Figure 5.9, this is depicted by the question marks (?).

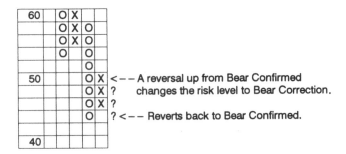

Figure 5.9   Bear Correction status.

Lessons from the Bullish Percent

As mentioned, my conviction in the Bullish Percent has only grown stronger through years of experience with different markets. You can gain this confidence level, too, by studying different market periods and how the Bullish Percent has reacted. If you take the time to read and study the market scenarios I am about to lay out, you will be miles ahead of the average investor in understanding how the markets work.

1987

I discussed the crash of 1987 earlier because the NYSE Bullish Percent Index saved our company and would have helped any investor avoid the crash if they had been following it. We were only 10 months old at Dorsey, Wright and had just begun to acquire some clients. We had decided when we started the company that our main market indicator would be the NYSE Bullish Percent Index. That index was the soulless barometer we would hang our hat on. If it had worked so well since it was developed in 1955 by A.W. Cohen, and was well founded in the irrefutable law of supply and demand, why should we look any further? On September 4, 1987, the indicator reversed into a column of O's and suggested we put the defensive team on the field. It was our Head Coach so we followed the signal without any reservation. From that day forward, our feature article in our "Daily Equity and Market Analysis Report" had to do with how to hedge a portfolio with options. The following month the market crashed, and I'll be the first to tell you we had no idea the decline would be so severe. Nonetheless, those who chose to follow our recommendations were prepared. The crash took no prisoners from *our* client base. This was a major confidence builder for us. We knew then, we were on the right track.

By the first week in November, the same indicator that had suggested defense on September 4, 1987, now suggested offense. This was just as tense as the sell signal the index had given us a couple of months earlier. All the newspapers, magazines, and TV shows were talking about depression, recession, 1929, no hope for

Wall Street, and on and on. The media did their part in scaring investors, right at the time our Head Coach (NYSE Bullish Percent)
told us to begin running plays. It was a great example of how the
market looks ahead. The Bullish Percent Index reversed up into a
column of X's and, once again, we knew of nothing else to do but
follow it. Those who followed our recommendation to buy, got
back in right at the bottom. I must add there was no brilliance on
our part for those calls on the market, it was the NYSE Bullish
Percent that did it. We simply followed its guidance like football
players follow the guidance of their coach. Ultimately, the most
credit should go to the late A.W. Cohen for creating this index in
1955 and to the late Earl Blumenthal for refining it. Along the
way, this method of analysis became a lost art that I revived in my
first book.

   After the crash, we put together a marketing piece consisting
of excerpts from our report pre- and post-crash. This marketing
piece in essence opened doors for us. From that day forward, the
NYSE Bullish Percent has been the mainstay of our market indicators. I have written many articles on it, and each time I write
about it I learn a little more. We have used this index to guide our
intermediate market action for 14 years now. We have seen it
work in bull, bear, and neutral markets. The more you learn
about this index, the more confidence you will have in your day-
to-day market operations.

1990

We really need to begin the discussion of 1990s market by going
back to 1989. In September 1989, the NYSE Bullish Percent hit 74
percent. Exceeding the 70 percent level put this important indicator into the red zone. In October 1989, everything changed. Six
percent of the stocks on the NYSE moved from buy signals to sell
signals and put the defensive team on the field. The initial move
down carried the NYSE Bullish Percent down to 38 percent in a
straight column of O's. By March, there was a slight reprieve. The
NYSE Bullish Percent reversed up from March until August when
on the day of the invasion of Kuwait, the NYSE Bullish Percent
reversed down into a column of O's putting us back on defense.

The thing about defense is you never know how bad it will be until it is over. For that reason, we always take the posture that it is better to preserve capital and lose opportunity than it is to lose money. Opportunity is easy to make up, but money is hard to make up. A 50 percent loss in a stock means you have to gain 100 percent just to get back to even. The NYSE Bullish Percent just continued to experience more sell signals and more sell signals until it was finally driven down to 18 percent in September. The Bullish Percent stayed at that level until November when it reversed up into a column of X's. I distinctly remember watching the financial news and hearing Alan Greenspan tell the American public that we were in a recession at the exact time our main market indicator was reversing up from oversold levels. The difference between economics and Wall Street is that economics reports on what is happening today, while the financial markets look ahead. The Bullish Percent was telling us that the recession was not just beginning, but rather it was nearing an end.

After the NYSE Bullish Percent reversed up from that 18 percent level to 24 percent, it rallied straight up to 70 percent. This is one of the few times the NYSE Bullish Percent has fallen to such an extremely low level and then rallied straight up to 70 percent. This is why we always take positions on any reversal from below 30 percent. Who knows when that move might end up going coast to coast? Usually we see an initial rally up off the bottom and then a retest that results in a higher bottom. When the NYSE Bullish Percent reached 70 percent, the risk management process started all over again. This points out how the Bullish Percent is an oscillator and not a trend chart, and why you cannot compare it to an index like the S&P 500. Keep the concept of a risk assessor firmly in your mind as you evaluate this chart.

1994

The market of 1994 has been dubbed the "stealth bear market." The indexes were holding up, coming in even for the year, but the sector rotation in the market was unbelievable. As one sector was getting hit, another was recovering from its selloff, the effect of this was to cancel each other out in the broad market indexes.

However, the individual stocks and many investors did not fare as well. The market during 1994 was one in which you came into the office and sat down and crossed your fingers that it wasn't your stocks that got taken out behind the shed and shot. The reality of the market was that 80 percent of the stocks on the NYSE were down 20 percent or more at some time during the year. The NYSE Bullish Percent was in a column of O's for eight months out of the year. That means for two thirds of the year we were playing defense. In 1994, the NYSE Bullish Percent started out the year at 66 percent. Is this good field position or bad field position to start out the year? Bad field position. By the end of the year, the NYSE Bullish Percent was at 32.1 percent. You might ask, "Why wasn't the Bullish Percent lower than 32.1 percent if 80 percent of the stocks were down 20 percent or more that year?" The reason is that many sectors bottomed at different points in time. Some sectors, like Drugs, bottomed out in the spring; others like technology, bottomed in the summer; and yet other groups bottomed out in December. While some sectors were moving to sell signals, others were moving to buy signals and those buy signals had the effect of canceling out some of the sell signals, thus keeping the NYSE Bullish Percent from getting down to a reading of 20 percent or lower. In the following list, you can see which sectors bottomed first and last in 1994. Nonetheless, what was the field position going into 1995? Good field position. In 1995, the NYSE Bullish Percent and other indicators had us playing offense for 70 percent of the year (36 weeks out of the year, the NYSE Bullish Percent was in X's), and certainly the market did quite well with the Dow Jones up 36 percent. In 1996, it was a similar story as the NYSE Bullish Percent was in X's 39 weeks that year, 75 percent of the time. The S&P 500 was up 20 percent that year. In 1997, the NYSE Bullish Percent was in a column of X's for 35 weeks or 65 percent of that year, and in general, it was another good year for stocks, except for the Asian flu crisis, which hit in October 1997. Before the market crumbled from the Asian flu, the NYSE Bullish Percent gave us notice having reversed in O's from the 72 percent level. That reading of 72 percent was the highest for the NYSE Bullish Percent since 1987.

When Sector Bullish Percents Hit Their Lows in 1994

Month	Sector	Low (%)
February	Nonferrous Metals	30
April	Drug	18
	Gaming	10
	Precious Metals	26
	Protection and Safety Equipment	32
	Telephone	30
May	Electronics	42
	Finance	26
	Food, Beverage, and Soap	36
	Forest and Paper Products	42
	Media	36
	Steel and Iron	26
June	Computer	30
July	Healthcare	34
September	Electronic Utilities	24
December	Aerospace/Airlines	32
	Autos and Auto Parts	30
	Banks	42
	Buildings	28
	Business Products	36
	Chemicals	40
	Household Goods	38
	Leisure	34
	Machinery and Tools	36
	Real Estate	26
	Restaurants	30
	Retailing	30
	Savings and Loan	42
	Gas Utilities	14
	Wall Street	22
	Waste Management	30
January 1995	Oil	32
February 1995	Oil Service	26

1998

The year 1998 showed another major change with respect to the NYSE Bullish Percent. What I find so interesting is that there are always different catalysts that seem to make the market rally or stumble but that doesn't matter to the NYSE Bullish Percent. Those catalysts are always rooted in the supply-and-demand relationship in the market, and that is what the NYSE Bullish Percent is designed to measure. I'll never forget the 1998 market. By April of that year, the NYSE Bullish Percent had risen to 72 percent. We began to see selling pressure build up as more stocks were going on sell signals versus buy signals. A change definitely was in the offing. Reversals from above 70 percent are particularly concerning. On April 1, 1998, we wrote in our daily research report, "It Wasn't Raining When Noah Built the Ark." I saw this euphemism on the marquee of a Baptist church as I was going to lunch one day. I felt as if the Pastor had put it up there for me to read. We always keep our eyes open on that marquee as we drive by because the Pastor of the church is incredibly creative with respect to his euphemisms. This one hit me right between the eyes because it was perfect with regard to what the market was on the verge of doing. We needed to have our professional clients begin to think about what they would do to protect their clients when this index moved to defense. Our intention was to get our clients to begin considering risk management/damage control—what to do when things go wrong. We could see the Bullish Percent was close to reversing to defense. It was like doing lifeboat drills on a cruise ship. The first thing you do when you embark on a cruise ship is participate in lifeboat drills that deal with what to do if the ship begins to sink. Our outlook was the same. Plan what to do if the market begins to sink so your portfolio won't go down with it.

By May 13, 1998, the NYSE Bullish Percent Index had reversed to a column of O's signaling defense. The index then marched straight down to 16 percent, which is an extremely washed-out condition. In July of that year, the Dow Jones rallied to all-time highs as did the Nasdaq, NYSE, and S&P 500. The trend charts of these indexes looked very good, but the reality of the situation was that more sell signals were piling up while a handful of stocks pulled these indexes to new highs. It was as if the generals were in the battle but the soldiers had left the field. Those who followed the Bullish Percent Index were dead on the money, playing defense while others who followed the trend charts of these indexes were on the wrong road with the offensive team on the field. This "major" rally that took these indexes to new all-time highs only lasted two weeks. Shortly after the highs were made, the market caved in. Or, should I say, those indexes caved in. The market had been declining since April 1998. As mentioned, the Bullish Percent eventually went down to 16 percent before we experienced a reversal during the month of September. Let's take a look at exactly what we said in that report of April 1, 1998, so you can get some more perspective on how our thought process evolves when we evaluate these indicators.

Plan Ahead: It Wasn't Raining When Noah Built the Ark*

I saw this quote the other day on the marquee of a Southern Baptist Church here in Richmond. Last October there were many brokers and investors alike out who were caught by surprise. For those of you reading our reports and following the indicators, October's pullback in the market was of no surprise to you. You knew the risk in the market was high as the NYSE and OTC Bullish Percents were at levels not seen since 1987—up at 76 percent and 72 percent respectively. You knew the bell curve was skewed heavily to the right-hand, or overbought, side of the ledger. In fact here's a quote from the summary of our "Technical Indicator Update" on October 16th. "The indicators remain positive but at such extended territory it behooves you to be cautious. The sector bell curve is skewed heavily to the right-hand side and the only way for it to get back to normal or oversold is to see sell signals given. . . . Be careful out there! We have many instances where pictures like the current sector distribution was the precursor of a 'Bad Moon Risin'.'" The picture today is beginning to look a lot like that of October 1997, and

---

*Excerpt from our *Daily Report*, April 1, 1998.

many other times in the market when we have seen a correction. Let's quickly recap where the indicators are now and compare that to some other tops in the market in the table below. As well, take a look at the bell curves from the following periods, too:

Percent Comparisons	Current	1997 High	1994 High	1989 High	1987 High
NYSE Bullish Percent	72.0%	76%	66%	74%	76%
OTC Bullish Percent	61.5	72	60 (late '93)	60	72
Optionable Bull Percent	73.2	74	62	No data	No data
Percent of 10	71.4	86	70	80	86
NYSE High-Low Index	87.6 (96.6% high)	96	88	94	96
OTC High-Low Index	86.7 (91.6% high)	94	80	84	No data

You are about to see something that looks like a bell curve. The symbols of the sectors we follow make up the body of the curve. Notice how the horizontal axis runs from 0 to 100 percent. This is simply a horizontal Bullish Percent Index with each sector placed on the percent line where it belongs in relation to it's own Bullish Percent. So you in essence see a large bell curve made up of individual sector bell curves; when viewed in the aggregate, they give you a great picture of the overall market. When the majority of sectors are skewed to the 70 percent side, the market is high. Conversely, when these sectors are skewed to the left side, the market is oversold. Now look at the progression of the market from 1987 on. What you will see is that all those markets have something in common. They all present the picture of an overbought market. This exercise demonstrates that March 1998 looks much like September 1987 and other markets that were very high and eventually resolved to oversold. In all cases, the picture became very skewed to the left side or the oversold side of the ledger. We cover more on sectors in the following chapters so you might want to earmark this page to go back to and study again.

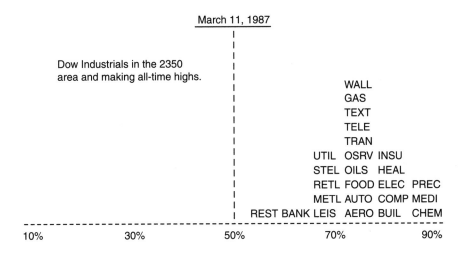

March 11, 1987

Dow Industrials in the 2350
area and making all-time highs.

```
                                    WALL
                                    GAS
                                    TEXT
                                    TELE
                                    TRAN
                          UTIL  OSRV INSU
                          STEL  OILS HEAL
                          RETL  FOOD ELEC  PREC
                          METL  AUTO COMP  MEDI
               REST BANK LEIS  AERO BUIL   CHEM
10%           30%         50%          70%         90%
```

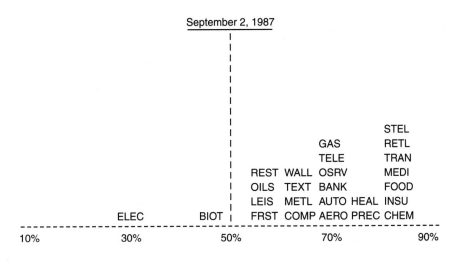

September 2, 1987

```
                                         STEL
                              GAS        RETL
                              TELE       TRAN
                   REST WALL  OSRV       MEDI
                   OILS TEXT  BANK       FOOD
                   LEIS METL  AUTO HEAL  INSU
         ELEC         BIOT    FRST COMP AERO PREC CHEM
10%           30%         50%          70%         90%
```

143

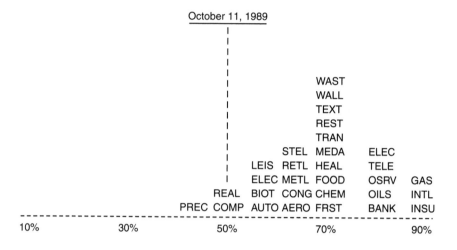

October 11, 1989

```
                                        WAST
                                        WALL
                                        TEXT
                                        REST
                                        TRAN
                              STEL  MEDA      ELEC
                         LEIS RETL  HEAL      TELE
                         ELEC METL  FOOD      OSRV  GAS
                    REAL BIOT CONG  CHEM      OILS  INTL
               PREC COMP AUTO AERO  FRST      BANK  INSU
```

10%   30%   50%   70%   90%

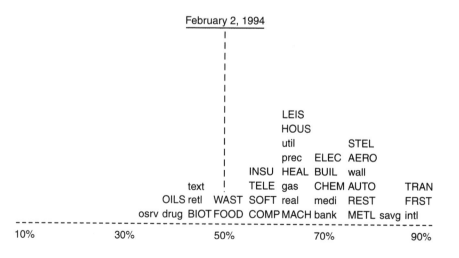

February 2, 1994

```
                                   LEIS
                                   HOUS
                                   util       STEL
                                   prec  ELEC AERO
                              INSU HEAL BUIL wall
                         text      TELE gas  CHEM AUTO      TRAN
                    OILS retl WAST SOFT real medi REST      FRST
                    osrv drug BIOT FOOD COMP MACH bank METL savg intl
```

10%   30%   50%   70%   90%

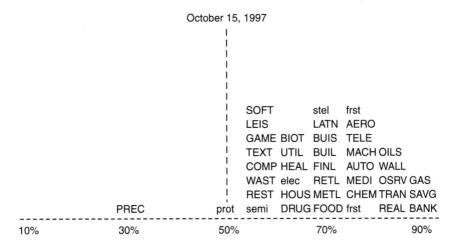

October 15, 1997

```
                          SOFT        stel    frst
                          LEIS        LATN  AERO
                          GAME BIOT   BUIS  TELE
                          TEXT  UTIL  BUIL  MACH OILS
                          COMP HEAL  FINL  AUTO  WALL
                          WAST  elec  RETL  MEDI  OSRV GAS
                          REST  HOUS METL  CHEM TRAN SAVG
              PREC   prot  semi  DRUG FOOD frst    REAL BANK
---------------------------------------------------------------
10%          30%          50%           70%          90%
```

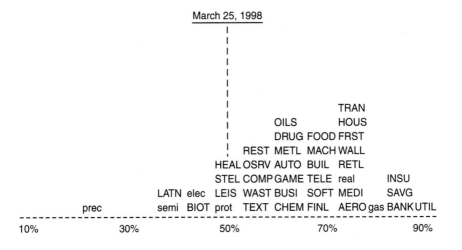

March 25, 1998

```
                                      TRAN
                              OILS        HOUS
                              DRUG FOOD FRST
                          REST METL MACH WALL
                    HEAL OSRV AUTO BUIL  RETL
                    STEL COMP GAME TELE  real     INSU
              LATN elec  LEIS WAST BUSI  SOFT MEDI    SAVG
         prec      semi  BIOT prot TEXT CHEM FINL  AERO gas BANK UTIL
---------------------------------------------------------------
10%          30%          50%           70%          90%
```

145

Look at the NYSE Bullish Percent at other market tops and you will notice that it is right up there with the highs seen before other market corrections. The same is true for the other indicators. When the Bullish Percents get near or move above the 70 percent mark, the availability of demand to push the market higher is diminished. You call your customer with a great idea. It's the newest widget-making company that will change the semiconductor industry. Your customer replies, "I love the idea. What should I sell to buy it?" You sell a stock to buy another and supply and demand cancel each other out. One day you start to sell but don't replace those sell tickets with buy tickets and that's what causes the Bullish Percent to reverse down. It's like a pressure cooker when you're above 70 percent. The top on the pot is rattling with the steam underneath. One day the steam gets to be too much and the top blows off. We don't know what the cause will be. It may be the Asian flu again or it may be another type of international crisis. What we do know is that the risk is high here and we must govern ourselves accordingly.

What does "govern ourselves accordingly" mean. It can mean many things to many people. NYSE Rule 405—Know your customer. What is right for one person may not be right for another. *There are many right answers.* If you are unaware that the indicators are in high-risk territory, you might just continue to buy stocks with unbridled enthusiasm. Most of us, though, would not take that tact. Here are some ideas that might make sense to your clients:

- Do nothing.
- Tighten up stop-loss points. As stocks start to give sell signals, you ensure that you don't give back too much of your profits. You might choose to just take partial positions off the table on the sell signal, but by doing that you have taken some defensive action.
- Take partial profits. One thing you might consider is selling a third of your position if you are up 30 percent or more. This gives you staying power with the rest of your position to handle a correction. The money you free up acts as a hedge and then you have that cash to reemploy once the indicators suggest you have a good buying opportunity again. As well, taking

partial profits will keep one stock from becoming too large a portion of your portfolio.

- Sell calls against partial or total positions. This takes the sell decision away from you. You take in premium which acts as a hedge against you, and you sell at the strike price. If the stock doesn't get called away, you keep the premium and can rewrite the calls. With this strategy, you must be willing to have the stock called away. If you are not willing to have the stock called away, then you're a closet naked writer.

- Buy protective puts on particular stocks. Let's say you own MBIA Inc. (MBI). The stock is at the top of its 10-week trading band, the weekly momentum just flipped negative, and the sector is extended and the next support is the 64 area with the stock currently trading around 76. Your client might be willing to accept the risk down to 70 but after that he wants someone else to carry the risk. You might choose to buy a six-month-out put struck at 70. That gives the client the right but not the obligation to sell his stock at 70 anytime between now and expiration no matter where MBI is trading. If the stock does in fact fall, you can always take the profits on the put and hold the stock.

- Buy protective puts on a portfolio. Ask anyone if he or she owns a put and the answer would likely be no. Ask the same people if they own a home or a car and you get a resounding yes. If you own a home or a car, you own a put. You own insurance on your home and car.

    Every six months, you send the insurance company a check to protect you for the next six months should there be an accident. Many people have portfolios worth more than homes and yet they don't even think to buy insurance on their stocks should there be an accident in the market. Let's say you have a portfolio worth $200,000 of blue chip names. Your client says he can handle a 5 percent drop in the market but after that he wants some insurance. The OEX is currently trading at 525. A 5 percent drop in that index would bring it down to 500. One way to hedge the portfolio is to buy puts on the OEX struck at 500. Each put that you buy protects $50,000 (500 times 100) of the portfolio. To hedge a $200,000 portfolio, you would buy 4 puts. The price you pay for the puts is like the car insurance premium you pay every six months to your insurance company. You hope you don't have to use it but if you do, you're sure glad you have it. Also, you don't have to buy protective puts on the whole portfolio. You can hedge just a partial portfolio.

- Buy only half positions here and average in the other half on a pullback. This allows you to at least get your foot in the stirrup in case we don't get a pullback. If the stock does pull back, then you can average in lower.
- Buy calls or leaps on stocks you want to own. Let the premium you pay be your stop-loss point and come back at expiration and see how you stand. The important thing to remember here is not to overleverage. If you normally buy 500 shares, only buy 5 calls; don't overleverage by buying 15. Keep the rest of the money in a money-market fund.

There are lots of ways to take a more defensive stance. What makes you different from the competition is you have a game plan. You have a soulless barometer to tell you what plays to run. Take a chart of the NYSE Bullish Percent to presentations with you and then do a technical portfolio review of the client's positions. Make a portfolio for him on our Internet page and then alert him whenever there is a technical change on the stocks he owns. This is your added value.

This is the type of research we put out each day. We try to make sense of the indicators. We never anticipate the anticipators; however, when we see changes in the offing we discuss what to do if the event does in fact take place. We always try to have the moves we would make in the chess game laid out for us ahead of time so that we don't act like a deer in the headlights when the change does take place. When the sector bell curve presented us with a situation like that of September 9, 1998 (p. 149), we knew what our course of action would be, given a washed-out, low-risk situation.

2000

The year 2000 was interesting, indeed. The NYSE Bullish Percent had been making lower tops since its peak in 1998 at 72 percent, and by February 2000 the NYSE Bullish Percent had fallen to

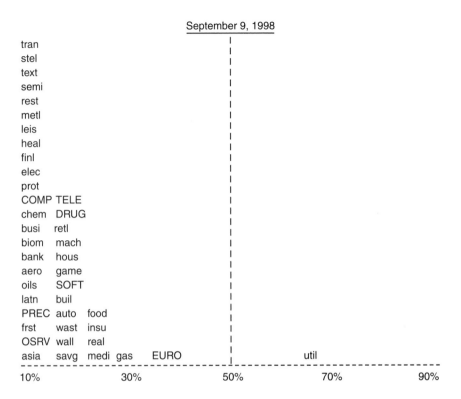

32 percent, just above the green zone or low-risk level. Then in March 2000, the NYSE Bullish Percent reversed up on the exact same day that the OTC Bullish Percent reversed down into O's. We had a situation in which we went from offense to defense on the OTC Bullish Percent while going from defense to offense on the NYSE. In March, we also saw some of our other relative strength indicators turning positive on the NYSE while turning negative on the OTC market (we discuss those indicators in Chapter 6). This call kept our clients underweighted in the OTC stocks and over-weighted in NYSE stocks while most of the investing public was doing just the opposite and getting killed. As mentioned, the years 1995 to 1997 saw the NYSE Bullish Percent in a column of X's 70 plus percent of the time keeping the offensive team on the field for those stocks for three quarters of the game. During 1998 and 1999, though, it was a different situation. During those years, the NYSE Bullish Percent was only in X's about half of the year. In other

words, we had the ball for 50 percent of the game and the market had the ball for 50 percent of the game. That's why it was so hard to make headway in the NYSE stocks during 1998 and 1999. But in 2000, we saw a switch back to investors having possession of the ball for 75 percent of the time.

One thing we have seen in the year 2000 is an increase in the volatility of the indicator, especially the OTC Bullish Percent. Some of this can be attributed to the advent of the Internet craze and technology stock proliferation. Over the past 45 years, there have been times when the index has only changed columns two times a year and most recently in this wild market, it's had changes six times a year. This volatility is not unprecedented. From 1960 to 1965, we had the same type of volatility with the index averaging six changes a year. That was during the close presidential race between Nixon and Kennedy. There was reason to believe there was voter fraud in that election. The Daley political machine was involved. We now have the same situation: A dead-even race between Bush and Gore, with Bush eventually winning. The Daley political machine is involved again and once again some people were clamoring there was voter fraud. We recently went through the impeachment trial of our President Clinton. During that span of years, 1960 to 1965, we witnessed the Cuban Missile Crisis, the Bay of Pigs incident and the assassination of President Kennedy. The Internet volatility is beginning to dry up somewhat as so many investors have been absolutely and unequivocally wiped out in 2000. At this writing the Nasdaq is down 50 percent from its high and that is over twice the percentage associated with a bear market. And, you know what? The media is acting as if nothing happened. It's business as usual. Investors in 2000 continued to buy the dip because "it always works out," and this time it didn't. Even though the volatility has increased significantly in the markets of late, the Bullish Percent concept is still the best method of evaluating the markets, hands down! After the 1960 to 1965 period, the volatility dried up and things came back to normal. Everything ebbs and flows.

Every few years, the NYSE Bullish Percent gives us some real opportunities by declining below the 30 percent level. It doesn't happen every year, but when it does, be prepared to buy.

The OTC Bullish Percent Index

The OTC Bullish Percent Index is important because of the plethora of high-tech, over-the-counter stocks we deal with each day. Chartcraft began the OTC Bullish Percent in 1981, and the same rules of reversals, box sizes, 70 percent high risk, and 30 percent low risk all apply to this one as well.

The OTC Bullish Percent Index is a compilation of the percentage of Nasdaq stocks that are on Point and Figure buy signals (see Figure 5.10). The OTC Bullish Percent Index (Figure 5.11) can give you a great deal of insight into what the technology stocks are doing. In 1982, the small stocks bottomed out much earlier than the large-cap stocks. By the time the big-cap stocks were ready to go in August 1982, the small stocks were already up 70 percent. The chart is read the same way as the NYSE Bullish Percent Index. When the index is rising in a column of X's, you have the football and should be running plays (buying stocks). Conversely, when it is in a column of O's, the OTC market has the football and you should be more concerned with defense (protecting your portfolio). The best sell signals come from above the 70 percent level and the best buy signals come from below 30 percent. Much of the time, the truth lies somewhere in the middle. Notice also how the OTC Bullish Percent tends to bottom out in the 36 percent to 34 percent level barring extreme washed-out levels like 1990, 1997, and 1998. This can be an important clue when evaluating the risk in the market.

The Nasdaq or OTC stocks have become much more important than they were years ago. When I was a broker in the 1970s,

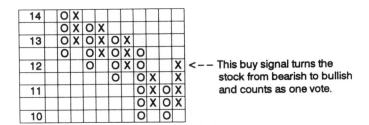

Figure 5.10 Bearish to Bullish.

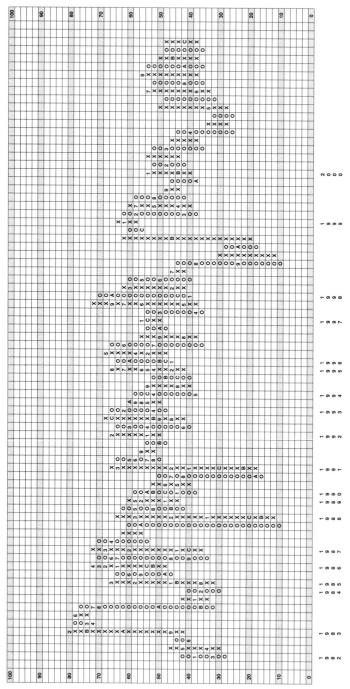

Figure 5.11 OTC Bullish Percent Index.

these stocks were considered poison. They were the lowest rung of the ladder and always considered high risk. Now we have Nasdaq stocks in the Dow Jones. Some of the largest cap stocks that trade are Nasdaq. I must say though, they are still volatile and in many cases are not suitable recommendations for investors who have a low risk tolerance. In the latter part of the 1990s, many investors who barely understood the mechanics of investing had totally overleveraged their whole portfolios with Internet stocks. The media as well as Wall Street analysts had convinced them these stocks could only go up.

Well, here we sit approaching 2001 and most of those stocks didn't go up, they blew up. I'll tell you something else. Just go back and view some of the recommendations by Wall Street fundamental analysts on these Internet stocks when they were at their absolute highs. You will break out in a cold sweat when you see the adoring reports at the top. Just the other day, Goldman Sachs took the stock Ask Jeeves Inc. (ASKJ) off their recommendation list after the stock dropped from 59 to 4. That's only a 93 percent decline from recommended to off recommended. They rate it Market Performer now. I guess if the market moves up 20 percent from here, Ask Jeeves Inc. should rise 20 percent. Of course, at 4, that would be 80 cents. How about this one. Just yesterday, Goldman took E-Toys off their recommended list when the stock declined under 1. This is why the technical analysis coupled with fundamentals is so important.

Chapter 6

OTHER MARKET INDICATORS

Since the first edition of this book was published in 1995, we have developed other indicators that dovetail beautifully with the long established Point and Figure indicators. With these new indicators, we still use the Bullish Percent concept. We simply apply this concept to the other aspects of a stock's technical attributes that we find essential. First, I want to discuss the indicators we have used for many years in our daily work in conjunction with the NYSE Bullish Percent. All our indicators are kept on our Web site (www.dorseywright.com) so you can refer to them in real time as you read this book. The Internet has truly revolutionized how we maintain and present our charting and portfolio system. You know, it doesn't seem that long ago we kept all these charts by hand. You can't imagine how many charts we updated daily. Doing them by hand was the only way to accomplish the task. How many charts do you think we updated each day? Each day before the advent of our computerized charting system with five analysts, we updated 2,500 charts by hand. Once we were able to computerize this process, getting my analysts to stop the hand charting was like pulling teeth. They loved seeing the stocks they updated. Every day each analyst had rotated the book he or she updated to another analyst. This way in one week, each analyst saw firsthand 2,500 charts. We did this for a decade before the Internet became popular. Today, the computer does the bulk of the updating but many of the analysts at Dorsey, Wright still update specific inventories of stocks by hand each day.

While we chart a lot of stocks each day, as we go through the indicators, we keep the number that we follow down to a handful. You have to keep it simple. We take those same indicators and apply them to each market, NYSE, ASE, and OTC, and the sectors; but we never gravitate from that handful of indicators. They define our work. We have no need to search for any other concept. We are, however, always looking for other ways to apply this same concept. It's like the hub of a wheel. This hub is the Point and Figure method of analysis with all the associated indicators. From this hub, we attempt to extend as many spokes as we can without ever leaving the concepts that define our company. Many investors make the mistake of trying to follow too many indicators or jump from one to another when one doesn't seem to work. Just about everywhere you turn, there is another indicator that someone assures you will make you rich. Just go to the chat rooms on the Net and you will be hit with a barrage of information and indicators that will both confuse and obfuscate the picture. The "Real Deal" is the irrefutable law of supply and demand. There is nothing else that causes price change.

Our most important indicators are the NYSE and OTC Bullish Percent Indexes, discussed in Chapter 5. These two Bullish Percents are our long-term coaches. Now let's take a look at our two most important short-term indicators—the Percent of Stocks Trading above Their Own 10-Week Moving Average Index and the High-Low Index. We calculate both of these indicators for the NYSE and OTC markets. For many years, the NYSE and OTC markets moved in tandem but the past two years saw many times where the two markets were split, moving in different directions. Because of the accuracy of these indicators, we were able to successfully negotiate the market when one index suggested offense and one index suggested defense. In fact, one of our absolute best calls was in March 2000 where the OTC Bullish Percent reversed to Defense and at the same time the NYSE Bullish Percent reversed to Offense. Our recommendation was to totally avoid the OTC issues and concentrate on the NYSE issues. Subsequently, the OTC stocks absolutely collapsed, and at the same time the NYSE stocks advanced. After a discussion of these short-term indicators, we will then look at some of the other ancillary technical indicators we watch.

The Indicators

The Percent of Stocks Above Their Own 10-Week Moving Average Index

This index has one of our most important short-term market indicators. It should be used in conjunction with the High-Low Index. As its name implies, the Percent of 10 is simply made up of the percentage of stocks on any index you are evaluating that are trading above their own 10-week moving average (see Figures 6.1 and 6.2). We keep this indicator for both NYSE and OTC stocks and each sector as well. It is as important to keep abreast of the short-term trend of the overall market as it is to keep abreast of the long-term trend. We use the same grid with this index that we use with the Bullish Percent Index. The vertical axis has a value of 2 percent per box and runs from 0 to 100 percent. The best sell signals come when the index rises above the 70 percent level, then reverses down below that critical level. In cases like this, there is a very high probability that the broad averages have begun a short-term correction. This is significant because the short-term often spills over into the long term. Conversely, the best buy signals come when the index declines below the 30 percent level, then reverses back up. In the case of the buy signals below 30 percent, the index does not have to cross that level on the upside to be valid.

What about changes between 30 percent and 70 percent? For example, say the Percent of 10 reverses up from below 30 percent changing the prevailing risk level to a short-term buy signal. The index then rises to 58 percent where it encounters supply and reverses into a column of O's. This reversal would only suggest that the short-term rally that was in effect is now on hold. It would not be a sell signal. However, since this index is short term, it moves like a sports car. An interruption in the trend, such as the one we are discussing could easily find the index back below 30 percent, where the whole process would start over. Let's say the index subsequently reverses back up and carries the index to the 74 percent level. It has now crossed that critical 70 percent line where any reversals that carry it down below 70 percent will change the signal from short-term buy to short-term sell. The same thing happens

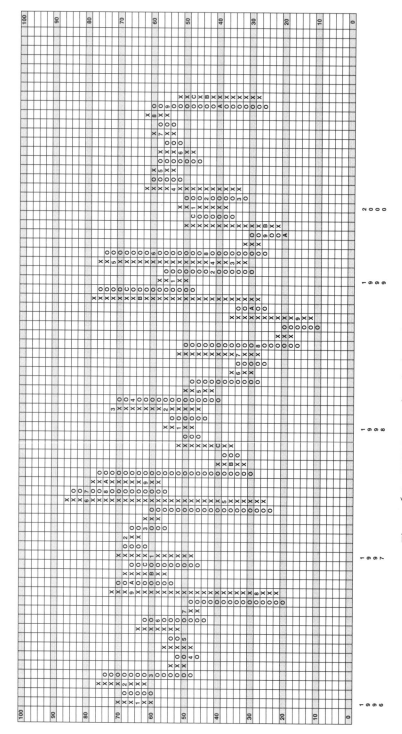

Figure 6.1 NYSE Percent of Stocks Above Their 10-Week Moving Average.

158

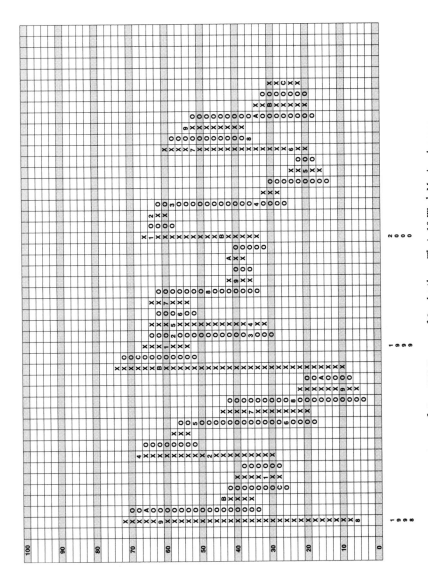

Figure 6.2 OTC Percent of Stocks Above Their 10-Week Moving Average.

159

when the index moves below 30 percent and reverses up; only at this end of the field, the signal turns to a buy.

This index is of great benefit when you are planning your trade. Investors, however, should never use the Percent of Stocks above Their Own 10-Week Moving Average Index as their sole indicator in making new stock commitments. Traders can effectively use it as a market timing indicator for short-term trades. If the main trend in the market is up as dictated by the New York Bullish Percent Index and the Percent of 10 is on a short-term sell signal, then expect the market to move lower near term. If the main trend is up and the Percent of 10 is on a buy signal, then you are in a market that is bull configured both short and long term. In the latter case, an investor would want to be fully invested. In the former case, an investor looking to make new commitments in the market might postpone buying stock, expecting to take advantage of near-term weakness in the market before making any commitments. I discuss this index again in later chapters.

The High-Low Index

This index is another short-term indicator that we use in conjunction with the Percent of 10. Again, just as with the Percent of Stocks Above Their 10-Week Moving Average, we keep a High-Low Index on both the NYSE and OTC stocks. If you wish, you can calculate this indicator yourself. Just take the daily NYSE (or OTC) Highs divided by the daily NYSE (or OTC) new Highs plus the Lows. Then take a 10-day moving average of this number and plot that figure on a grid exactly like the Percent of 10 (see Figures 6.3 and 6.4). The vertical axes will extend from 0 to 100 percent. We evaluate it the same way as the Percent of 10. The two critical levels are 30 percent and 70 percent. Buy signals come from reversals up from below 30 percent. Sell signals come from reversals from above to below 70 percent. Buy and sell signals can also come by exceeding a previous top or bottom respectively. Reversals from above 70 percent suggest that there is a trend change from more stocks making new highs to more stocks making new lows. Conversely, when the index reverses up from below 30 percent, it tells us the number of stocks making new lows is drying up considerably.

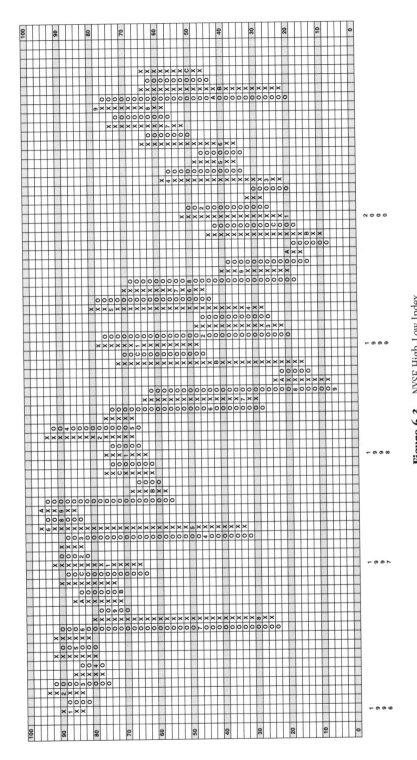

Figure 6.3 NYSE High-Low Index.

161

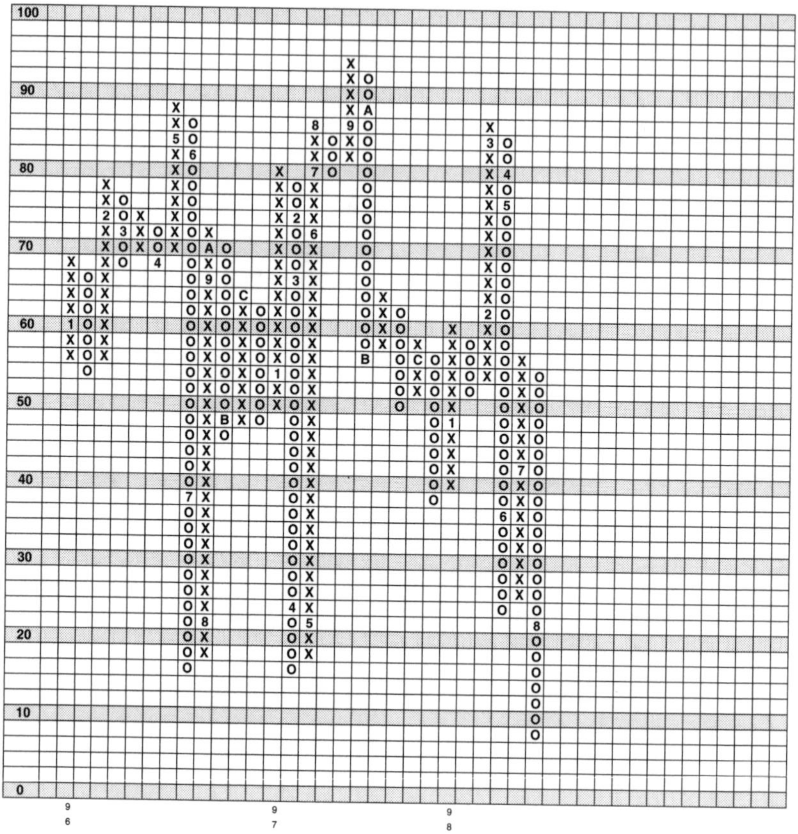

Figure 6.4   OTC High-Low Index.

There are a couple of other things we want to point out about this indicator. First, it can go above 70 percent and remain above that level for some time, even months at a time. Second, this indicator can rally move to extremes, hitting 90 percent or higher and also falling to 10 percent or even lower. Third, when the NYSE High-Low Index goes below the 10 percent level, it is a sign of a very washed-out market. Think about it for a second. To get to 0 percent we would have to see 10 consecutive days of no stocks hitting new highs. Reversals up from 10 percent are usually good buying opportunities. Following is a study on the NYSE High-Low and the times it has been below 10 percent.

NYSE High-Low Readings below 10 Percent—Very Washed Out Condition

Date	Moved below 10%	Dow Reading	Low Reading	Dow Reading	Upside Reversal	Dow Reading
March 1980	3-6-80	828.07	0.9%	800.94	4-10-80	791.47
September 1981	8-31-81	881.46	2.0	849.98	10-7-81	868.72
June 1982	6-7-82	804.03	5.5	795.57	6-24-82	810.41
February 1984	2-17-84	1148.87	7.5	1134.21	2-28-84	1157.14
May 1984	5-29-84	1101.24	5.3	1124.35	6-11-84	1115.61
July 1984	7-18-84	1111.64	5.5	1096.95	8-2-84	1166.08
October 1987	10-20-87	1841.01	0.7	1938.33	1-4-88	2015.25
January 1990	1-31-90	2590.54	8.9	2590.54	2-7-90	2640.09
May 1990	5-2-90	2689.64	9.7	2689.64	5-7-90	2721.62
August 1990	8-15-90	2748.27	3.4	2613.37	9-18-90	2571.29
November 1994	11-23-94	3674.63	5.4	3746.29	12-21-94	3801.80
August 1998	8-31-98	7539.07	4.2	7615.54	9-23-98	8154.41
October 1999	10-21-99	10297.69	7.7	10302.13	10-29-99	10731.76

The Percent of Stocks Above Their Own 30-Week Moving Average Index

The Percent of 30 is a longer term index that we follow religiously on a weekly basis. It is constructed by calculating the percentage of stocks on the NYSE that are trading above their own 30-week moving average (see Figure 6.5). This long-term index does not give many signals; we use it in conjunction with the other indicators. Like the other indicators, buy signals come when the Percent of 30 exceeds a previous top or goes below 30 percent and then reverses up. As well, the sell signals come when the indicator falls from above 70 percent to below 70 percent or exceeds a previous bottom. An interesting aspect of this indicator comes from Dan Sullivan of the Chartist newsletter. He found that when this indicator goes above 80 percent and then falls below 60 percent, it will see 40 percent before it sees 80 percent again. This has happened 12 times, and each time the 80%-60%-40% rule has worked out. The last time it happened was

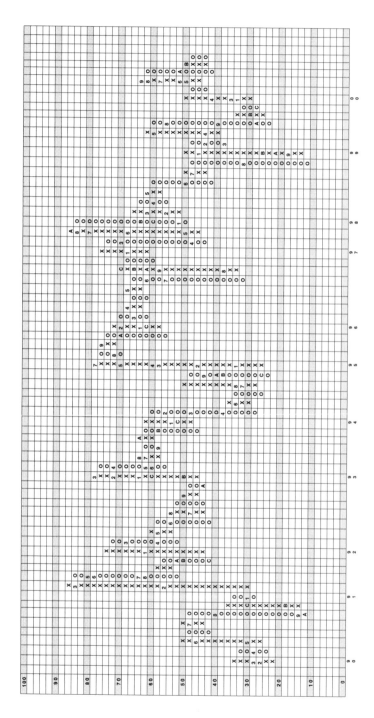

Figure 6.5 NYSE percent of stocks above their 30-week moving average.

in 1997. Keep this study in the back of your mind. It will come in handy one day.

The Advance-Decline Line

The Advance-Decline Line is a nonprice measure of the trend of the market. It is based on the number of issues advancing and declining and not on the price of these issues. Every day, the difference between the issues advancing and the issues declining is calculated. If more issues advanced than declined, the difference is added to the preceding day's total; if more issues declined than advanced, the difference is subtracted from the previous day's total. We keep Advance-Decline lines for the NYSE, ASE, and Nasdaq markets. We look at the Advance-Decline indicators in two respects. First, we look to see if the level is above that of 10 days ago. If it is, then we say that market's Advance-Decline line is positive on a short-term basis. Second, we look at a Point and Figure chart of the Advance-Decline line. If the chart is on a buy signal, we say the Advance-Decline for that market is positive longer term. If the chart is on a sell signal, we say the Advance-Decline for that market is negative longer term. In addition to looking for double tops and double bottoms on the chart, we also take into account high pole and low pole warnings. We like to look at Advance-Decline lines because they, like the Bullish Percent, give each stock one vote. While the Dow Jones or Nasdaq Composite may be going down, what are most of the stocks doing? The Advance-Decline lines give us insight into the "true market" and not just an index of 30 stocks or so.

Percent Positive Trend

When evaluating any stock, in addition to looking at the chart pattern, we also place a lot of importance on the overall trend of the stock and its Relative Strength chart. We have married the positive trend and Relative Strength concepts with the Bullish Percent concept that we know works so well. We began keeping these indicators in 1997 so these charts are not very long, but we have certainly seen their value in the 1998 top and in 2000 again. First, let's look at how we incorporate positive trend and Bullish Percent and then we'll cover Relative Strength.

The Percent Positive Trend chart, or as we like to call it in-house, the PT chart, measures the percent of stocks within a particular market or sector trading above their Bullish Support Lines. So let's say there are 100 stocks in a sector and 50 of them are trading above their Bullish Support Lines. This would give us a reading of 50 percent. If this number is increasing, it tells us more stocks in the sector or market are turning to positive trend charts and supporting higher prices. Conversely, if we see a net 6 percent change of stocks that were in positive trends now in negative trends, it speaks volumes about the change in trend for the sector to negative. It is this battle between the two trends that eventually causes one or the other to win the match and reverse. It is the reversal that warrants our attention.

As outlined earlier, whenever we initiate a new position, we try to stack as many odds as possible in our favor and one of the

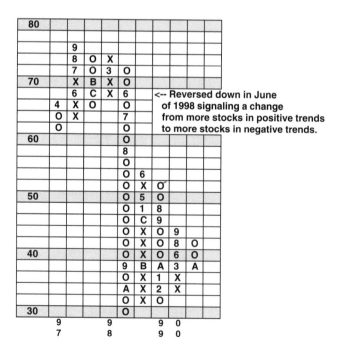

Figure 6.6 PTNYSE (percent of stocks with positive trend charts).

primary things we look at is "What is the overall trend of the stock?" We want to focus our buying on those stocks trading above their Bullish Support Line. In the aggregate, we want to focus on those areas of the market that are showing more and more stocks moving to a positive trend or trading above their Bullish Support Line. We can easily see whether this is happening by looking to the PT chart.

In March 1998, the PT chart for the NYSE was at 74 percent (see Figure 6.6). That meant 74 percent of the stocks on the New York Stock Exchange were above their Bullish Support Lines and in a positive trend. In June 1998, 6 percent of the stocks violated

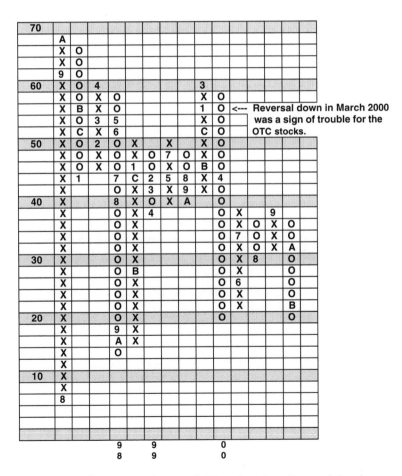

Figure 6.7   PTOTC (percent of OTC stocks with positive trend charts).

their Bullish Support Lines. This change was enough to reverse the PTNYSE chart down into a column of O's telling us a change was coming for the NYSE stocks. This change signaled a trend change from stocks trading above their Bullish Support Lines to more being in a negative trend, trading below their Bearish Resistance Lines. In other words, more stocks were heading down I-95 South. In February 2000, the PTNYSE chart was down to 32 percent meaning only 32 percent of the stocks on the NYSE were above their Bullish Support Lines. In March 2000, the PTNYSE chart reversed up, while the same week the PTOCT (Percent of Stocks with Positive Trend Charts for the Nasdaq/OTC Market) reversed down (see Figure 6.7 on page 167). This told us a major switch was occurring—more stocks with downtrends on the OTC or Nasdaq, while more positive trend charts should start appearing on the NYSE. This game really gets to be fun when you understand how the players are moved around the board. It's like a big chess game.

Percent Relative Strength in X's

Another important attribute we want to see in any stock we purchase is that the Relative Strength chart is in a column of X's, showing the stock is currently outperforming the market. Taking the same logic of the PT charts, we want to focus on those areas of the market that are showing more and more stocks in a column of X's on their Relative Strength charts. Within each industry group, we calculate the number of stocks whose individual Relative Strength charts are outperforming the market on a shorter term basis. Though Relative Strength signals on average last two years or more, a change in columns on the Relative Strength chart lasts generally six to eight months, and we find it very useful to evaluate stocks based on their RS chart's most recent column. If the RS chart is in X's the stock is outperforming on a nearer term basis; if it is in O's, it is underperforming the market on a nearer term basis.

This RSX percentage is also plotted on a grid from 0 percent to 100 percent, like the PT indexes, and when this indicator is in X's and moving higher, it suggests that area of the market or sector is performing better than the market on a shorter term basis.

We refer to these charts in-house as RSX charts because we use the prefix RSX before the market or sector symbol to call up the chart on our Web site. For example, RSXNYSE is the Percent of Stocks in the NYSE universe that have their Relative Strength charts in a column of X's.

With the RSX charts, we saw a specific divergence between the NYSE and the OTC markets, too. The RSXNYSE chart had been rising since March 22, and you can see this in Figure 6.8. The index rising in a column of X's is telling us more and more stocks within the NYSE universe are outperforming the overall market. At the same time, take a look at the RSXOTC chart (Figure 6.9). Here you can see that the number of stocks within the OTC universe that have Relative Strength charts in a column of X's was at 52 percent in March, and is 28 percent currently. This

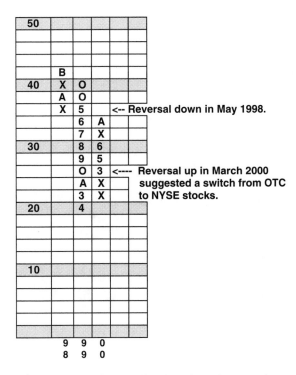

Figure 6.8 RSXNYSE (percent of stocks with RS charts in column of X's).

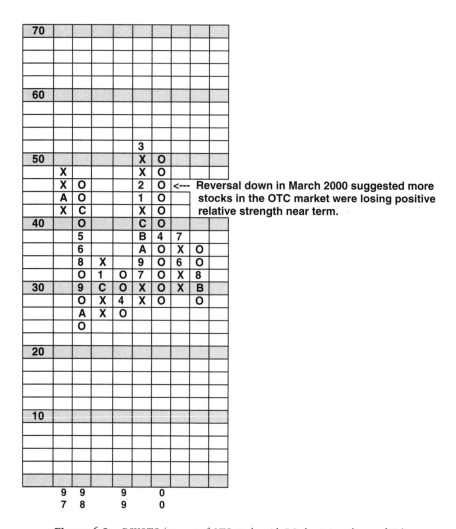

Figure 6.9   RSXOTC (percent of OTC stocks with RS charts in column of X's).

shows us that more and more OTC stocks are reversing back down into a column of O's on their RS charts, or are underperforming the market. To support the fact of relatively stronger NYSE stocks and weaker OTC stocks, look at the cumulative advance-decline lines. From March 22, 2000, through November 27, 2000, we saw a cumulative 5,241 more decliners than advancers on the NYSE market, while at the same time there have been a cumulative 64,618 more decliners than advancers on the OTC market! That shows you how much better the NYSE stocks held up in the year 2000.

You can also notice that the RSXNYSE chart reversed down in a column of O's in May 1998 and remained in that column of O's until March 2000. Remember the consumer stocks during this period and the bank stocks? Both are very heavily congregated in the NYSE universe. During this time, many bank stocks got cut in half, and that's if they were lucky. From its 1998 highs to its 2000 lows, Bank of America (BAC) fell from the 88 area to the 38 area. Coca-Cola (KO), which had been such a great performer since 1994, got cut in half from its highs of 88 in 1998 to a low of 44 in early 2000. At the same time, the RSXOTC chart was in X's and rising. During this time, the meteoric rise in technology stocks continued as the technology bubble got larger and larger. I'll never forget trading stocks like Hyseq (HYSQ) during this time period from 16 to 100 or Redhat (RHAT) from 25 to 125. But boy when that bubble burst, it burst. Stocks that were trading at 150 (you had to use a 5-point-per-box scale just to compress the chart so it was readable), are now trading below 5. As I write this, I feel like a part of history. In the years to come as I talk with my grandchildren, I can envision saying, "That's right, I was a part of that phenomenal bull market in technology and witnessed the blood bath after the bubble burst." The beauty of all this is that the charts guided investors willing to look and heed, just as an experienced captain guides an Exxon Tanker safely out of the harbor.

Percent Relative Strength on Buy Signals

The Point and Figure Relative Strength buy and sell signals are long term in nature, lasting on average two years. Within a market or an industry group, we calculate the percentage of stocks whose Relative Strength charts are on buy signals. This percentage is then plotted on a grid from 0 percent to 100 percent. When it is in a column of X's and rising, it means more stocks underlying that sector are getting stronger versus the market on a long-term basis. This indicator is much slower moving than the Percent Relative Strength in X's and the Percent Positive Trend.

When changes in the Percent Relative Strength on Buy Signals (RSP charts as we call them in-house) do occur, however, they are important (we talk some more about this chart in Chapter 7). In Figure 6.10, you see the chart of the Percent Relative Strength on Buy Signals for the OTC (RSPOTC). Notice that along with the RSXOTC and PTOTC charts, the RSPOTC chart reversed down in April 2000. This was yet another sign that this area of the market was in for a rough ride.

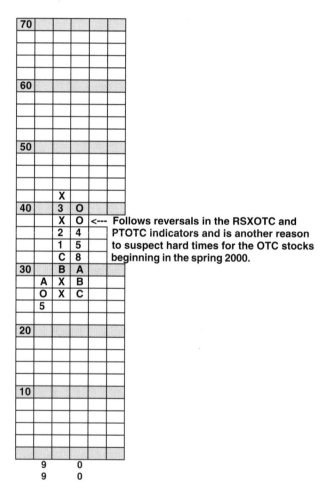

Figure 6.10   RSPOTC (percent of OTC stocks with RS charts on a Buy Signal).

Bullish Sentiment Index

Mike Burke of Chartcraft/Investors Intelligence created this index long ago. He receives hundreds of newsletters each week. He reads them all and categorizes them in either the bullish, bearish, or correction camp. His theory is that when everyone is on one side of the ship, it is best to go to the other side. Most money managers never outperform the broad averages—they have, in essence, become contrary indicators. When the majority of investment advisers are bullish, the market has a high probability of going in the opposite direction, and the opposite is true when there is a high level of bearish advisers. When the majority are looking for a correction, the current trend will probably continue. Chartcraft/Investors Intelligence puts these numbers out each week.

Bearish Sentiment Index

This index is the exact opposite as the Bullish Sentiment Index. It just gauges the percentage of investment advisers that are bearish. When the majority are bearish, expect the market to turn and to see prices rise.

Summary of the Indicators

Now let's stop for a second and allow this discussion to seep in. We have talked about several different concepts and indicators that can be applied to the NYSE and Nasdaq markets as well as to sectors. Each week to keep this information straight in my mind, I sit down and fill out the Market Indicator Summary form shown on page 175. We do the same type of exercise on our Web site, but I still find that writing something by hand is especially helpful. It just makes what is going on in the market more real when you write it down instead of just looking at it on the computer screen.

Once I have the Market Indicator Summary form filled out, then I evaluate it. You would be surprised that there are very few changes. Making changes in the overall bias of the indicators we have outlined here is like moving an aircraft carrier, not a jet ski. But when those changes occur, it is important to heed them and take action where necessary. If you become very comfortable with these indicators and the types of strategies you want to employ when changes do occur, you won't have the "deer in the headlights syndrome." You will intuitively understand what used to baffle you. Those of you who play golf have probably read some of Dr. Robert J. Rotella's works. He was the Director of Sports Psychology at the University of Virginia and is a consultant to many professional golfers; he also writes extensively about golf. One of Dr. Rotella's tips that stayed with me was, "It is more important to be decisive than to be correct when preparing to play any golf shot, particularly a putt." Life on Wall Street means that you will not be correct every time. However, you must not let that keep you from sticking to your game plan, and you must not allow yourself to second-guess your tactical moves. One of the problems with pursuing perfection is hunting for the perfect method. Trying a new system each week will not get you to your goal. It requires remaining focused on one method and maintaining consistency and discipline. You may find that Fibonnaci numbers, Gann angles, or astrology works for you; and that is fine. But, once you find the method that you are comfortable with, you must stick with it. We find the Point and Figure method works the best for us because it is firmly cemented in something we can easily understand and know is true—the irrefutable law of supply and demand. If you begin to second-guess your play book, you are doomed to lose the game. Take those principles you have practiced and implement them when the time comes. Remain true to yourself, win, lose, or draw. Nothing is right every single time but the objective is to be more right than wrong and to stack as many odds in your favor as possible.

When you are evaluating the following form each week, think about some of the scenarios that might occur. If there are more indicators in X's and rising for each market, then I know I have the football and can run plays. If the indicators are in X's but all near the 70 percent level, then I know the risk is high and I need to make sure the defensive players are well rested and ready to come on the field at a moment's notice. If the majority of the indicators are in O's and falling, that tells me we have a weak market and I

Market Indicator Summary Form

Indicator	NYSE Market	Nasdaq Market
Bullish Percent		
Percent of Stocks Above Their 10-Week Moving Average		
High-Low Index		
Percent of Stocks Above Their 30-Week Moving Average		
Advance-Decline Line		
Percent of Stocks with Positive Trends		
Percent of Stocks with RS Charts in X's		
Percent of Stocks with RS Charts on Buy Signals		

should continue to employ wealth preservation strategies. If the indicators are in O's but all below 30 percent, then I need to begin formulating shopping lists of ideas to begin buying once the indicators reverse up. What you will find is that some indicators move faster than others, and when major changes in the market occur, it is like a puzzle coming together. When you dump out a puzzle on a table, it is a hodgepodge of pieces. Once you get those corner pieces in place and the border set, however, the picture becomes much clearer. That's the way the indicators work.

Bond Market Indicators

Interest rates are a critical ingredient in investors' decision making. They weigh the advantages of holding interest rate-bearing securities against holding equities. As rates rise, investors typically move out of stocks and into interest-rate-bearing securities. This disintermediation causes excess supply in the equity markets driving prices lower. This is a simplistic explanation of how interest rates affect the stock markets. Books have been written on the subject. For our purposes, we simply want to get a handle on whether we expect rates to rise or fall. Again, we endeavor to keep things simple. There are only a few indicators we use daily. What we really do is simply update the charts each day by hand and that forces us to keep track of what is going on in the bond market.

The Dow Jones 20 Bond Average

This is one of our main long-term bond indicators. The Dow Jones 20 Bond Average is simply placed on a Point and Figure chart (Figure 6.11). The box size is 0.20 per box. The average moves slowly and does not often give signals, but when they occur, you must pay close attention. Buy signals can be given two ways—a double top buy signal or a low pole warning. Recall that a low pole warning occurs when a stock or index makes a "pole" of O's down and then retraces that pole by more than 50 percent. A column of O's can constitute a pole if it exceeds the previous column of O's by at least three. Sell signals can also occur two ways—a double bottom sell signal or a high pole warning. A high pole warning is evident when a stock makes a pole of X's up (the column of X's must exceed the previous column by at least three X's) and then retraces more than 50 percent of that move upward.

Figure 6.12 shows the infrequency of signals in the long-term bond indicator. Since 1992, there have only been 16 signals in the Dow Jones 20 Bond Average. Of those signals, 11 were profitable. That is being right almost 75 percent of the time, not a bad percentage; these signals kept you out of bonds in the disastrous 1994 and 1999 markets and in them for the nice rally in 1995. Heck, think of it this way. Alex Rodriguez, the baseball player, will make over $250 million over the next 10 years for being "successful" only 30 percent of the time. Think what he would make if he were successful 75 percent or 80 percent of the time? The point is that not every signal, whether buy or sell, will be right but you want to play each one accordingly. When you play a game of five-card stud, if you receive two aces as your first two cards, what are you going to do? You are going to bet because at that time you have the best hand possible. The odds are good then. Of course, you are going to receive three more cards and that will

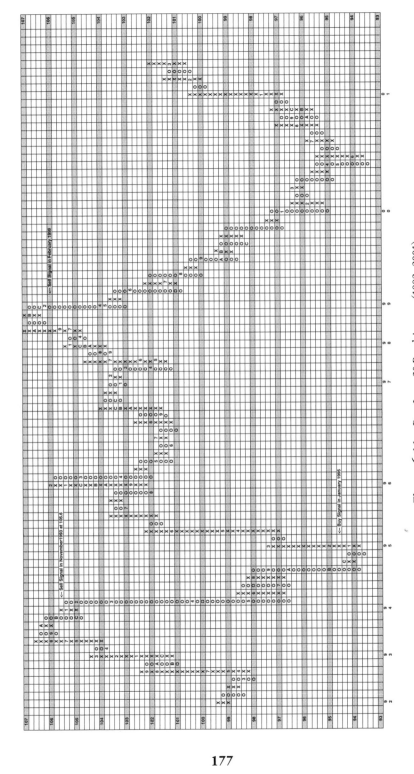

Figure 6.11 Dow Jones 20 Bond Average (1992–2001).

May 1992	Buy Signal	99.2	
October 1993	Sell Signal	105.6	+6.4
October 1993	Sell Signal	105.6	
January 1995	Buy Signal	94.6	+11.0
January 1995	Buy Signal	94.6	
July 1995	Sell Signal	102.8	+8.2
July 1995	Sell Signal	102.8	
September 1995	Buy Signal	103.0	−0.2
September 1995	Buy Signal	103.0	
March 1996	Sell Signal	103.8	+0.8
March 1996	Sell Signal	103.8	
August 1996	Buy Signal	102.0	+1.8
August 1996	Buy Signal	102.0	
January 1997	Sell Signal	103.0	+1.0
January 1997	Sell Signal	103.0	
June 1997	Buy Signal	102.6	+0.4
June 1997	Buy Signal	102.6	
February 1999	Sell Signal	106.0	+3.4
February 1999	Sell Signal	106.0	
February 2000	Buy Signal	96.4	+9.6
February 2000	Buy Signal	96.4	
March 2000	Sell Signal	95.6	−.8
March 2000	Sell Signal	95.6	
June 2000	Buy Signal	94.6	+1.0
June 2000	Buy Signal	94.6	
September 2000	Sell Signal	96.0	+1.4
September 2000	Sell Signal	96.0	
December 2000	Buy Signal	97.2	−1.2
December 2000	Buy Signal	97.2	
February 2001	Sell Signal	100.4	+3.2
February 2001	Sell Signal	110.4	
March 2001	Buy Signal	101.6	−1.2
March 2001	Buy Signal	101.6	

Figure 6.12 Buy and sell signals for the Dow Jones 20 Bond Average.

decide the ultimate outcome. In other words, you are going to bet the hand every time, but you won't win every single hand. But you keep the odds of success in your favor.

In our daily *Equity Market Report* back in October 1993, I said that if this bond index gave a sell signal it would suggest that rates were about to rise and anyone who had an adjustable mortgage should lock in the current rate. I watched the sell signal given in November 1993, and the index was dead on the money. Did I lock in my adjustable mortgage? No. There I sit praying for lower rates. The moral to the story is, trust the indicators. The bottom came when the Dow Jones 20 Average broke a double top buy signal at 94.6 in January 1995. Many of you might remember the news coming out at this time about Orange County. I think of the Orange County debacle as the cover story for the bottom in the bond market. Remember, the news media report on what is happening today, not what's going to happen in the future, and that is what the markets are concerned with. Watching the indicators helps put us in the right trend before it makes it to the cover of the magazine.

Most recently in the Dow Jones 20 Bond average, we saw a sell signal on February 2, 1999, when the Dow Jones 20 Bond Average was right back up in the same area where it topped out in 1993 (Figure 6.11). At this time, the cover story on *Time* magazine was "The Committee to Save the World." It was a picture of Alan Greenspan, Larry Summers, and Robert Rubin. This was a major statement to us to move out of bonds or at least hedge positions, to look at our financial related equity positions, to make sure we had stop-loss points set. The Dow Jones 20 Bond Average fell from 102 on that sell signal down to a low of 93.4 before beginning to regroup—it was even a worse decline in bonds than in 1994.

Commodities

We look at commodity charts as well. These charts can provide some important guidance on raw materials that in turn affect stock prices. One of the charts we watch closely is that of West Texas Intermediate Oil (Figure 6.13). In March 1999, this chart showed that the trend changed back to positive for the first time

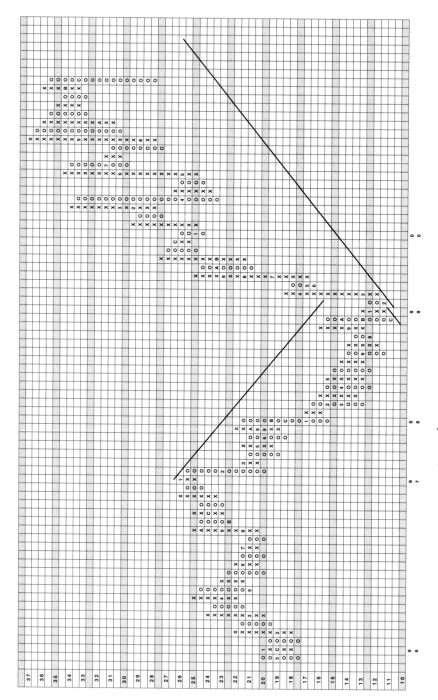

Figure 6.13   West Texas Intermediate Crude Oil.

in years. This told us that we should expect higher crude oil prices and doing a price objective based on that buy signal yielded 33. Now, when I told that to people, they wanted to put me in a straitjacket. This major buy signal in West Texas Crude also caused us to take a look at Oil and Oil Service stocks. The sector Bullish Percent, which we discuss in Chapter 7, was below the 30 percent level and suggesting low risk in the group. That led to a great move in these stocks.

Other commodities that we find helpful to watch are Gold and Silver for some helpful insight on Precious Metals stocks. We also keep a chart of London Gold which is plotted on a Point and Figure basis, not a Bullish Percent basis. As well, we watch Copper in relation to copper-related stocks like Phelps Dodge (PD). Recently we were evaluating a chart of Starbucks (SBUX) and also looked at the chart of Coffee to see if there was anything to glean from that.

When we evaluate our main bond indicator, the Dow Jones 20 Bond Average, we also look at bond futures to see if they correspond. Typically when the Dow Jones 20-Bond Average is giving a sell signal, bond futures are also breaking down and giving sell signals. Conversely, when the Dow Jones 20-Bond Average is moving to a buy signal, bond futures, too, are usually breaking out on the upside. There are two other indexes that you should be aware of— the 30-Year Yield Index (TYX) and the 10-Year Note Index (TNX). Both of these indexes measure *yields*. They will be moving in the opposite direction of the Dow Jones 20-Bond Average or bond futures. Options can be bought on the TYX or TNX to play a change in yields.

Chapter 7

SECTOR ANALYSIS

Sector Analysis with Bullish Percent Indexes

The same Bullish Percent concept that is applied to the NYSE and OTC markets can be applied to sectors within the market. This application expands our ability to evaluate the pieces of the puzzle. The puzzle is the whole market, made up of many sectors. We look at these sectors as the pieces of the puzzle. Sector analysis is probably the most important consideration when investing. Sectors are like the schools of fish you might have seen on the Discovery Channel. These schools dart quickly in one direction or the other, but what is amazing is how a whole school of fish moves perfectly together on each turn, as if some sixth sense tells each individual fish what the group is about to do. Sector rotation tends to behave the same way. Economic stimuli tend to affect all the stocks underlying the sector causing them to move in unison. Sector analysis is one of the most important yet least analyzed parts of the market. We place tremendous emphasis on sector rotation in our daily work. I have said in previous chapters that about 75 percent of the risk in a stock is associated with the market and sector, and only 25 percent is stock-specific risk. Stocks don't just jump about with no rhyme or reason. Moves tend to be orchestrated.

Another analogy keeps coming to mind. I picture a herd of wildebeest romping across the African plains. They move in unison, first in one direction, then another. A few of the herd get out of sync, but the majority tend to move together. Sectors operate the same way. Wall Street tends to follow the actions of the herd. First the sector's supply-demand relationship changes and more buyers begin to cause the stocks in that particular sector to rise. As the sector moves up, other institutions are alerted that the move is on, and they climb on board. Eventually the mainstream financial media catch wind of a sector move underway and begin to write articles about how the industry has made a turnaround and should have clear sailing ahead. This draws in the individual investors just in time to catch the top. By the time the articles appear in magazines about how great the industry is, almost everyone is in who wants to be in leaving little available demand to force the industry up much further. The last group in is the unsuspecting public, who use newspapers and magazines as their primary source of stock market research. *Time* magazine has a cover story about XYZ Company rated "Company of the Year." Mr. Jones, who sees this major statement on the cover of this mainstream magazine, calls his broker and buys the stock, virtually drying up the last available demand for the sector. Everyone is now in who wants to be in. The magazine cover signaled maximum saturation of positive information about this company. At this point, all it takes is the slightest selling pressure to start the downturn. With little demand left, it only takes a small amount of supply to turn the situation around. Once the public is in, virtually no one is left to do the buying. Remember that prices move as a direct result of supply-and-demand imbalances. If there are no more buyers left to cast their vote, supply, by definition, must take the upper hand. The sector then begins to lose sponsorship and moves to an oversold condition where everyone who wants to be out of the sector is out, and the whole process starts anew. It's actually beautiful how these natural rhythms evolve. When you think of the seasons changing, or the produce in the supermarket coming in and out of season, think of sector rotation as I do.

You know, I mentioned magazine covers. Watch them carefully. The next time you are in the airport, look at the magazine rack and see if you can find a widely read magazine that makes a major statement on its cover about some sector of the market— something like "The Banking Industry Is in Trouble." If you find one, buy the magazine and keep it. Actually, just keep the cover. Normally, the trend in that sector will continue to move for a couple of months in the direction the cover suggests, as the last Joneses buy their shares. Give that sector eight months, and you will find its behavior has a high probability of being opposite of that suggested on the magazine cover. The reason for this is that the cover stirs Mr. Jones and Ms. Smith into action and while all the Joneses and Smiths are busy reacting, the sector moves in the forecasted direction. Once these investors are in and the door slams behind them, there is no more buying or selling pressure (whichever the cover suggests) left to sponsor the sector. The forces of supply and demand slowly begin to change, and the sector takes the opposite tack. Try it—you will be amazed. It's simply human nature.

To put some quantitative research on why sector rotation is so important in stock selection, I want to discuss an interesting study done by CDA Weisenberger. In this study, they had four hypothetical investors invest $1,000 starting in 1983; each had a different set of investment rules. The first investor used a buy-and-hold strategy. The second timed the market. The third and fourth investors both used sector timing. The study looks at each one of the theories over a 15-year time period, 1983 to 1998.

Mr. Buy and Hold started with $1,000 and just bought the S&P 500 and held that original investment through thick and thin; his account grew to $11,817. That is certainly not a bad return. The next investor, the market timer did even better though. For the purposes of the study, Mr. Market Timer was omnipotent enough to know every month when the S&P 500 was up and stayed invested for those months; and when the S&P 500 was going to show a loss for that month, he was not invested. Using these rules, Mr. Market Timer turned his $1,000 into $73,373! The third investor was Mr. Good Sector Timer. Like, Mr. Market Timer, Mr. Good Sector Timer was omnipotent about the fate of sectors in the marketplace. Every year he looked into the crystal ball and knew exactly what sector was going to be the best performer for the coming year. By putting his money into the best performing sector each year, his account swelled from the original $1,000 to $115,006 by the end of 15 years. Spectacular performance to say the least. Finally, the last investor was Mr. Poor Sector Timer. This poor soul didn't have fate on his side and invested in the worst performing sector each year. His portfolio had dwindled to $172 by the end of 15 years. You can graphically see these results in Figure 7.1.

While all these investors are fictitious and certainly no one would ever be able to have the 100 percent accuracy that Mr. Market Timer and Mr. Good Sector Timer had, the study points out that market and sector timing are extremely important in investing. Being able to identify strong sectors and weak sectors can enable one to gain an advantage over just buying and holding without regard for sector rotation. One doesn't even have to be close to getting every sector move correct to outperform the buy-and-hold theory. The investor who perfectly timed the market saw his portfolio rise more than $100,000 based on the same original investment of $1,000 that was made by Mr. Buy and Hold.

When evaluating sectors, you must be a contrarian. You must find the courage to buy stocks in sectors that are out of favor. You must avoid the crowd. This is extremely difficult as it goes against human nature. We tend to gravitate to the crowd. You go to your neighborhood supermarket. It's payday and you are sure the store will be crowded. When you arrive at the store, you see

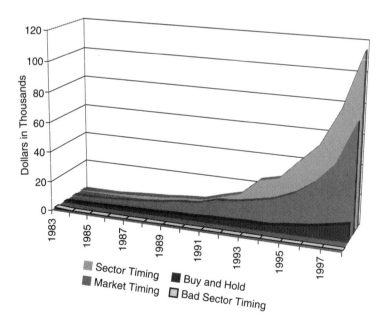

Figure 7.1   CDA/Weisenberger Study—perfect market timing versus perfect sector timing.

that a major incident of sorts has captured everyone's attention. There is a major crowd around this incident. Do you go with the crowd to see what is happening or do you take advantage of an empty store while the other shoppers are crowded around the incident outside? The sector Bullish Percent indexes force you to go into the store and shop while you can with no interference. You will be able to have your pick of the best produce, best meats, not wait in line at the deli, and have first choice in the marked-down meat section. On top of that, you will be able to check out with no line and all because you went against the crowd.

That contrary view of things is exactly what Earnest Staby was talking about in the mid-1940s. As mentioned earlier, trend charts always look most bullish at market tops and most bearish at market bottoms. The Bullish Percent indexes force you to be more negative at tops and more positive at bottoms. Once you see more than 70 percent of the stocks underlying the market or a sector go on buy signals, you are in a condition where just about everyone is in who wants to be in. When translated into supply and demand, it simply suggests that the availability of demand has been spent. If this is the case, then an investor should be less enthusiastic about buying stock in the market or that sector when the index is at 70 percent or higher. When the index is near the 30 percent level or lower, it's time to put your buy list together.

When I was a stockbroker, I went with the crowd. It was easier to do business that way. Even though I was at a major wirehouse with highly paid fundamental analysts who were literally hit or miss (you never knew which), my primary source of research was the *Wall Street Journal* and *Barron's* weekly financial newspaper. When those didn't yield enough ideas, I listened to the broker next to me pitching a stock. All of us got ideas the same way, and as you may have already guessed, the process was lackluster at best. Our training back then was basically in sales and not much else. It really hasn't changed much since then either. Now the emphasis for many stockbrokers is on raising money and giving it to a "professional manager" to manage, knowing full well that over 75 percent of all managers and mutual funds never outperform the broad averages. The broker's place in this equation is to manage the manager for a fee. Somehow I seriously doubt this type of fee will last much longer. What is a broker to do, though? Most brokers have no plan of action one way or the other. Don't get me wrong, there are many craftsmen out there indeed; and many of them subscribe to the Point and Figure method. The investor's job is to find a broker who has a solid game plan that includes not only buy strategies but also sell strategies. I assure you, you will not find one by going to a branch office of any firm and asking for the broker of the day. Good stockbrokers who have all the skills to manage the money themselves are a rare breed these days. When you find one, stick with that broker. If you need one, just e-mail us (DWA@dorseywright.com), and we can supply the name of a craftsman who lives near your area. Most of our clients understand the concepts in this book and use them in their daily market operations. There are still no guarantees but I assure you, I would want a broker who at least had the principles of this book firmly in mind. This is his operating system, just like Windows 98. There is no question about it, wealth is still created in the stock market. But as we also found out in 2000, the market is the fastest place to lose wealth if your portfolio is not managed properly. The year 2000 was a real eye-opener for most investors. Recently, I had a Sunday morning call at my home from an independent broker in New Jersey who has decided he would be better off having the Money Management arm of Dorsey, Wright handle a number of his accounts. The market has just taken the wind out his sails. Not only has it taken a strong understanding of Point and Figure Technical Analysis to negotiate this market the past few years, it has also taken a good understanding of how to use the options product to help manage the volatility and risk of the markets.

We run Bullish Percent calculations on numerous sectors as well as international sectors. In Chapter 5, we discussed the NYSE Bullish Percent Index in detail. The same principles apply here. You might think these concepts are universally known, but they aren't. It's still a lost art. I was watching a new Wall Street show the other night called *The Street*. I was totally surprised that on the show they shouted over the broker's intercom, "The Point and Figure Charts are now updated." It really floored me when I heard this. How did Hollywood ever learn about the Point and Figure concept and feel it was important enough to create an audio that all the viewers of the program could hear? I was so surprised because very few individuals and professionals on a relative basis understand these concepts. After reading this book, you will join a very elite group of investors. You would be hard-pressed to find a broker, outside our client list, who understands this philosophy and has reached what we would call craftsman status. The reason is simple, it takes some education and dedication to understand it, and most investors and professionals are not interested in going that extra mile to become a true craftsman. Those of you who are reading this book are a rare breed indeed. You are learning a lost art.

Everything you learned in Chapter 5 on the Bullish Percent Index applies here, so I'm not going to rehash the discussion. If you find you do not understand this concept thoroughly, go back to Chapter 5 and reread it. Sectors employ the same concept, but the number of stocks in the sector universe is smaller than that of New York Stock Exchange or Nasdaq universe. Because of the smaller number of stocks in sector Bullish Percents, they tend to move faster than the NYSE Bullish Percent. To construct a statistically valid Bullish Percent, a sector should have a minimum of 100 stocks. If you have less than 100 stocks, then one stock's buy or sell signal could move the Bullish Percent 6 percent. Just as the broad market Bullish Percents have six different risk levels, so do those of the sector. The best way to get a handle on using this concept as well as other indicators for sectors is to take an example and go through it. Let's take a look at a sector Bullish Percent chart and outline on the chart where the pertinent changes took place.

Electric Utility Bullish Percent

In Figure 7.2, you can see the Electric Utility Bullish Percent. Many people would regard this as a sleepy sector, not worthy of consideration because "it doesn't move enough." That really is not the case at all. This sector, like others, has provided good opportunities over the years. In 1994, the Electric Utility Bullish Percent chart fell to 24 percent. This is down into the "Green Zone," "Promised Land," or "oversold" territory. The fall to 24 percent had come after the Electric Utility Sector Bullish Percent reached

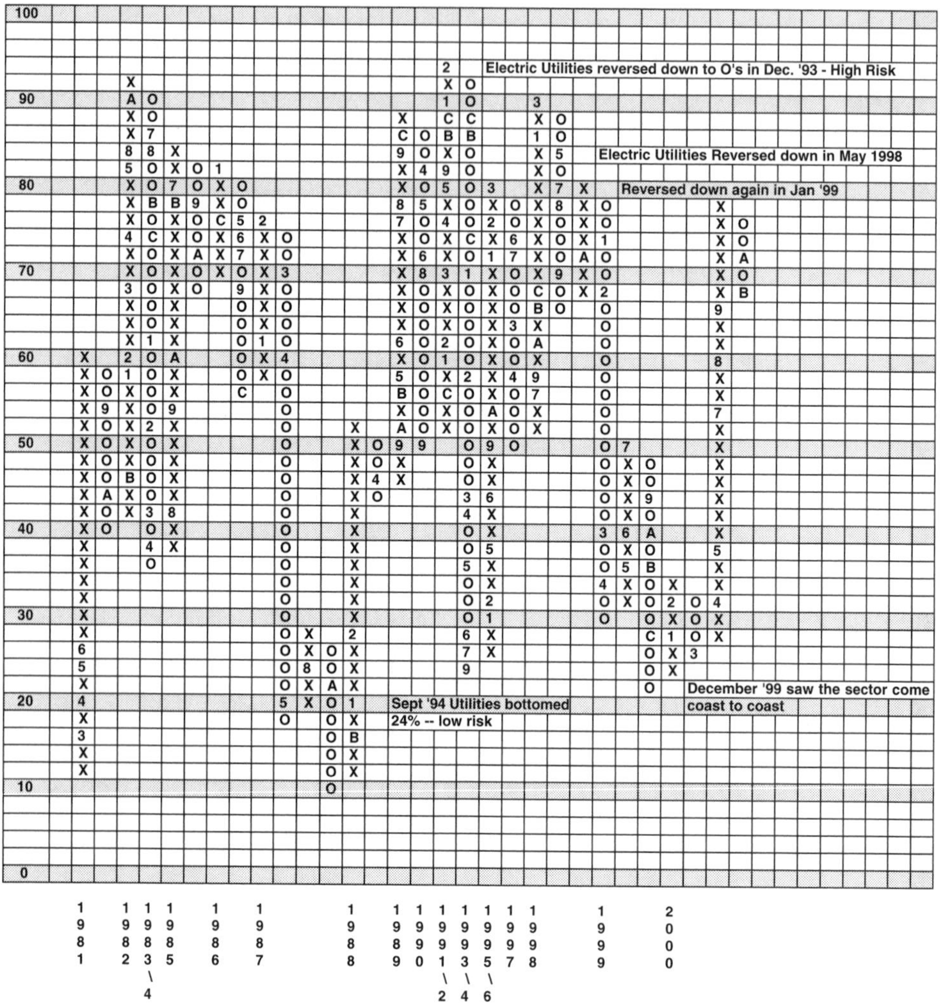

Electric Utilities reversed down to O's in Dec. '93 - High Risk

Electric Utilities Reversed down in May 1998

Reversed down again in Jan '99

Sept '94 Utilities bottomed 24% -- low risk

December '99 saw the sector come coast to coast

Figure 7.2   Utilities—Electric.

as high as 94 percent in February 1993 and then reversed down in December 1993. The reversal down in December 1993 into O's suggested that you bring the defensive team on the field with respect to Electric Utilities. In your portfolio, you would have wanted to examine the Electric Utility stocks you owned on a fundamental and technical basis. If the individual stock had deteriorated on either account, then action was warranted. Remember that a reversal down from above 70 percent puts the sector on defense and suggests high risk. If you owned Electric Utility stocks in December 1993, you had a high-risk position in your portfolio. To mitigate that risk, you would have several choices. You could set a stop-loss point at which you were not willing to give back any more. You could have taken partial profits off the table, thus reducing your exposure to the sector. You could have bought protective puts on your Electric Utility positions giving you the right to sell that stock at a specific price at a specific time in the future. Again, the whole point would be to reduce risk in an otherwise high-risk sector. If you will also recall from Chapter 6, the Dow Jones 20 Bond Average gave a major sell signal in November 1993. Do you see how this is all coming together and the pieces of the puzzle begin to fall into place? Well, the Electric Utility Bullish Percent fell all the way down to 24 percent by September 1994. Sometimes, sectors fall in a straight line and other times they move down like a staircase with each rally producing lower highs and each sell-off producing lower bottoms. From the February 1993 high in the PHLX Utility Index (UTY) to the September 1994 low, the UTY was down 27.5 percent. That's a utility index, mind you, down 27.5 percent!

Now continuing forward in time, in January 1995, the Electric Utility Bullish Percent chart reversed up to X's meaning we bring the offensive team back on the field with respect to the sector. As well, the Dow Jones 20 Bond Average (DJBB) had just given a buy signal, the first since the November 1993 sell signal. This information would have meant you go to your fundamental inventory of Electric Utility stocks and find those also controlled by demand to initiate new positions in. You could have also bought calls on the UTY index. Today, Utility iShares are available allowing you to buy a school of utility fish instead of owning just one fish. Just as there are numerous ways to be defensive, there are numerous ways to be offensive, too. Sometimes one of the things we do in our Dorsey, Wright Profit Sharing account when a sector reverses up from a low level is buy not just one name within that sector, but two. We do this for a couple of reasons. First, when a sector is reversing up from an oversold condition and has some other factors going for it, we overweight that sector. Let's say typically we take a 5 percent position in a sector. If the sector Relative Strength is strong and things are lining up great for the sector, then we might take an 8 percent position. By purchasing two names in the sector, it allows us some extra flexibility when we feel the indicators warrant scaling back in the sector. Second, it seems like Murphy is always hanging around the corner. The Electric Utility stock we would choose to buy would be the one with some type of noose around its neck that doesn't allow that stock to rally while the rest in the group take off like a rocket. We just had that happen to us with the Healthcare sector. The sector was shaping up, but the overall market was showing signs of weakness so we just put on one position. Our pick was Medtronic (MDT), and the stock hasn't hurt the portfolio but it just didn't participate like so many others in the group.

Just as the move down in 1993 for Electric Utilities was very sharp and steep, the upmove for Electric Utilities in 1995 was powerful. The sector Bullish Percent rallied from 30 percent on the reversal up into X's straight up to 80 percent. During this time frame (January 1995 to March 1996), the PHLX Utility Index (UTY) was up 21.7 percent. Again, not a bad move for a "slow" sector like Electric Utilities, and that return doesn't include any dividends.

Let's continue to look at the Electric Utility Bullish Percent chart for the year 1998. In March 1998 the sector Bullish Percent was at 90 percent, near those 1993 highs of 94 percent. Now look at that chart again and say out loud whether you think this is a high-risk or low-risk time to buy Electric Utility stocks. It's a high-risk time. With a reading above 70 percent on a Bullish Percent chart, it tells us that most of the people who want to be in the sector are already in. The availability of demand to continue to push the sector higher is extremely limited. In May, the sector Bullish Percent reverses down to O's and falls to 66 percent by September. Then in October 1998, the Electric Utility sector reverses up to X's at 72 percent. The sector is back in X's, but the field position is 72 percent. What would you do? Would you go out and enthusiastically buy Electric Utility stocks the way you would when the sector is reversing up from below 30 percent? Probably not. In fact, definitely not. A sector Bullish Percent may be in a column of X's, but the field position is not good;

have patience, it will come back to a better level. They all do. Or, if you have to have a presence in that sector, take just partial positions, not full positions. By January 1999, the Electric Utility Bullish Percent was back into a column of O's at 72 percent. Now, let's bring another piece of the puzzle into the equation. The Relative Strength chart of the UTY was in a column of O's. The Percent of Stocks with Relative Strength Charts in X's for the Electric Utility sector (RSXEUTI) was in a column of O's reversing down from 70 percent too. As well, the Percent of Stocks with Positive Trend Charts for the Electric Utility sector (PTEUTI) was still in X's but at 84 percent. Here's the breakdown of the indicators for the Electric Utility Sector in January 1999:

Summary of Indicators for Electric Utilities in January 1999

Sector Bullish Percent	In O's; reversed down at 72% after making lower top
Sector Relative Strength	In O's; reversed down in October 1998
RSPEUTI	In X's
RSXEUTI	In O's, reversed down in October 1998 from high of 70%
PTEUTI	In X's at 84%

These indicators tell me the majority are in O's and another is at very extended levels. The picture points to a high-risk status for the sector. For any sector that I am evaluating, I like to take the preceding five indicators and write down where everything stands. It really makes a clear, black and white picture for me to evaluate the sector. Either the majority are positive or the majority are negative and it only takes a minute to gather the data on our Web site. You can see that the picture was beginning to show a high risk for the Electric Utility sectors in January 1999 and suggested action if you owned these stocks.

By December 1999, the Electric Utility sector had fallen to 22 percent, the lowest level on the chart since the October 1987 crash carried the group down to 10 percent. That move from October 1998 to the December 1999 lows saw the PHLX Utility Index (UTY), fall 28 percent. Now, let's take a snapshot of the

Electric Utility sector when the sector Bullish Percent is reversing up to X's in January 2000.

Summary of Indicators for Electric Utilities in January 2000

Sector Bullish Percent	In X's; reversed up at 28% after low of 22%
Sector Relative Strength	In O's
RSPEUTI	In X's
RSXEUTI	In X's, reversed up from low of 10% highs were 70%
PTEUTI	In O's; at 38%—high was 84%

You can see here that the Electric Utility indicators had flipped from having three negative to now having three positive, enough for new positions. In April 2000, the sector Relative Strength reversed up for the group and the PT chart followed in June. So if you were not comfortable enough to enter a full position in Utilities in January, then you could have added to positions in the spring. In the year 2000, the Electric Utility sector was the best performing group, up about 40 percent in the face of a Nasdaq Composite down 50 percent from its highs.

Looking at the position of the Electric Utility Bullish Percent in November 2000, we see that the sector Bullish Percent was now in O's at 68 percent. As you are already catching on, this suggests to us high risk in the group. The sector Relative Strength, RSP, RSX, and PT charts all remain positive but they are beginning to give up some ground. Since you can look at the history of the Electric Utility Bullish Percent chart and see that the move has generally run out of steam when the sector Bullish Percent gets into the upper 70 percent range or beyond, a prudent thing to do would be to begin scaling out of positions and taking partial profits off the table. Set stop-loss points so you make sure those hard-earned profits don't turn into losses.

Telecommunications Bullish Percent

In Figure 7.3, on page 196, you can see a chart of the Telecommunications Sector Bullish Percent. Notice that this sector

Bullish Percent chart has a lot more movement in it than the Electric Utility Bullish Percent chart. However, that doesn't make it any less effective. This sector really got clobbered in 2000, so let's take a look and see if there were any warning signs. I like to think of the sector Bullish Percents as children. They each take on their own personalities. For example, the Drug Sector Bullish Percent chart tends to top out around 68 percent and bottom out in the 34 percent to 36 percent area. This sector generally does not get down to extremely washed-out levels of 10 percent or 20 percent very often at all while other sectors like Biotech and Semiconductor can get to 80 percent and above and down into the teens. Now in looking at the Telecommunications Sector Bullish Percent chart, notice in March 2000, the sector reversed to O's from the 70 percent level putting the defensive team on the field and with poor field position. At that time, here is where the composite picture of the sector presented itself. These charts are shown in Figures 7.3 to 7.7 (pages 196–200).

Summary of Indicators for Telecommunications March 2000

Sector Bullish Percent	In O's; reversed down from 70% high
Sector Relative Strength	In O's
RSPTELE	In X's (note that it reversed down in April)
RSXTELE	In O's, reversed down from 78%
PTTELE	In O's; reversed down from high of 84%

This showed that Telecommunications was a very high-risk area of the market. That certainly was the case for 2000 as many of these stocks were hit to the point that they were down 75 percent, and 90 percent from their highs by the end of November. Of course, these stocks did not go straight down. There were bounces along the way, but the important thing to note is that while sometimes the sector Bullish Percent reversed into X's, it was not accompanied by a reversal up in the RSPTELE (Percent of Telecommunications Stocks on Relative Strength buy signals) or the RSXTELE (Percent of Telecommunications Stocks in a column of X's on their RS charts) charts.

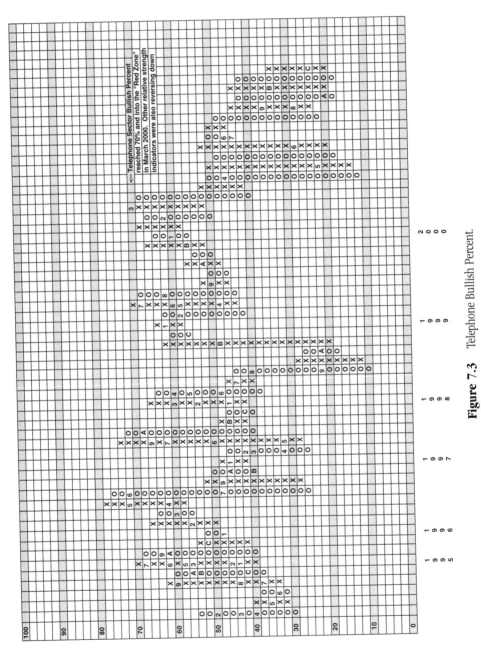

Figure 7.3 Telephone Bullish Percent.

196

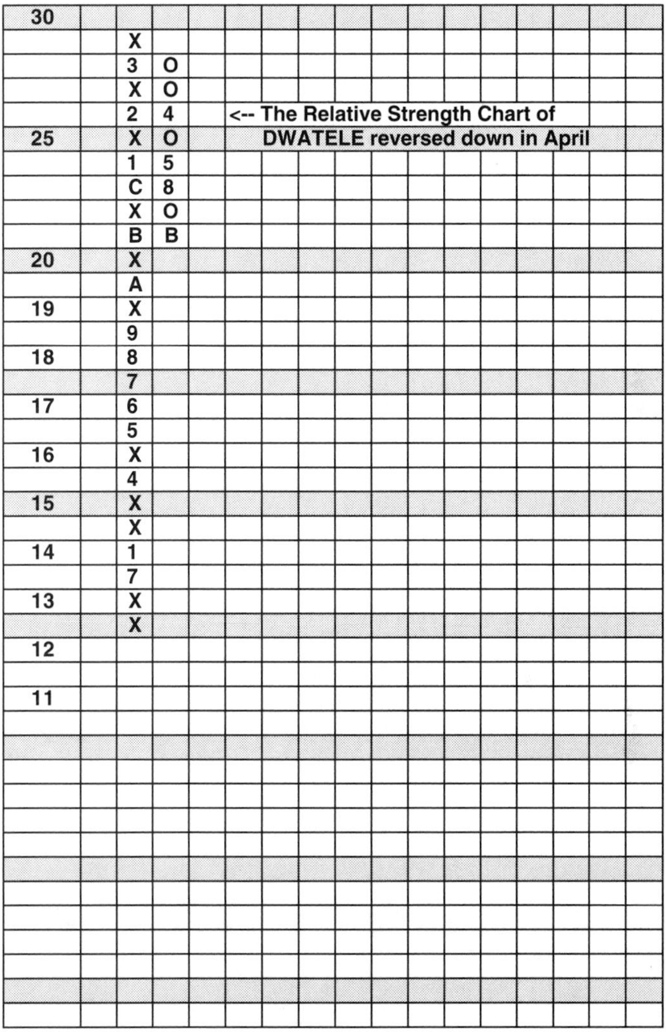

Price			
30			
	X		
	3	O	
	X	O	
	2	4	<-- The Relative Strength Chart of
25	X	O	DWATELE reversed down in April
	1	5	
	C	8	
	X	O	
	B	B	
20	X		
	A		
19	X		
	9		
18	8		
	7		
17	6		
	5		
16	X		
	4		
15	X		
	X		
14	1		
	7		
13	X		
	X		
12			
11			

Figure 7.4 DWA Telephone Index (DWATELE) Relative Strength chart.

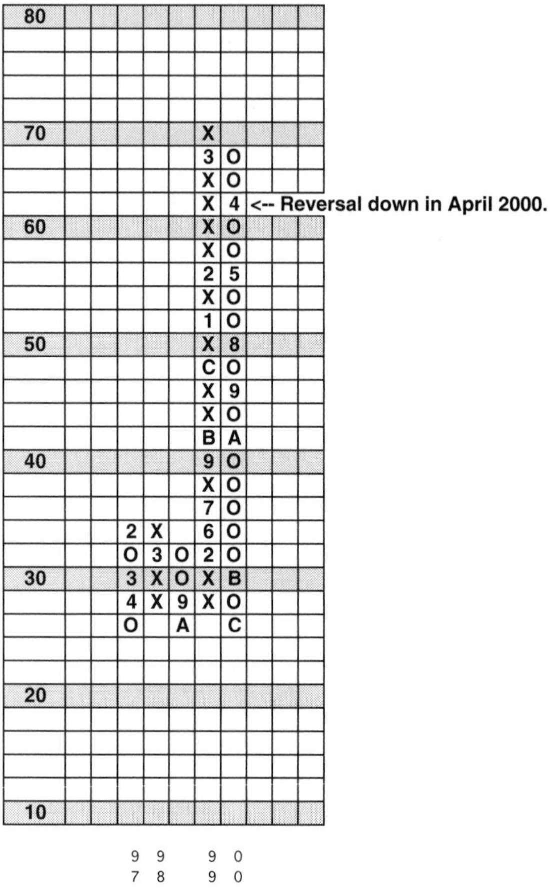

Figure 7.5   Percent of Telephone Stocks on a Relative Strength Buy Signal (RSPTELE).

Summary

To evaluate sectors in the market, we look at the following indicators:

- *Sector Bullish Percent.*   Percent of Stocks on a Point and Figure Buy Signal within a sector.
- *Sector Relative Strength.*   How this sector is performing compared with the overall market.

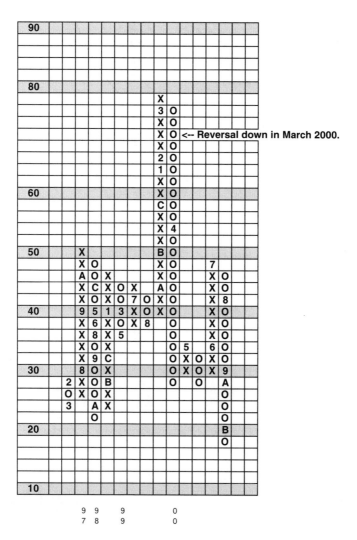

Figure 7.6 Percent of Telephone Stocks in a Column of X's on the Relative Strength Chart (RSXTELE).

- *Sector RSP Chart.* Percent of Stocks within a sector on a Point and Figure Buy Signal on its Relative Strength chart.
- *Sector RSX Chart.* Percent of Stocks within a sector in a column of X's on its Relative Strength chart.
- *Sector PT Chart.* Percent of Stocks within a sector trading above their Bullish Support Lines.

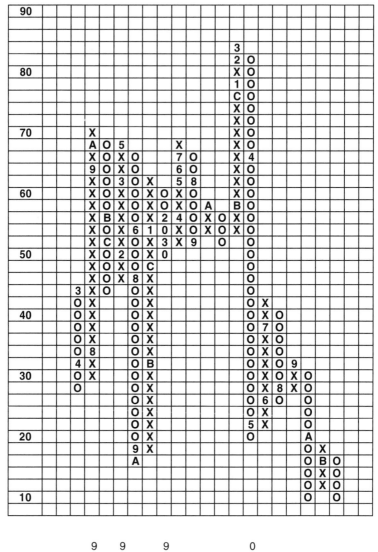

Figure 7.7 Percent of Telephone Stocks with Positive Trends (PTTELE).

For each of these indicators, not only do we look to see if the chart is in X's or O's but we want to consider the field position. When the majority of these indicators are positive, that sector should be a market leader and it is where we would concentrate most of our new money going into the market. Once the sector no longer has the majority of indicators in its favor, then we must begin to think about defensive strategies. New positions in sectors where the majority of indicators are not positive suggest we should expect trading rallies only, not market leadership qualities.

Sector Bell Curve

In Chapter 5, we reprinted an article from one of our daily reports. In that report was a discussion of the sector bell curve. Let's take a minute here and discuss the sector bell curve in more detail. This is one of the tools we use a lot. There are basically just two things we know from the study of economics or statistics that we can apply to the stock market. First, we have supply and demand. When there is more demand than supply, the price will rise and conversely when there is more supply than demand prices will fall. We depict the supply and demand in the marketplace by recording the price (the net of all supply and demand) of a stock in a logical, sensible, and organized manner, the Point and Figure chart. Second, we have the statistical concept of the bell curve with an overbought, oversold, and normal level.

One way we use the bell curve concept is to take the different sector Bullish Percent charts we follow and plot them on a bell curve. Every sector will always trade between 0 percent and 100 percent because every stock in the sector can either be on a buy signal (100%), on a sell signal (0%), or some combination thereof. Typically, we publish the sector Bullish Percent readings in a vertical format with the Y-axis on the left going from 0 percent to 100 percent like that of the Electric Utility Bullish Percent in Figure 7.2. With the sector bell curve, we take the vertical axis and make it the horizontal axis. Then, the first four letters of each sector Bullish Percent are plotted on the curve. If the sector abbreviation is in upper case, then the sector Bullish Percent chart in question is in X's and moving to the right of the curve. Lower case letters indicate the sector Bullish Percent is in O's and moving to the left of the curve. Plotting each of the sectors on a bell curve in this fashion gives us a composite picture of the risk in the market. Sometimes, as in July 1999, the curve will get very skewed to the right-hand side indicating an overbought market. Sometimes, as in October 1999 or December 1994, it will get very skewed to the left-hand side indicating an oversold market. You know that old adage, a picture is worth a thousand words. Well, that's what I think of the bell curve. In one quick picture, I can see whether the market is normally distributed, mostly overbought, or mostly oversold.

The Sector Bell Curve of February 2000 was interesting and unusual. In the February 9, 2000, curve there are some sectors, mostly NYSE denominated, on the oversold, left-hand side of the curve. On that same curve, we see that on the right-hand side, it is populated by technology stocks, mostly OTC or Nasdaq denominated. In general, if you limit yourself to buying in sectors that are bullish and around 50 percent or lower, it forces you to buy when the risk is low and be more defensive when the risk is high. This is an excellent way to get a composite picture of risk in the market.

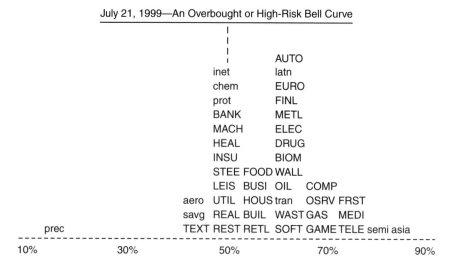

July 21, 1999—An Overbought or High-Risk Bell Curve

October 20, 1999—An Oversold or Low-Risk Bell Curve

```
        stee                       |
        rest                       |
        prot                       |
        osrv                       |
        leis                       |
        latn                       |
        food                       |
        busi                       |
        savg       biom            |
        chem       util            |
        heal text  medi            |
        auto tran  drug            |
   inet bank hous  fina  elec      |
   insu retl real  soft  metl      |
   aero buil wast  frst  oil  tele gas
 wall semi mach comp game asia prec EURO
------------------------------------------------------
10%          30%         50%         70%         90%
```

February 9, 2000—A Bell Curve with Both Upside and Down Opportunities

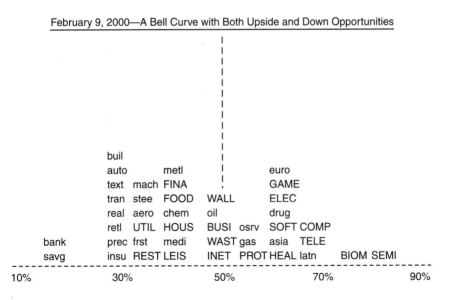

```
                                   |
                                   |
                                   |
                                   |
                                   |
                                   |
                                   |
                                   |
        buil                       |
        auto       metl            |    euro
        text mach  FINA            |    GAME
        tran stee  FOOD    WALL         ELEC
        real aero  chem    oil          drug
        retl UTIL  HOUS    BUSI osrv  SOFT COMP
   bank prec frst  medi    WAST gas  asia  TELE
   savg insu REST  LEIS    INET PROT HEAL latn   BIOM SEMI
------------------------------------------------------
10%          30%         50%         70%         90%
```

Deus ex Machina[*]

I'm convinced that the power of the mind is God's greatest gift to us. I'm also convinced that the secret to unlocking that power lies in belief. Belief, I contend, is the *deus ex machina,* or the magic elixir that can transform a mediocre athlete into a world-class competitor. The same can happen for an investor. A friend called recently to tell me his investing had changed dramatically since he embraced the Point and Figure principles coupled with the fundamentals. His account is growing, but more importantly his confidence has doubled because he now believes in himself and his ability to make money and manage risk in his account. That word *belief* is so powerful, it's life transforming. Confidence comes from education and experience, and it's confidence that is the key to a stable, long-lasting investing portfolio. If you believe in yourself, there is nothing you can't do! That includes sports, business, and your personal life.

Over my years of competing in sports on a world level, I have a formula I have used for success. It goes like this: Conceive, Believe, and Achieve. It's simple but profound. I'm sure most of you have conceived yourself as being great at one time or another. That is very important. When I was a little boy, I always saw myself as being great, actually awesome. In fact, I was always visualizing myself kicking Larry Holmes's butt or breaking Hank Aaron's home run record. I never had a problem conjuring up images of myself doing something spectacular. The problem was that, in my heart, I really didn't believe I could reach such heights. There is a big difference in conceiving yourself as being great and actually believing that you are going to be great. It's when you truly believe you can be great (and that you are going to be great), that you are within reach of being great. Your goals are within reach. At this point, you have the vision of how to arrive at that goal. Belief is the deux ex machina that transforms mediocre to excellence. Believing in yourself opens the doors for success. The consequence is that you don't know what heights you can hit.

---

[*]This section was written with the assistance of Judd Biasiotto, PhD.

I like to tell the story about the chicken and the eagle. It's an old Indian fable about a young brave who took an egg from an eagle's nest and put it into a chicken's nest. When the egg hatched, the eagle thought he was a chicken. As the eagle grew up among the chickens, he learned their way of life. He pecked the ground for food, scratched the dust, and made vocal sounds like the chickens he lived with. One day he looked into the sky and saw an eagle soaring above him. He flexed his wings and said to his mother, "I wish I could fly like that." "Don't be silly," his mother said. "You're a chicken—only eagles can soar so high in the sky." Feeling foolish and convinced that his desire to fly was futile, the eagle went back to scratching and pecking in the dirt. He had, for all practical purposes, become a chicken because he believed he was a chicken. Never again did he question his role on earth.

It is all a matter of perception. The eagle couldn't fly, not because he lacked the natural ability, but rather because his belief was, "I am a chicken, and chickens can't fly." To fly, he needed to alter his perception of himself. He had to recognize his God-given abilities, and/or change his mind-set concerning these abilities. He had to believe in himself. Although our perceptions of reality determine what we believe, what we believe determines what we are and will become. If we perceive ourselves to be like the traders in the movie *Wall Street,* then that is the type of account we will have. I know this because that is exactly what happened to me. I would overleverage positions and engage in strategies with a low probability of success. It wasn't until years later that I began perceiving myself as a money manager and risk manager and, you guessed it, serious wealth began to accumulate.

As human beings, we tend to act appropriately to what we believe to be true, regardless of what is actually true or false. We are the product of conditioning in much the same manner that a computer is the product of its programming. For 14 years now, I have seen brokers and investors transformed from chickens to eagles. I once was a chicken. There is no worse feeling than coming into work each day, worrying about which stock will be the next one to take the pipe on a great fundamental recommendation. The feeling of being out of control permeates your thoughts. The best stocks you own, you never have enough of, and the worst, you always have too much. You sit at your desk, staring at the screen, not knowing how to make up the losses. You become painfully aware you are a chicken in an eagle's world, but you don't know how to become an eagle. These feelings build and eventually you give up control. You settle for chicken status and lose hope of ever flying in your career. Over the years I have seen countless others have the vision of becoming an eagle and go for it. They realize that they can't do it with their current knowledge so they do whatever it takes to obtain that knowledge. Knowledge is power and as they gain more knowledge, they gain more confidence and belief that they will become an eagle. This confidence and belief is contagious and people want to follow the confident.

The transformation in my life from chicken to eagle happened when I read the first paragraph of the introduction to the book *The Three Box Reversal to Point & Figure Technical Analysis*, by A.W. Cohen. It is out of print now. I came to realize that as a broker I only had half the equation to work with. Fundamentals answer the question what to buy; but technicals, equally important, answer the question when to buy and sell it. One without the other is like playing the piano with only one hand. Overnight I soared like an eagle. I had become reacquainted with the irrefutable law of supply and demand. A simple economic law that I had studied in the university for four years hit home the second time around. I transformed myself that moment from chicken to eagle. This transformation lead to the development of Dorsey, Wright & Associates. Time and again, I have seen brokers and investors reach the same revelation after reading the first edition of this book and employing its principles with their already good fundamental work. When it comes to Wall Street, we at Dorsey, Wright have more eagles as clients than can be found anywhere else. What type of bird do you want to be in your investing career?

Chapter 8

MANAGING RISK
IN A PORTFOLIO WITH
OPTIONS AND EXCHANGE
TRADED FUNDS

Let's begin with a nice, easily understood discussion of the options product. It doesn't have to be complicated. These are arrows you must have in your "risk management quiver." The option business can be as complicated or simple as you want to make it. I have spent a lifetime making it simple. I developed and managed an options department for a broker-dealer for the better part of a decade. I've seen it all. I learned one thing for sure during that period—the more complicated the option strategy, the lower the probability of success. The year 2000 truly pointed out the need for solid risk management skills. After the year 2000, I looked back on how I did with the accounts I directly managed. It was an eye-opener. The gains I made in these accounts were primarily due to selling calls against long stock positions that year. Selling calls also cushioned the blow in stocks that turned out to be poor performers. Unless you owned a utility stock in 2000, you had rough going. Whoever would have thought Utilities would be the premier performer for the year? Technology stocks were slaughtered that year and the uncertainty surrounding the unprecedented presidential election stalemate exacerbated the demise of that group. If there ever was a year perfectly designed for the skilled risk manager, it was 2000. You know something else? Many investors saw their 401(k)s take a body blow that year and have come to the realization that sometimes it's better to have the "pie on the table" rather than "pie in the sky." This whole book is about risk management techniques. Options are simply one of the tools we use to help us in this task. Too many investors have bought into the media's game plan of simply buying for the long haul. In the year 2000 alone, we have seen companies like Priceline Dot Com (PCLN) decline from 150 to 5. Lucent Technologies (LU), a premier company, faded from 80 to 6 without the benefit of a split. Cisco Systems (CSCO) declined from 70 to 14, and the story goes on and on and on. I would have to call the year 2000 "The Year of the Risk Manager."

Let's take a look at some option strategies that might make sense in your portfolio. There are basically two appropriate strategies for the individual investor. One is buying calls or puts as stock substitutes; the other is using puts as an insurance product to protect portfolios against disastrous declines in the overall markets. Using options as a vehicle to speculate wildly in the market will surely result in losses in the long run. In the short run, anything is possible.

I have taught many classes on options to both stockbrokers and individual investors and have written numerous articles on the subject. The key to understanding options is understanding the definitions of a put and call. All option strategies hinge on these definitions. No matter how difficult the strategy, if you break it down into its pieces and evaluate each piece separately, you will find options are no more difficult than basic arithmetic.

We'll start with the definitions. Learn these well enough to write them down from memory. If you ever get confused with any particular option strategy, stop, write the definition down, and evaluate each piece of the strategy separately. This is exactly how I learned options. I took a legal pad home on weekends and practiced breaking strategies up into pieces. I would then evaluate the pieces at expiration when there was no time premium left in the option, and before I knew it, options became second nature. It can be just as easy for you. Just remember, keep it simple.

Call Options

Definitions

Call Option (Buyer)   This is a contract that gives the buyer the right to call (buy) 100 shares of the underlying stock covered by the contract, at a stipulated price (exercise price) and at a stipulated time in the future (expiration date), in return for paying a premium to the seller of that call. Numerous exercise prices are attached to each stock. They generally go in 2½-point intervals up to 22½ and in 5-point intervals above that level.

Call Option (Seller)   The seller of a call option contracts to sell 100 shares of the underlying stock covered by the contract, at a stipulated price (exercise price) and at a stipulated time in the future (expiration date). The seller receives the premium (cost of the option) from the buyer.

The Call Buyer

The buyer of a call has tremendous leverage because of the ability to control a large amount of stock for a very small amount of money. Leverage is what draws investors to this arena. Let's say Red Hot Inc. is currently around the $60 level. A call option to buy Red Hot at 60 for the next 6 months costs $4 per share. Each contract represents 100 shares so the total cost, not including commissions, is $400. One hundred shares of Red Hot at 60 costs $6,000. To control that dollar amount of Red Hot for 6 months costs $400. You can see that the leverage can be quite high. Let's say you bought the call option we were just discussing. At expiration, Red Hot is at 80. What is your call worth? Here is where basic arithmetic comes in handy. Let's go back to the definition. The call buyer has the right to call stock away from the seller at a stipulated price. In this example, it is 60. At expiration, or any time before, you can exercise that right—you paid for it. If Red Hot at expiration is 80 and you have the right to buy the stock at 60, the value of the call is $20 ($80 − $60 = $20) × 100 shares per contract or $2,000. Since you paid $400 for the call, subtract the cost of $400 from your gross profit and you get a net profit, not including commissions, of $1,600. That is a 400 percent gain on the money you put up.

What if Red Hot instead went down to 55? If you held the contract until expiration, it would be worthless. Why? It would be worthless because you have the right to pay 60 and the stock is at 55. If you wanted to own the stock, you would be better off just buying it in the open market. Leverage is a double-edged sword. Your loss in this case is 100 percent. Where most option traders go wrong is overleverage. A word to the wise: Never buy more contracts than you have an appetite for round lots of the underlying stock. It's a quick way to the poorhouse. Early on in my career as a stockbroker, I routinely allowed my clients to overleverage themselves. The standard number of option contracts most clients aspire to is 10. It's just a round number and each point of profit equals $1,000 if you buy 10 contracts. Think of the preceding Red Hot example. You could just as easily put up $4,000 for 10 contracts as you did $400 for 1 contract. With 10 contracts, you are now controlling 1,000 shares of Red Hot at 60. This is $60,000 worth of stock. The $4,000 is probably less than investors usually put up to buy stock. The difference in this example is, you are buying calls on 1,000 shares of stock. If your normal appetite for stock is, let's say, 300 shares, you have just overleveraged yourself by 700 shares even though you spent less money than you would normally spend when buying the underlying stock outright. Such transactions lead to financial disaster. The net result could be that the stock goes down, the $4,000 is lost, and the investor claims the option product is too speculative and is responsible for losing a good percentage of his inevitable capital. It wasn't the option product at all, it was the investor's desire to overleverage. Take my advice, if you are a 300-share buyer of stock, never buy more than three contracts. Manage your leverage.

Okay, how might buying call options make more sense than buying the underlying stock? Many investors simply don't have the money to buy the many good stocks that trade over $100 a share. Take, for example, Marsh & McClennan (MMC) now trading at 123. This is a high-quality insurance stock that has been around for years. Let's say Mr. Jones normally buys stocks in the

$50 to $60 range. Just because MMC is out of his price range doesn't mean he can't take a position in it. If Mr. Jones is normally a 200-share buyer, he might consider buying a deep-in-the-money call option with a strike price of 100. At this writing, it is trading around 33. The deep enough in-the-money call carries a delta of 1. In other words, the call option will move point for point with the underlying stock. If MMC moves up 1, the call option will move up 1. So at a price of 33, the cost will be $3,300 per call. That number is calculated by multiplying 100 shares (each contract of an option equals 100 shares) × $33 (going price per share of the contract) = $3,300 for one contract representing 100 shares. Mr. Jones now controls 100 shares of MMC for $3,300. Had he bought 100 shares outright, it would have cost him $12,300. He now has his normal complement of stock, and is in a high-quality insurance stock of his choosing for less money than it would have cost him to buy the stock outright. The call option expires the third Friday of June. He has six months to hold the call option that gives him the right to take 100 shares of MMC away from the Options Clearing Corporation at anytime during the contract life at $100 a share.

Now let's see what happens at expiration at different prices. If MMC did absolutely nothing from now until expiration, the call option Mr. Jones bought would be worth $23 a share. How did that happen? Mr. Jones lost $10 a share. Remember the call cost $33 and had a strike price of 100. Add $33 to $100 and you get a stock price of $133. In essence, Mr. Jones was paying $133 for the stock from the outset. If the stock stayed at 123 without any movement, the difference between the strike price of $100 and the stock price of $123 is $23. Simple arithmetic. Now let's see what happens if the stocks rises as he expects it to. The stock at expiration is at 167. The call option must be worth $167 − 100 = $67. He paid $33 so his profit is $67 − $33 = $34. That translates into a 103 percent gain! What if he bought the stock? The return would be $44 or 36 percent return. That's what you call bang for your buck. Now let's look at a disaster. The stock opens at $80 one day and stays there until expiration. The loss is $33 per share to Mr. Jones. But had he bought the stock, he would have a loss on paper of $43. He's still better off with the options. Now think of how you might construct a whole diversified portfolio of call options. Just for the fun of it, put one together and go through the same exercise we just did with MMC. Oh, yeah, it might just be better to buy calls than the underlying stock.

The Covered Call Writer (Seller)

The seller of that call is generally interested in capturing the premium income of the call, and is willing to give up the stock at the exercise price if the buyer of the call chooses to exercise the contract and take the stock. The individual investor should stick pretty much to the basics when writing or selling covered calls. Professionals use numerous exotic strategies that work for them simply because their transactional charges are almost nonexistent. One strategy the individual investor often uses effectively is the covered write. This strategy is simply an income-producing strategy in which the investor selling the call is willing to forgo potential upside appreciation in the stock in return for the premium income generated by selling the call. Let's use the Red Hot example again. You own Red Hot at 60 and feel the stock is likely to move sideways for a while. You might choose to sell a 6-month call against your stock. Using the previous example, you would receive $400 in cash for selling the 6-month call struck at $60 (transaction fees are left out for simplicity). The $400 goes in your pocket now. You have received payment for contracting to give up your 100 shares of stock at $60 per share if the buyer of that contract so desires. If Red Hot rises to $80, you will not benefit in the gain. Your sales price will be $60. You knew that going in. If Red Hot declines, the $400 received may partially or totally offset the loss. Your break-even price is $56 ($60 − $4 = $56). If at anytime during the life of that contract, you would like to negate it, you can simply buy the same contract back. You will be at the mercy of the market and may pay more than you received, but the option to cancel is still open to you.

   In our daily research, we regularly recommend covered writes and base our selection on several guidelines. The first rule is the stock must be one that we believe is going up in price. In other words, the stock is trading above the Bullish Support Line with strong Relative Strength. Next, we look at the return for selling the call. For us to recommend a covered write on a stock, the annualized called return should be 20 percent, the annualized static return should be 10 percent, and the downside protection should be 4 percent.

One more thing to remember about covered writing. I want to bring you back to your Statistics 101 class in college. Remember the old bell curve? The bell curve is made up of 6 standard deviations. In the stock market business, we call them volatilities. Another way of discussing these areas is to use the word zones. You can take a bell curve and divide it up into six equal zones or standard deviations. Using men to construct a bell curve, we might find at the far right side of the curve are very tall men, who might become basketball players. On the far left side, we would find the opposite, men are very small in stature. In the center, we will find the majority of men, right around the 5-foot-8 to 5-foot-11 height. These so-called normally tall men take up the two zones surrounding the center of the bell curve. This area would encompass one zone to the left of center and one zone to the right of center. This area takes up 68 percent of the curve. This holds true of anything we evaluate statistically including stocks. Usually, stocks tend to stay around the center of their Normal Distribution or bell curve. We find that 68 percent of the time any stock we evaluate will stay within one zone or standard deviation above or below trend, or the center of the curve. In other words, stocks are usually just middlin', kind of hanging around the center of the curve. What this means then is that the strategy that will prove successful 68 percent of the time is a neutral strategy like covered writing. So there you have it, a statistical reason to consider covered writes.

Now let's discuss the downside of this strategy. Any stock you buy should have all the attributes of a stock you expect to rise, even if you intend to sell calls against that position. What often happens is in a total covered writing program, the good stocks' appreciation is capped off by the sale of the calls; and the downside risk of the stocks poised for a down move is only partially mitigated by the premium received by selling the calls. In a strong bull market, covered writing is not the appropriate strategy. I often use the covered write in markets where I feel we are likely to move sideways. I also like to sell calls against long stock when the stock rises to the outer tail of the bell curve suggesting some sort of breather is in order. You can see this bell curve on the right side of every stock chart on our Internet system (www.dorseywright.com). These are great guides.

Put Options

Definitions

Put Options (Buyer)   The buyer of a put has the right to put (sell) stock to the writer of that put, at a stipulated price (exercise price), for a stipulated time in the future (expiration date), and for that right must pay a premium to the seller of that put.

Put Options (Seller)   The seller (underwriter) of the put stands ready to buy stock at a stipulated price (exercise price) for a stipulated time in the future (expiration date), and receives the premium from the buyer.

The put option is the most versatile option tool available. It is also the most misunderstood. There are primarily two strategies that make sense to individual investors; buying puts as short sale substitutes and buying puts as insurance against severe declines in their portfolios. Let's look for a second at what a short sale is.

Selling Short

Many investors will not sell short. It is simply contrary to most investors' optimistic outlook on things. A completed trade in the stock market consists of a purchase and sale of the underlying stock. Most investors are familiar with buy first-sell later transactions. The short sale entails selling first and buying later. In the end, both ingredients are present for a completed trade, the purchase and sale. Short sellers simply make a bet the stock will decline rather than rise. They borrow the stock they want to sell short through a brokerage firm promising to replace the stock at a future date. Normally, the replacement comes through an open-market purchase of the stock they sold. It may be at a profit or a loss depending on whether the stock subsequently rose or declined following the sale. Short sellers are also liable for any dividends on the stock they borrow. Short sellers are important in the scheme of things because they provide liquidity to the marketplace, thus helping other market participants facilitate their trades.

Actually, stocks decline faster than they rise. A study done by Purdue University shown in the first edition of this book, points out mathematically how stocks decline at a faster rate than they rise. "When things go to Hell, they go to Hell in a hand basket." This suggests you are better off selling short in a bear market than you are going long in a bull market. Why then do so few investors take advantage of selling short? Aside from the pessimistic view you must have on the market, there is theoretically unlimited risk in a short sale. If you buy a stock, it can only go to zero, and some do as we found out in the dot-com world of "who needs net profits, all we need is page hits." There is no limit to how high a stock can go. The difference in buying a stock versus selling a stock short is that your risk is defined when you buy a stock and undefined when you sell short. Most investors prefer to stick to the known side of the equation. Short sales must also be done in a margin account. My late mother, like many investors, refused to go on margin no matter what. She still remembered how her father got wiped out as a result of margin (overleverage) in the 1929 crash. There is a tool, however, that can make the short sale more palatable to the individual investor.

Put Options as Short Sale Substitutes

How about using puts as short sale substitutes? Remember the definition of a put? It gives the buyer the right to sell stock at a certain price until the expiration date of the contract. Let's say you bought a put on Red Hot with an exercise price of $60 and an expiration date 6 months hence. For that right, you pay a premium of $4 × 100 shares or $400. (We'll use the same numbers as we did in the call example to keep things simple.) At the end of that period, Red Hot is at 45. If you have the right to sell Red Hot at $60 and it is currently selling in the market at 45, the put option must have some value. That value is the difference between what you can get by selling the stock versus what you must pay to buy the stock. What you could do is buy 100 shares of Red Hot at the current market price of 45 and then exercise your put option to sell at 60. Your profit is $15 per share. Although you could go through those paces, very few investors do. If Red Hot is at 45 at expiration, your put with an exercise price of 60 will be worth $15. All you have to do is sell your option.

I have purposely left out examples prior to expiration because other variables such as time to expiration, volatility, and the prevailing risk-free interest rate come into play to determine the value of the option above its basic intrinsic value. Since this book is not designed to focus on options, and I feel simple is best, I will leave the complexities of options for you to explore in textbooks devoted entirely to the subject.

What if Red Hot did not go down but instead went up 15 points? It's simple—your put option would expire worthless if you held it to expiration. Why? Go back to the definition. The buyer of a put option has the right to sell stock. In this case, it is at a price of $60. If Red Hot rose to 75, you would have to buy stock at $75 and then exercise your right to sell at $60. No one would do that, so the contract would expire worthless. Your loss as the put buyer would be $400—that's it—no matter how high Red Hot went.

This is the main difference in risk versus the outright short sale. In a bad situation, your risk is defined by the amount you paid for the option. In a short sale, the pain just gets worse as the stock goes against you. If you want to talk about sleep deprivation, short sales will do it. Remember, any time during the life of the contract you can sell that put at whatever the market price is at that time. You do not have to wait until expiration to sell the contract. You can sell it 15 minutes after you buy it if you choose. In this example, the put provided a way to participate in an expected down move in Red Hot with a defined risk of the premium paid. In this way, put buying can be much more palatable to the individual investor than selling short.

Selling Puts—The Underwriter

The put sellers are a special breed of investors who in many cases really don't understand what they are getting into. Describing what happened to put sellers in the fast-paced 1980s, much less the 1990s, will add flavor to my explanation of this strategy. During the 1980s, the option business ran rampant. The market just continued to go up, so the easier it got, the more speculative investors became. Selling put options slowly but surely began to expand in popularity until it reached its height in 1987. Someone once said whenever a speculative bubble is formed, a pin is not far away. The pin became evident in October 1987. The decade of the 1980s was an amazing period for the option product. It was like Dodge City with the sheriff on vacation.

I was once a featured speaker at an American Stock Exchange Options Colloquium. The AMEX held this forum each year to give the options experts in the world the opportunity to share their profound research with other practitioners in the investment business. I was proud to be accepted as a speaker at such a high-powered conference and gave a presentation on the merits of naked straddle writing on index options. I discussed how conservative the strategy was and how the then margin rules helped augment the returns when Treasury bills were put up as collateral for the strategy. I break out in a cold sweat when I think of this speech, which I gave before the 1987 crash. Prior to 1987, virtually no one expected a decline of that magnitude—not in one day. Anyone following my grand plan found out in short order how painful selling put options on indexes could be. In fact, anyone selling any puts found it distasteful at best. We live and learn, but what a hard lesson this was.

What is the investor's motive for entering into this type of strategy? The put seller is simply the underwriter of a stock market insurance policy. For your car, an insurance seller might be Aetna Life and Casualty, Allstate, USAA, or any of a hundred other insurance companies. Sellers of a put or insurance are simply stating they are perfectly willing and capable of underwriting the risk outlined in the contract. In the case of the car, the insurance company is willing to buy your car from you, less your deductible, if you have an accident. In the case of the put, the insurance underwriter is willing to buy your stock from you at the stipulated price if your stock has an accident. Naturally the net you will receive is less the cost of the insurance or put. The put writer or underwriter is seeking to capture the premium on the contract just as an auto insurer does. It is the premium income from the sale of the contract that interests the underwriter, not capital gain. The success of an insurance company hinges on diversification, and lots of it. The insurance company knows it will have to pay off a certain amount of policies, but not the majority. Put writers typically can't get the diversification they need to act as an insurance company in the investment business. Typically, put sellers speculate that the stocks they sell puts on will not have an accident. In 1987, all stocks had an accident on October 19. If all the automobiles in the United States were to have an accident on the same day, the insurance industry would be wiped out. Put sellers in October 1987 were wiped out. Almost all put writers at that time were undercapitalized and totally unprepared for the consequences of contracts they had promised to fulfill. Wall Street was in total disarray, and it was rumored that some brokerage houses would go under. I know of numerous cases where people lost their whole life savings and more. This created a rash of lawsuits on Wall Street from brokers who demanded payment for the losses generated by the crash and from customers who sued the broker for allowing them to engage in an investment that was unsuitable for their investment objectives and temperament. Overnight, the option product went from being the darling of Wall Street to being a product that was to be avoided at all costs. Wall Street has a tendency to overdo things. The repercussions are still with us. Some brokerage firms will not allow new brokers to engage in option trading until they have been in the business for three years and still others require an act of Congress to open an account that does uncovered option strategies. This leaves tremendous opportunity for professionals to specialize in this versatile product.

Most investors blame the trouble on the option product itself, but the real problem was overleverage, not options. I guess you could call it basic greed. Recently, we have had another bubble burst. It had to do with overleverage again. This time, it was primarily confined to bond derivatives (another name for option products). Major losses were taken by so-called conservative bond funds. In fact, a hedge fund called Comprehensive Capital, run by Nobel Laureates absolutely melted down overleveraging in derivatives. This was so serious the Federal Reserve had to concoct a bailout plan. The losses were mind boggling. Again, the culprit was overleverage, not the option product. I recently saw a cartoon of a homeless man sitting on a sidewalk with a cup begging for change. He had a sign beside him saying "No Derivatives Please." For the purposes of this chapter, I want to present some basic ideas on how you can successfully trade options.

Before the crash of 1987, it seemed everyone wanted to get into the game regardless of expertise. I can remember an elderly couple coming into our brokerage firm and telling their broker they wanted to increase their retirement income by selling uncovered put options. They would collateralize the puts with the fully paid Treasury bills they had in their brokerage account. You see, they had heard of this strategy at their bridge club. Apparently, other members of the club had been employing the strategy very successfully. It would work well as long as the market, and the stocks they sold puts on, kept going up. A major decline in the market and stocks in general would spell financial disaster for most of them. I remember being called by the branch manager of our firm to discuss this situation. This was a sharp manager and was able to head off a potential disaster. He did not allow them to employ the strategy.

You know the interesting thing about this? The uncovered put sale is the same risk equivalent of the covered write discussed earlier. Yes, it certainly is. Let's look at two examples for a second. Let's say you bought XYZ company at $50 per share. Now you decided to turn the position into a covered write. You sell the January 50 call for $5. You have just given the call buyer of the contract you sold the right to take that stock away from you at $50 per share and in return he gave you $5 cash per share. Let's say the stock declines to 0. What is your risk? The answer is $45. Why? You paid $50 for the stock and took in $5 in premiums by selling the January 50 call option. That is $50 – $5 = $45. Okay. Now let's look at selling the uncovered put. XYZ is at $50; however, instead of buying the stock and selling the call you choose to simply sell the January 50 put now trading at 5. Again the stock declines to 0. What is your risk? Since the put contract said you stood ready to buy the stock at 50, the holder of the contract exercised his right to sell you XYZ at 50. Since the stock went to zero, you lost $50. But you were paid $5 to enter into the contract. So you only lost $45, just as you did in the covered write. Interesting isn't it. It's just a little arithmetic.

Puts as Insurance Policies

To explain puts from a different angle, the buyer of insurance, let me ask you a question. Do you own a put, Yes or No? Let me ask you one more question. Do you own a car? If the answer to the second question is yes, you own a car, then the answer to the first question is also yes, you own a put. If you own a car, you also own some insurance on the car. Puts are simply insurance policies. A put option gives the buyer of the put the right to sell stock at a certain price for a certain time period by paying a premium (cost of the put) for this right. Your insurance policy on your car effectively says you can do the same thing. Let's say you have an accident that leaves your car a total wreck. Your insurance policy will pay you for that wrecked car. Your policy states in the event of an accident, the insurance company will pay you a stipulated amount of money covering the extent of the damages. The insurance policy stays in effect for a certain period of time, let's say 6 months, at the end of which time you must renew or cancel the policy. For the right to own that insurance policy, you pay a premium to the underwriter or seller of that policy, the insurance company. When I was a teenager, I had an accident in my father's car that bent the frame. The car couldn't be repaired. The insurance company paid us book value for the car minus the deductible. I actually think we made out on that deal. My dad didn't.

The put option is no different. Since put buyers have the right to sell stock (underlying stock) at a certain price (exercise price) for a certain period (expiration date), they are entering into a contract very similar to the one you have on your car. Option contracts always represent 100 shares of stock. Let's say you buy Philip Morris at $60 per share. Let's also say you want to protect against a major decline in the market that will undoubtedly include Philip Morris. You might consider buying a 6-month put option with an exercise price of $60. The put might cost you $3 for each 100 shares of stock or $300 (in the previous example, we used $400). Option prices change daily as time to expiration as well as other factors change. If Philip Morris declined to 50 over the next 6 months, you could notify your broker you would like to exercise your put contract that stipulates you can sell Philip Morris at $60 per share. You might also decide to hold the stock and simply sell the option for the gain. In our example, Philip Morris had an accident and declined to $50 per share. By exercising your put contract, you would be able to sell 100 shares of Philip Morris at 60. With the stock now at 50, you could protect yourself by $1,000. Now what did it cost you to get that protection? The cost was $300 ,so your net protection was $1,000 − $300 = $700. If Philip Morris didn't have an accident and remained at 60 or higher, the put policy would simply lapse. When we buy insurance policies, we always hope we don't have to use them. So to recap, the put buyer can also be interested in insuring his portfolio rather than making a bet the stock will decline.

The key to successful option trading is successful stock trading. You must be right on the stock before you can be right on the option. Before you select an option to buy, you must first go through the steps outlined for stock selection in the previous chapters of this book. You cannot even consider an option until you have done your homework on the underlying stock.

The following definitions will help you to understand options more thoroughly:

Delta The amount an option will move in relation to a one-dollar move in the underlying stock.

Exercise Price The stated price to buy the underlying stock in a contract, generally fixed at 22½-point intervals below 22½ and at 5-point intervals above 22½.

Expiration Date Date on which the option contract expires. The owner of an option can sell the contract at any time before expiration at prevailing market prices. The seller of an option may repurchase the option he sold at prevailing market prices.

Option Premium Value of the option determined by market forces, including underlying stock's volatility, risk-free interest rate, time to expiration, and underlying stock's dividend.

In-the-Money In the case of a call, an exercise price below current market prices of the underlying stock; in the case of a put, an exercise price above current market prices of the underlying stock. (If it sounds confusing, go back to the definitions of puts and calls earlier in this chapter.)

Out-of-the-Money   In the case of a call, an exercise price above the current market price of the underlying stock; in the case of a put, an exercise price below the current market price of the underlying stock.

At-the-Money   In the case of both put and call, an exercise price and underlying stock price that are the same.

Intrinsic Value   With reference to the premium of an option, the amount the option is in-the-money. If IBM was at 65 and an October 60 call was trading at $6, we would say that $5 of that $6 represents intrinsic value (amount in-the-money) and $1 of that $6 represents time to expiration. If the stock just sat there until expiration, the call option would eventually be worth the exact amount it was in-the-money—in this case, $5.

Time Premium   The value of an option above its intrinsic value. If there is no intrinsic value, the total cost of the option represents time to expiration.

Again, the key to successful option trading is successful stock trading. If you are wrong on the stock, you will be wrong on the option. All we want the option to do is replicate the stock as much as possible. Once you have selected the underlying stock, then and only then can you consider the option. This is where the term *delta* comes into play. The deeper the put or call is in-the-money, the higher the correlation to a point-for-point move with the underlying stock.

Rule of Thumb for Deltas

Here is a general guideline for deltas: An option that is 5 points in-the-money will have an option delta of approximately 75 percent. In other words, you can expect about a ¾-point move in the option for each 1-point move in the stock. An option that is at-the-money will approximate a delta of 50 percent, and an option that is 5 points out-of-the-money will have a delta approximating 25 percent. Computers can fine-tune the delta down to ⅒ of a percent, but who needs to know exactly what the delta is when market forces keep that figure in constant flux? Just try to stay in the ballpark and you'll be fine.

When I was a broker, we usually bought options by price. Our selection typically had nothing to do with how the option would move in relation to the underlying stock. If a client had $1,000 available to buy options, we bought the exercise price that fit that client's pocketbook. Keep in mind that back in the 1970s and early 1980s we didn't know much about options. We flew by the seat of our pants. Let me give you an example. In the previously stated rule of thumb, I said that a strike price 5 points out-of-the-money would carry a delta (amount the option will move in relation to a 1-point move in the stock) of approximately 0.25. Let's say IBM is at $60 per share and I choose to buy a 3-month call with an exercise price of 65. The exercise price is 5 points above the current price of the stock. We say it is 5 points out-of-the-money since "the money" is the current price of IBM. The delta of this call option will be around 0.25. If IBM moves up $1, my option will move up 0.25. At expiration, IBM must be trading at $65 for this 3-month call to be worth nothing. Think back to the definition. The buyer of a call has the right to call stock away from someone at a stipulated price. If the price is, in this case, $65 and the stock is currently at $65, there is no advantage to holding the call at expiration. Thus its value is zero. This is a situation where the investor was dead right on the stock and dead wrong on the exercise price selection. Here are five of my rules of the road:

1. *Always buy in-the-money calls or puts because the delta is relatively high.* Remember you want the option to look as much like the stock as possible. Some strategists recommend you buy two at-the-money calls instead of one in-the-money call to replicate the move in the stock. Think about that statement for a moment. We said in the rule of thumb that an at-the-money call had an approximate delta of 0.50. If you bought two options with a delta of 0.50 you would have a delta of $0.50 + 0.50 = 1$. This would give you a move in the combined options of 1. As the stock rose, moving further in the money, the deltas would increase thus giving you a greater than 1 move in the calls versus the stock. The only problem with this is that if the stock sits still during the life of the contract (which often happens), the total premium paid will be lost. Since a deep in-the-money call is almost all intrinsic value, the time premium will be minimal. Thus if a stock stays

neutral during the life of the contract, the majority of the option's price will remain intact. In my estimation, this aspect of an in-the-money call is more important than gaining any added delta from the purchase of two at-the-money calls.

2. *Never overleverage.* Only buy as many contracts as you would otherwise buy round lots of the underlying stock. Keep the remaining money you would have invested in the stock in the money market fund. Overleverage is a very common mistake made by options traders.

3. *Buy time.* Time is the silent killer of options, the Grim Reaper. Always go out longer than 6 weeks because time premium decays most rapidly beginning around 6 weeks to expiration. Since you are keying off a move in the underlying stock, be sure your option does not expire before the stock has had a chance to work out.

4. *Stop losses.* There are two ways to look at an option trade. The simplest is to look at the premium you pay for the put or call as your stop. Had you bought the underlying stock, you would have been willing to take a certain loss up to your stop point. You can consider that loss you would have taken in the stock as the premium you pay for the option. If the stock does not move in your favor, you simply hold until expiration. This gives you second and third chances to succeed. Lots can happen to a stock over a 6-month period. Another possible loss-limiting strategy would be to sell the option at the point you would normally stop the loss in the stock. Since you are attempting to create a position in the option that is similar to the stock, treat the option as if it were the stock. This might save you 50 percent of the premium, but you also give up the chance to make it back later on. I have a tendency to play it both ways depending on the situation.

5. *Keep it simple.* The more sophisticated, the lower the probability of success. Remember, you cannot consider an option before you have done all the work on the stock first.

In evaluating which option to buy, the market is your first consideration. Who has the ball? Buying calls in a bear-configured market will be difficult at best. On the other hand, bear-configured markets are conducive to put buying. Be sure you know who has the ball before you jump into the game. Check the short-term picture. It might be best to hold off the purchase of calls when the short-term indicators are bearish. Remember, time is the silent killer of options. Timing is everything here. The long-term trend might be bullish while the short-term trend is bearish. Have both the long and short term going in the same direction before you buy an option. Evaluate the Sector Bullish Percent Indexes before you select the stock. In the case of a call, the sector should have the offensive team on the field, preferably with strong Relative Strength readings, and below the 50 percent level for optimum conditions. In the case of a put, the sector should be on defensive and preferably have weak Relative Strength, and the sector Bullish Percent should reside above the 50 percent level.

Once the sector is selected, find a stock within the sector that is fundamentally sound. Simply check to see if a Wall Street firm is recommending the purchase of this stock. The best place to start is with your broker. Most have numerous correspondent firms' research and can answer this question in a moment. This goes a long way in ensuring the stock is fundamentally sound. Along with the fundamentals, it's nice to see some insider buying in the stock (like the president buying his own stock). This is not essential, but it's nice to have.

After you have selected the list of fundamentally sound stocks, check the Point and Figure chart patterns and select the best and strongest looking stock. Be sure the stock is on a buy signal and is trading above the Bullish Support Line.

Exchange Traded Funds and Asset Allocation

It was about 8 years ago that I told one of the major exchanges to forget options on indexes, simply securitize the index and trade it as if it were a stock. This fell on deaf ears. About eight years later, we are seeing a proliferation of Exchange Traded Funds (ETF). First, the American Stock Exchange began trading the SPDRs (Standard & Poor's Depository Receipts). In essence, you can simply buy the S&P 500 with one order and without being charged for mutual fund management. You could also sell it short or write calls against it. Needless to say, the product set sail. More indexes followed with the Dow Jones Diamonds (DIA) also trading actively as well as the Nasdaq 100 Index (QQQ). Next came Amex Sector Select SPDRs and the Merrill Lynch HOLDRS which were baskets of stocks made up of particular sectors. Next came the Barclays Global Investors iShares. The iShares have over 50 different index funds that you can buy and sell just like stock. Each share represents a portfolio of stocks designed to closely track a specific stock index. iShares are managed by Barclays Global Fund Advisors, a subsidiary of Barclays Global Investors, N.A. These Exchange Traded Funds offer investors a way to buy into a whole index rather than focusing on a single stock. The HOLDRS have a little different twist in that you actually are buying the whole basket of stocks individually and you must buy in 100 share lots. SPDR's, Diamonds, QQQs, Sector Select SPDRs, and iShares can be bought in 1 share lots. A great source of information on the ETFs is the American Stock Exchange's Web site (www.amex.com). You can also find information at www.ishares.com and www.holdrs.com. I personally find myself gravitating more and more to the indexes. As previously discussed, at least 75 percent of the risk in any particular stock is the sector and the market. These investment vehicles, ETFs, allow the investor to drop one step in the investment process. Time and again, in the year 2000, I saw individual stocks crater one after another. If you didn't live through it, you wouldn't believe it. It was like the Demolition Derby.

Since a sector is made up of many stocks, one disaster only marginally affects the sector itself. It's like buying a whole school of fish, all moving in the same direction. Sectors tend to do the same thing. The same economic stimulus that affects one stock is likely to affect them all. If our sector work suggested we buy technology, we could simply go to the iShares and buy the technology sector in the same way we would purchase an individual stock. Let's say Real Estate was the play as it was in 2000. Instead of trying to pick one REIT, we could purchase the whole sector. Conversely, when things begin to look bad for a sector, all stocks are likely to feel the heat. Here is a great example of how we research sectors and present our findings to you in our daily work. Susan Morrison, my top stock market analyst at Dorsey, Wright, did the following write-up on the Box Makers. Because she uncovered the problems she saw with this sector and explained them in a logical, organized, understandable fashion, anyone who read the piece and followed the advice, avoided the Silver Bullet. By December, these stocks were drawn and quartered. What Susan tried to point out is the need to think through a certain situation to the end. So few investors have the ability or the desire to do this. This comes from our September 26, 2000, daily report.

Thinking beyond the First Step:
The Box Makers*

The first step can be "a doozy," as they say, and Friday's market action was certainly no exception to that adage. For many investors, the carnage that chipmaker Intel (INTC) instigated through an earnings shortfall preannouncement came as a complete surprise. But was that announcement a phenomenon, in and of itself, or was it the first of an onslaught in earnings preannouncements? Yesterday's *Investor's Business Daily* ran an interesting cover story that led us to delve further into the INTC collapse, and question whether this isn't a proverbial shot over the bow. The article cited that this announcement had little to do with the declining Euro and European demand, as the Company has stated, but rather a reflection of slowing PC sales. Approximately 75 percent of Intel's sales are from PC chips, according to the article, which supports the declining growth rate that troubled traders last week.

An interesting observation that can be taken from Friday's action was that while many chip-stocks gapped down on the open, they rallied back in the afternoon. Intel remained battered and bruised, even though many of its peers were able to regain their composure after the initial panic selling had subsided. The cause of this dynamic may have been that INTC controls the PC market with AMD, but consumer electronics and broadband communications products drive many of the Semiconductor producers that held their own. The later areas continue to produce high sales growth according to Drew Peck, an analyst with SG Cowen Securities Corporation, and should leave many Semiconductors well

---

*Excerpt from the *Daily Equity Report*, September 26, 2000.

positioned. While this may be good news for many of you looking to play the semiconductor sector on the long side, there is another edge to the Intel sword.

Think about a story of a young hellion throwing a rock through the baker's window, as explained in "Economics in One Lesson" by Hazlett. On the surface, we dismiss this as a childish stunt with few repercussions; easy enough. However, a simple understanding of supply and demand, along with the foresight to see past the first step in any economic process, will lead us to the conclusion that this is a financial blow to the tailor. It is the tailor that would have had the business of the baker, had the baker been able to buy the suit of clothes he planned to buy from the tailor had he not lost the $250 deductible insurance fee when the insurance company replaced the window. Most people, when reading this little fable, initially think no real harm has been done as the insurance company covers the loss. This example doesn't even take into consideration the theoretical increase in insurance premiums everyone will have to pay in the future because of this one thoughtless act by a child. By the same thought process, we must look down the road and consider the possibility that Intel's earnings shortcoming is not simply a rock through the baker's window. If PC sales are indeed slowing, this is not strictly an INTC quagmire, this is an issue that could loom over the Computer Box Maker's heads as we enter the next earnings season. Remember that while the INTC breakdown caught many traders by surprise, the technicals gave us warning signs to exit positions before the hurricane hit Thursday afternoon. The stock had given multiple sell signals on its trend chart, and violated its Bullish Support Line as well. The writing was on the wall for INTC, so now we look to see if the scribes have sent warnings forth elsewhere. As we mentioned earlier, 75 percent of Intel's sales are from an industry which it controls 85 percent of the supply: Personal Computer chips. The PHLX Computer Box Maker Index (BMX) is our primary indicator of how the PC community is performing as a group. If we look at the trend chart for this index, we see that a triple bottom violation of the long-time Bullish Support Line has recently been broken at 200. The chart is in Figure 8.1, along with a table outlining many of the prominent names within the index. You will note that many of the blue-chip names included here have already given sell signals and violated support

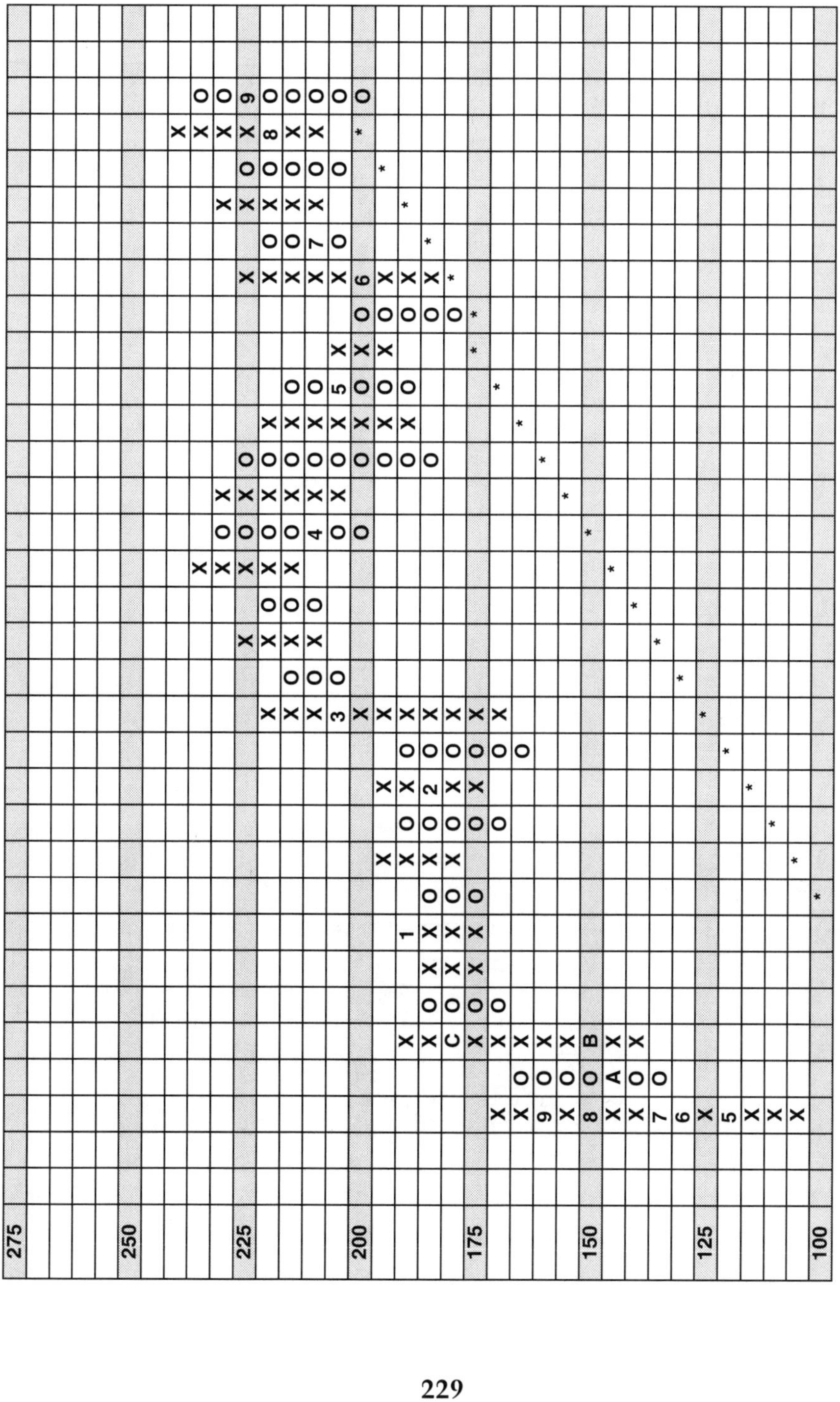

Figure 8.1 PHLX Computer Box Maker Index (BMX).

lines on their trend charts. Many of you likely have positions in one or some of these stocks, you need to evaluate these positions closely. Do not let one mistake blow-up a portfolio because it was neglected. Just as with INTC, many investors likely ignored initial sell signals, but those who heeded the advice of these signals were able to move to the sidelines before Friday. Stocks such as CPQ and IBM continue to hold up on a technical basis, but should be watched closely for signs of deterioration. Charts and Comments follow.

Technical Data on Boxmakers

Symbol	Recent Price ($)	RS Sig (DOW)	RS Col (DOW)	RS Sig (Sector)	RS Col (Sector)	Trend	P&F Sigl	Momentum
AAPL	52.19	Buy	X	Sell	X	−	Sell	−
CPQ	29.63	Sell	X	Buy	X	+	Buy	−
DELL	35.94	Buy	O	Sell	O	−	Sell	+
GTW	55.50	Buy	X	Buy	O	−	Sell	−
HWP	103.94	Buy	O	Buy	O	−	Sell	−
IBM	124.00	Buy	X	Buy	X	+	Buy	−

Technical Data on Box Makers

Charts and Comments

[AAPL] Apple Computer (53.625) enjoyed a late summer rally, garnering sponsorship to move from a triple top at 52 to recent highs at 64. The month of September has yet to show the same returns however. AAPL has posted two sell signals, the most recent being a double bottom at 54 that was followed by a violation of the Bullish Support Line at 50. Those long here may use a recent bounce to 55 to lighten/stop positions. Near-term, weakness may loom as weekly momentum has just flipped negative (see Figure 8.2). *Tom Dorsey's note: Apple is trading at 14 on December 7, 2000. It wasn't long after this report that the stock opened one day, down 50 percent.*

[CPQ] Compaq Corp (28.600) continues to hold up on a technical basis having recently broken out of a big base. The stock remains on a buy signal with good support in the mid-20s. Those

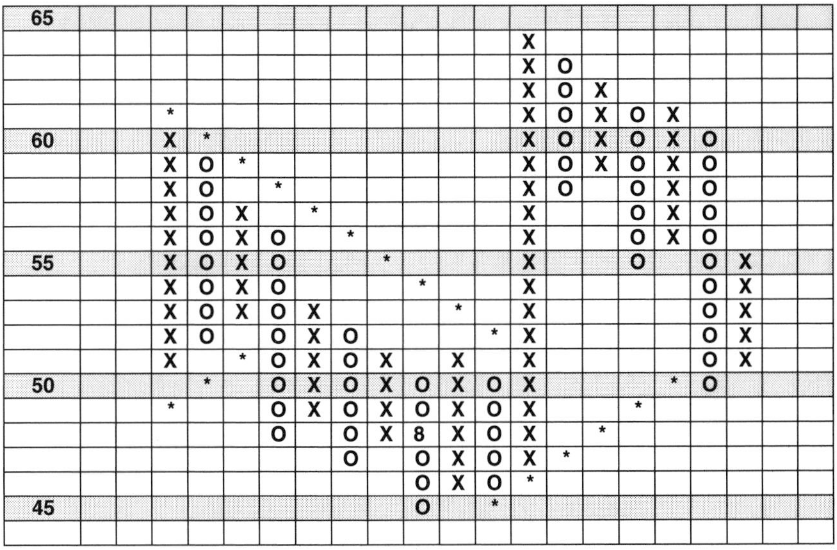

```
65 |
   |                                          X
   |                                          X  O
   |                                          X  O  X
   |         *                                X  O  X  O  X
60 |      X  *                                X  O  X  O  X  O
   |      X  O  *                             X  O  X  O  X  O
   |      X  O     *                          X  O     O  X  O
   |      X  O  X     *                       X        O  X  O
   |      X  O  X  O     *                    X        O  X  O
55 |      X  O  X  O        *                 X        O     O  X
   |      X  O  X  O           *              X              O  X
   |      X  O  X  O  X           *           X              O  X
   |      X  O     O  X  O           *        X              O  X
   |      X     *  O  X  O  X     X           X              O  X
50 |         *     O  X  O  X  O  X  O  X           *  O
   |      *        O  X  O  X  O  X  O  X        *
   |               O     O  X  8  X  O  X     *
   |                        O     O  X  O  X  *
   |                              O  X  O  *
45 |                              O     *
   |
```

Figure 8.2   Apple Computer Inc. (APPL).

long here can maintain a stop loss of 23, a spread triple bottom violation of support. Relative Strength remains in a column of X's versus the overall market (see Figure 8.3). *Tom Dorsey's note: Compaq is trading at 19 on December 7, 2000.*

[DELL] Dell Computer (34.375) continues a series of lower tops and lower bottoms, and overall bearish trend. Continue to avoid this stock here as it continues to be a market and sector laggard (see Figure 8.4). *Tom Dorsey's note: Dell is trading at 18 on December 7, 2000.*

[IBM] International Business Mach (121.375) continues to exhibit sound technicals here as the stock remains on a buy signal, with RS in a column of X's. The stock recently went to new highs at the 134 area before pulling back to the middle of the 10-week trading band. Okay to hold long positions here with the first sign of weakness being a move to 108, a double bottom. Longer term, a move to 99 will violate a large area of consolidation, okay to stop there (see Figure 8.5). *Tom Dorsey's note: Although IBM on December 7, 2000, is trading at 97 it went as low as 87 following this report.*

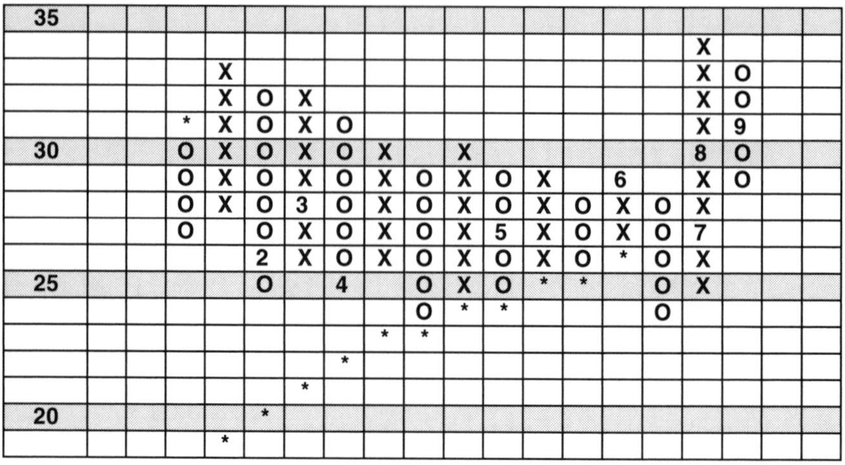

Figure 8.3 Point-and-figure chart

35															
												X			
		X										X	O		
		X	O	X								X	O		
	*	X	O	X	O							X	9		
30		O	X	O	X	O	X		X			8	O		
		O	X	O	X	O	X	O	X		6	X	O		
		O	X	O	3	O	X	O	X	O	X	O	X	O	X
		O		O	X	O	X	O	X	5	X	O	X	O	7
			2	X	O	X	O	X	O	X	O	*	O	X	
25		O		4		O	X	O	*	*		O	X		
					O	*	*			O					
				*	*										
			*												
		*													
20	*														
	*														

Figure 8.3 Compaq Computer Corp. (CPQ).

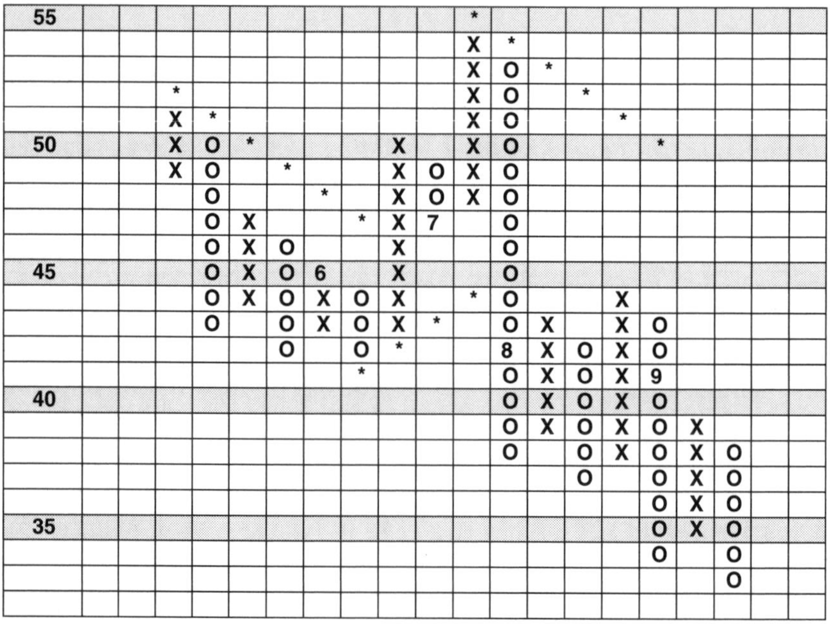

Figure 8.4 Point-and-figure chart

55								*							
							X	*							
							X	O	*						
		*					X	O		*					
		X	*				X	O			*				
50		X	O	*		X	X	O				*			
		X	O		*		X	O	X	O					
			O			*	X	O	X	O					
			O	X			*	X	7		O				
			O	X	O			*	X		O				
45			O	X	O	6		X		O					
			O	X	O	X	O	X		*	O		X		
			O			O	X	O	X		O	X	X	O	
			O			O		*	8	X	O	X	O		
								*	O	X	O	X	9		
40									O	X	O	X	O		
								O	X	O	X	O	X		
								O		O	X	O	X	O	
								O		O	X	O			
										O	X	O			
35										O	X	O			
										O		O			
										O					

Figure 8.4 Dell Computer Corporation (DELL).

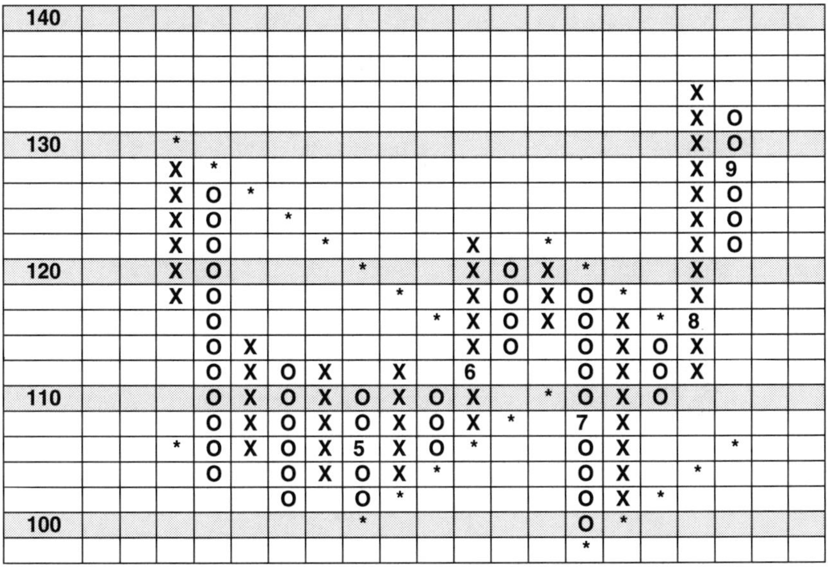

140																		
															X			
															X	O		
130		*													X	O		
		X	*												X	9		
		X	O	*											X	O		
		X	O		*										X	O		
		X	O			*			X		*				X	O		
120		X	O					*	X	O	X	*			X			
		X	O						*	X	O	X	O	*	X			
		O							*	X	O	X	O	X	*	8		
		O	X						X	O			O	X	O	X		
		O	X	O	X		X	6					O	X	O	X		
110		O	X	O	X	O	X	O	X		*		O	X	O		
		O	X	O	X	O	X	O	X	*			7	X			
	*	O	X	O	X	5	X	O	*				O	X			*
		O			O	X	O	X	*				O	X		*	
					O		O	*					O	X	*		
100							*						O	*			
							*						*				

Figure 8.5   International Business Machines (IBM).

[GTW] Gateway (56.710) has now given two consecutive sell signals, the most recent being a double bottom at 62 that followed a lower top. Okay to lighten up on positions here as the stock has bounced to 57 recently. No new positions here (see Figure 8.6). *Tom Dorsey's note: Gateway is trading at 17 on December 7, 2000. This was a major killer like Apple.*

[HWP] Hewlett Packard (101.375) recently broke down to violate the Bullish Support Line with a spread double bottom at 102. The stock is now in an overall downtrend, and those long may look to use yesterday's bounce to lighten up on positions. RS is already in O's and weekly momentum has recently turned negative (see Figure 8.7). *Tom Dorsey's note: Hewlett Packard is trading at 66 on a presplit basis on December 7, 2000.*

There are investors who have whole portfolios of computer stocks. They believe the story the media has fed to investors: "Buy for the Long Term." The problem is the media hasn't even thought of the investors who are retiring in 6 to 10 years. They don't have long term to wait for their portfolio to return what has

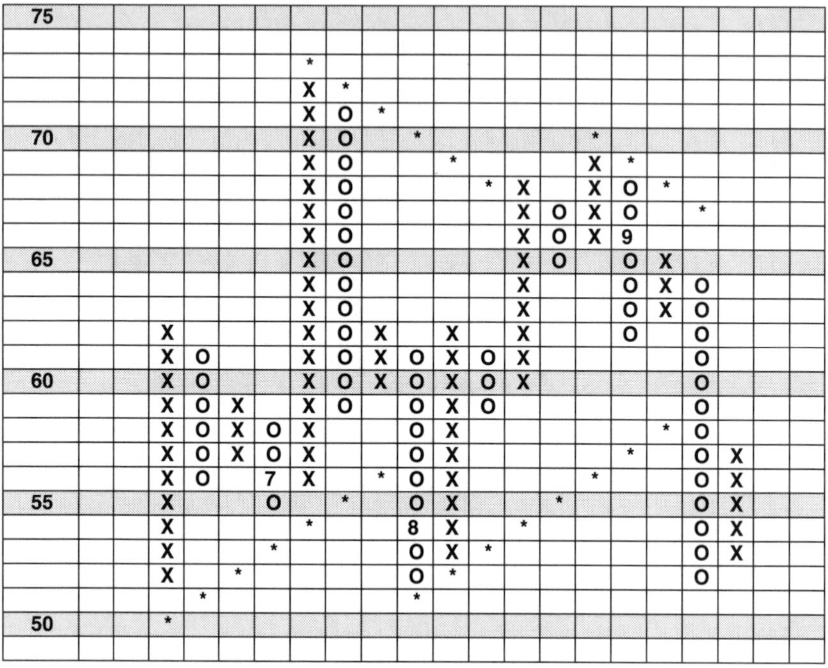

Price																
75																
74																
73								X	*							
72								X	O	*						
71								X	O		*					
70								X	O			*			*	
69								X	O				*	X	*	
68								X	O			*	X	X	O	*
67								X	O			X	O	X	O	*
66								X	O			X	O	X	9	
65								X	O			X	O	O	X	
64								X	O			X	O	X	O	
63								X	O			X	O	X	O	
62			X					X	O	X		X	O	O		
61			X	O				X	O	X	O	X	O	X	O	
60			X	O				X	O	X	O	X	O	X	O	
59			X	O	X			X	O	O	X	O	O			
58			X	O	X	O	X			O	X			*	O	
57			X	O	X	O	X			O	X				O	X
56			X	O	7	X		*	O	X			*		O	X
55			X			O		*	O	X		*			O	X
54			X				*	8	X		*				O	X
53			X			*		O	X	*					O	X
52			X		*			O	*						O	
51				*					*							
50	*															

Figure 8.6   Gateway, Inc. (GTW).

been the average rate over the past 80 years. What they need most of all is *risk management and preservation of capital.* The article by Susan Morrison provides a perfect example of managing risk. Anyone with retirement on the horizon, who had a portfolio of these stocks, and did not manage risk, would be looking at a very different retirement than he had hoped for. This is reality. Managing risk is what this book is all about.

There are many ways an investor might have managed risk in the preceding portfolio. Put options, as discussed earlier, would have been a perfect way to insure the portfolio without having to sell any of the stocks. Yes, there is a cost for the insurance, the price of the puts, but that is a very small price to pay for the protection that could have kept your 401(k) or IRA or any other account almost intact. Another way to protect the portfolio would have been to place stop-loss orders at particular levels.

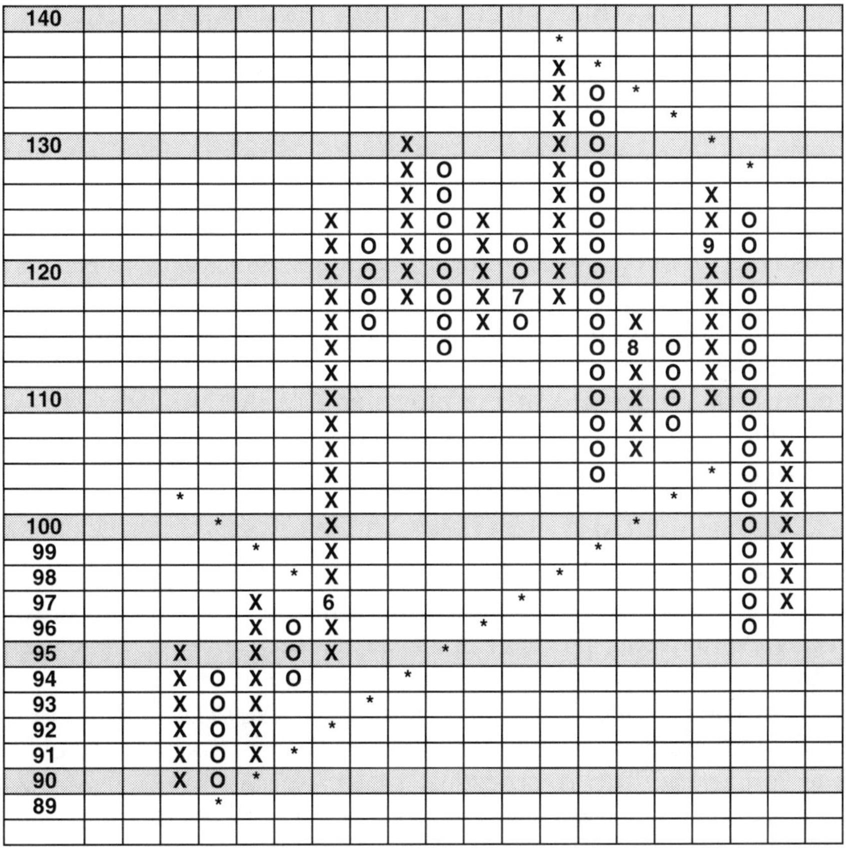

Price	1	2	3	4	5	6	7	8	9	10	11	12	13	14	15	16
140																
											*					
											X	*				
											X	O	*			
											X	O		*		
130							X				X	O			*	
							X	O			X	O				*
							X	O			X	O		X		
						X	X	O	X		X	O		X	O	
						X	O	X	O	X	O			9	O	
120						X	O	X	O	X	O			X	O	
						X	O	X	O	X	7	X		X	O	
						X	O		O	X	O		O	X	O	
						X					O	8	O	X	O	
						X					O	X	O	X	O	
110						X					O	X	O	X	O	
						X					O	X	O		O	
						X					O	X			O	X
						X					O			*	O	X
		*				X								*	O	X
100			*			X						*			O	X
99				*		X					*				O	X
98					*	X				*					O	X
97				X	6				*						O	X
96				X	O	X		*							O	
95		X		X	O	X	*									
94		X	O	X	O		*									
93		X	O	X		*										
92		X	O	X	*											
91		X	O	X	*											
90		X	O	*												
89			*													

Figure 8.7   Hewlett Packard (HWP).

The investor might also have simply bought a put on the Box Maker Sector (BMX) that trades on the Philadelphia Stock Exchange. That would have hedged the total risk of a portfolio overweighted in the "Box Makers." In fact, the Box Maker Sector (BMX) declined during the same period from 240 to 125, or 48 percent. So you would have calculated the dollar value of the portfolio of "Computer Box Stocks" and then bought an equivalent number of BMX (Computer Box Maker Index) at-the-money puts trading on the Philadelphia Stock Exchange. Yes! You can actively manage risk no matter what the media tries to tell you.

Practical Applications of Exchange Traded Funds

Now let's take a little different look at how these ETFs might be used. A word to the wise, the diversification in these index-based products can be misleading. The Nasdaq 100 Trust (QQQ) naturally comprises 100 stocks, so you might think you are receiving the diversification of 100 issues. That's not the case. The Nasdaq 100 is a capitalization weighted index and therefore some stocks are more important in the calculation of the index than other stocks. As we are writing this, the top 10 stocks in the QQQ account for 38.6 percent of the movement of the Nasdaq 100 and the top 20 stocks account for 53 percent of the movement in the Nasdaq 100. That means when you purchase the QQQs you are essentially purchasing a basket of 10 to 20 stocks, not 100 stocks. Purchasing the QQQs to get a basket of 10 technology stocks is a great way to play the technology movement, but you must be aware of what exactly you are purchasing so that you can accurately evaluate the position. Because the QQQs are a capitalization weighted index, it makes sense to evaluate the stocks moving the index in addition to looking at the OTC Bullish Percent. Remember that the OTC Bullish Percent is a one stock—one vote index. The 10 stocks that carry the most weight in the QQQs may look great while the majority of OTC stocks are heading lower. In the S&P 500, the top 10 names account for 24 percent of the movement of that index while the top 20 names account for 36 percent of the movement in the index. Or, said another way, 4 percent of the stocks in the S&P 500 carry 36 percent of the weight of the index.

Another reason to investigate the stocks in each ETF before buying is that the name can be misleading. For example, the iShares Healthcare Index (IYH) suggests that you are purchasing a group of healthcare stocks. However, on investigating the top 10 holdings, they account for 67 percent of the momentum in the index. Nevertheless, those 10 stocks are large cap drug and biotech names, not stocks like Medtronic (MDT), Guidant (GDT), Boston Scientific (BSC), or United Healthcare (UNH). So again, make sure you know what you are purchasing. There are several great Web sites for information on these ETFs including www.amex.com, www.ishares.com, and www.holdrs.com. When you bring up an ETF on our Web site, you can click a button and get the top 10 holdings and a technical summary of the top 10 holdings. In Figure 8.8, we have listed the market index based ETFs available at the time this book was written, and in Figure 8.9 we have listed the sector index based ETFs available at the time this book was written.

As you can see, there are quite a few; some would even suggest that you don't have to go further then these ETFs to construct a worthy portfolio. One thing we do know is that over the years 80 percent of all money managers and mutual funds in the world never outperform the S&P 500. One could begin constructing a

Market Index Funds	Symbol
Dow Jones Diamonds	DIA
S&P 500 SPiDR's	SPY
Midcap SPiDR's	MDY
Nasdaq 100 Index	QQQ
iShares Dow Jones US Total Market Index Fund	IYY
iShares Russell 1000 Index Fund	IWB
iShares Russell 1000 Value Index Fund	IWD
iShares Russell 2000 Growth Index Fund	IWO
iShares Russell 2000 Value Index Fund	IWN
iShares Russell 3000 Growth Index Fund	IWZ
iShares Russell 3000 Value Index Fund	IWW
iShares S&P 500 Index Fund	IVV
iShares S&P 500/Barra Growth Index Fund	IVW
iShares S&P 500/Barra Value Index Fund	IVE
iShares S&P 400 MidCap Index Fund	IJH
iShares S&P 400/Barra Growth Index Fund	IJK
iShares S&P 400/Barra Value Index Fund	IVE
iShares S&P SmallCap 600 Index Fund	IJR
iShares S&P SmallCap 600/Barra Growth Index Fund	IJT
iShares S&P SmallCap 600/Barra Value Index Fund	IJS
streetTRACKS Dow Jones Global Titans Index Fund	DGT
streetTRACKS Dow Jones US Large Cap Index Fund	ELG
streetTRACKS Dow Jones US Large Value Index Fund	ELV
streetTRACKS Dow Jones Small Cap Growth Index Fund	DSG
streetTRACKS Dow Jones Small Cap Value Index Fund	DSV

Sources: www.amex.com (1-800-THE-AMEX); www.ishares.com (1-800-ISHARES); www.streetTRACKS.com (1-866-S-TRACKS); www.holdrs.com.

Figure 8.8   Available Exchange Traded Funds.

Sector Index Funds	Symbol
HOLDRS	
Biotech	BBH
Broadband	BDH
B2B Internet	BHH
Internet	HHH
Internet Architecture	IAH
Internet Infrastructure	IIH
Market 2000+	MKH
Pharmaceutical	PPH
Regional Bank	RKH
Semiconductor	SMH
Software	SWH
Telecom	TTH
Utilities	UTH
Select Sector SPDR	
Basic Industries	XLB
Consumer Services	XLV
Consumer Staples	XLP
Cyclical/Transportation	XLY
Energy	XLE
Financial	XLF
Industrial	XLI
Technology	XLK
Utilities	XLU
iShares Dow Jones US	
Basic Materials	IYM
Chemical	IYD
Consumer Cyclical	IYC
Consumer Non-Cyclical	IYK
Energy	IYE
Financial	IYF
Financial Services	IYG
Healthcare	IYH
Industrial	IYJ
Internet	IYV
Real Estate	IYR
Technology	IRW
Telecommunications	IYZ
Utilities	IDU
streetTRACKS	
FORTUNE e-50	FEF
Morgan Stanley High Tech 35	MTK
Morgan Stanley Internet	MII

Sources: www.amex.com (1-800-THE-AMEX); www.ishares.com (1-800-ISHARES); www.streetTRACKS.com (1-866-S-TRACKS); www.holdrs.com.

Figure 8.9   Sector index based Exchange Traded Funds.

portfolio by putting a portion of the portfolio in the SPYs. Then, augment that with other sector ETFs. Let's say that the following sectors had a majority of their indicators, Bullish Percents, and Relative Strength indicators as positive. Each of these strong sectors could be paired up with an ETF. If the sector went to having the majority of its indicators negative, then you would remove that ETF from the portfolio. As a sector rotated up to having the majority of its indicators positive, then you would add the appropriate ETF to the portfolio. This would be a very viable, manageable program that would keep you in the leading sectors and out of the weak sectors. Sometimes, there may not be an ETF for a particular sector, for example, Restaurants don't have an ETF. Therefore, you might want to purchase an individual stock. Let's take a sample market scenario of the following sectors being positive and what ETF would make sense to play a move in that sector:

General Mkt Exposure	S&P 500 SPDRs (SPY).
Mid Cap Index	S&P Mid Cap SPDRs (MDY).
Bank Sector	iShares Financial Services.
Insurance Sector	
Forest & Paper Products Machinery & Tools Chemicals	They are all "heavy" sectors, so the iShares Basic Materials Sector (IYM) would be appropriate.
Electric Utilities	iShares Utility (IDU)—would choose these over the Amex Sector Select Utility SPDRs since they are mostly telephone utilities.
Semiconductor Sector	Merrill Lynch Semiconductor HOLDRs (SMH).
Food & Beverage Sector	There isn't a good ETF for this sector so would instead choose to buy a couple of stocks in the sector that were showing good Relative Strength versus the market and their peer group.
Euro Gives a Buy Signal while the Dollar Gives a Sell Signal	iShares Euro 350 Index Fund would provide the International exposure to benefit from a rise in the Euro and a decline in the dollar.

Tell me this portfolio doesn't look appealing! You can mix and match as your research and strategy suggests. Just look at the diversification you have in this portfolio. You can also hold out more cash for individual stocks. Now don't think that just because you have great asset allocation here that you don't have to manage risk. You do! Let's say the NYSE Bullish Percent, our main coach, went above 70 percent just as in April 1998 then reversed down as it did on May 13, 1998. We would go to defense. This might mean we would go to 50 percent cash in all indexes and buy at-the-money puts on the individual stocks. Or, we could consider hedging the indexes that have options attached. Some do, some don't. I keep looking up at that portfolio and think, "Boy, that looks nice." Often when the time comes to go to defense on our portfolios, we tend to act as if we were a rabbit in the headlights of a car—frozen. We know what the indicators are telling us, but we just can't find the strength to execute. This time is always different. This happened to me while I was getting my Private Pilot License. I was flying near San Diego. I was lost and inexperienced. I knew if I could only get to the coast I'd simply turn left and arrive safely at Brown Field. Ahead of me was nothing but blue. I knew it was the ocean even thought my compass said I was flying southeast. I knew I was flying west. I just knew it. Well, the compass was right and I ended up having to land the plane with virtually no fuel in a horse pasture 18 miles south of Tecate Mexico. I had crossed the border without knowing it all during the time I thought I was flying west as my compass said I was flying southeast. When your compass tells you defense, don't choke—execute. The article I wrote with Judd Biasiotto, who is a sports physiologist, might help you avoid choking.

Choking: Tips for Controlling the Terror of Coming Unglued[*]

We tend to think of choking as something that happens in sports. Like the time you were in Little League and the game came down

---

[*]Thomas Dorsey and Judd Biasiotto, PhD, Excerpt from the *Daily Equity & Market Analysis Report*, June 9, 1999.

to your "at-bat." The adrenaline starts running, you get weak in the knees, and thoughts of failure dance through your mind. "Strike one," the Umpire shouts. You were frozen, unable to swing the bat. The fast ball flies past you, knee high. Two more shots at it. The next ball is pitched, you are not going to let this one whistle past you this time. You swing and miss by a mile, "Strike two." This is it. Two strikes, no balls and you're about to blow it. Your team needs you desperately, at this moment. The pitch from the crowd and your team mates, yelling "you can do it Tom," is rising and your adrenaline is rising too. No balls, two strikes, and you can't afford to let even a marginal pitch past. The worst thing would be to go down without a swing on the third strike. Time seems to downshift to slow motion. The pitcher is as determined to strike you out as you are to hit the ball. It's hard to swallow, and sweat beads appear on your forehead. You are about to choke. The ball is pitched, it's a slider, low and to the outside. You swing. All of a sudden, the ball isn't where you thought it was, it curves to the right. You swing for the fence. Nothing but air and the refrain from the umpire, "Strike three, you're out." *You choked.*

Choking is not only associated with sports. The same thing can easily come in this business. I've choked many times in the past. When I was a broker and operating without a plan, it was easy to choke. Clients came to me for advice that I was unprepared to give. Especially when I first came back from training school. It's not on paper anymore. It's for real. This is real, hard-earned money your client is entrusting to you. You were a whiz trading on paper but in the real world you start getting sick to your stomach. "What if I lose this money for my client?" On paper it's simple. I just select the right portfolio and let it "happen captain." If I'm wrong, so what, nobody gets hurt. Now if I'm wrong someone does get hurt. The market has been going down, I'm scared as hell as the business periodicals all are saying we're in a recession. My client wants ideas and I'm frozen. I begin to think conservative. Maybe I'll recommend something that just can't get hit. I remember the first premise of advising is "do no harm." Okay, I'll go with utilities, REITs, and a few high-yield consumer stocks that have low volatility. I'll also keep 30 percent Treasuries. You choked! The NYSE Bullish Percent just reversed up from below

30 percent, the Utility sector and the REITs just reversed down from above 80 percent (fictitious accounts and fictitious examples only) and Cyclical stocks are all washed out and their RS charts are reversing up from low levels. As the market takes off, your customer is losing money because you put him in low volatility stocks that were about to correct for the first time in two years. One month down the road, your customer is wondering if you have a clue. You realize you don't.

Let's talk for a second about controlling that phenomenon called choking.

1. *Put things in perspective.* In sports one must remember it's just a game. From the start put sports into perspective and you'll enjoy them more. Work hard, compete hard, but don't worry about winning or losing. The investment business is the same. Keep it in perspective. Work hard, compete hard (remember the market is your competitor and ready to take your money away from you as quickly as possible), but don't let the thoughts of winning or losing cloud your judgment. I bet you've all had a portfolio of stocks that was down for one reason or another. You desperately needed a winning trade so your luck might change. You let winning cloud your vision. You bought what you thought would be the stock that would make it right but you ended up making it worse as the stock you selected to get you right, got you wrong.

2. *Don't be afraid to make a mistake.* No one is successful all the time. Even Michael Jordan missed the last second shot now and then. Actually he missed it more often than you may think—about 50 percent of the time. When it came to crunch time, though, Jordan still wanted the ball. His shooting percentage when the game was on the line didn't bother him, because he knew that hit or miss, there was plenty more shots to take. That's the best lesson to learn—no matter what happens there is always another day.

3. *Be prepared.* When preparing for competition (you compete with the market every day) give it everything you have. The secret is to be overly prepared. When I was a broker I was unprepared and totally willing to begin selling the stock my quote machine mate was selling. I did not know how to be prepared. We

simply did what the home office told us to do. Evander Holyfield has a wonderful philosophy about preparation. When he was to fight Mike Tyson for the first time he was asked by a sports reporter if he was nervous or scared. Holyfield said "I never get nervous when I'm in the ring, because I'm always prepared physically and mentally when I get there. I do everything I can in training. I work as hard as I can. When it comes time to fight, I know I've done my very best. When you have done your very best there is no reason to be nervous. Generally the people who get nervous and choke are the people who are unprepared. And if I lose, I can live with it, because I gave it everything I could." Without a doubt, confidence that comes from preparation is the "real deal." I got a call from a broker I talk to frequently from Everen in California. He just closed a $12 million account because he was prepared. He had this whole program laid out in understandable form and closed the account. He told me he was driving home from that meeting and he said "I've never felt more confident in my whole career as I do now." He also said he was readopting the title Stockbroker. He's going after another $10 Million account next week and my bet is he wins it. He's prepared, confident, and that is as contagious as the flu. Whether you are an individual investor or a broker, come to work prepared.

4. *Focus on the moment.* One of the best ways to choke is to think about how important the contest is that you are competing in. When competing, focus on the task at hand. Don't worry about the outcome of the contest or what can be won or lost. Focus on the task. When the mind is totally focused, all doubt is pushed aside. In short, your body will cease to experience a body that is inhibited by the distractions of your mind. Over time you will learn that if you maintain this type of focus, the outcome of the event will take care of itself. All too often investors focus on what the "market" as dictated by the Dow Jones is doing. They live in fear that we are entering a bear market as the newspapers would suggest at times and lose sight of their stock picking prowess. They focus on the outcome of the contest and forget their focus on the individual stock. Focus on the pieces of the puzzle and the puzzle itself will come out all right. Focus, focus, focus.

5. *Develop a consistent behavioral pattern.* As previously mentioned, the response of fear is generally associated with

cognitive involvement. Usually, it's your thoughts that bring about the physiological symptoms associated with fear and/or choking. In other words, before every lift in a powerlifting event you attempt, go through the same ritual—chalk your hands, take two deep breaths, visualize your lift, take two more deep breaths, grab the bar, and then attempt to lift. I always go through the same routine in competition. Each behavior should follow the next without interruption so that you would only have time to focus on the behavior that you are engaging. By becoming more systematic about your lifting, you will decrease negative thinking and thereby decrease your chance of choking. When investing, it is always best to have some consistent behavior patterns you go through when evaluating a portfolio or stock. What is the overall market risk, offense or defense, and field position? How does the sector distribution look, skewed to the overbought side or oversold side or normal? What sectors are oversold and what sectors are washed out? Within those sectors, what is my inventory of stocks (derived by fundamentals)? From that inventory, what stocks meet my technical criteria? When I select a stock, what will I do if things go right and what will I do if things go wrong? Lastly, execute the plan without fail.

6. *Look at the worst-case scenario.* Sometimes in life we simply screw up. Sometimes in this business we simply screw up. Some of you out there might have screwed up a time or two in your portfolio. There is nothing you can do about it. In most cases when you have the wrong stock, you believed in the fundamentals, got married to it and behold, it collapsed. Instead of riding it into the dirt, it is usually best to sell the stock and replace it with another stock with the opposite fundamental and technical attributes. Once you have taken corrective action, never look back, only forward. It is best to determine what you will do from the onset if the worst case scenario does appear. Determine just what is a worst-case scenario from the onset of the trade, not some time after things get bad. This way you have a plan.

7. *Look for the silver lining in each situation.* There is always good in every situation no matter how bad it seems. You just have to look for it. When you make a misstep in the investment process it generally costs you some money. You as the investor must learn from your mistakes. Find out if you did

everything you could have done before buying the equity. Find out why it went awry and what you can do not to make that same mistake in the future. It takes time in the investment business to gain whiskers, and don't ever mistake it, this is a business. Much of what we learn comes from the school of hard knocks. They can't teach this in the University. You have all been involved in bad situations in the investment business. Make the situation better by learning from your mistake. No matter how dark the cloud, there is always a silver lining. Learn these things and you are on your way to becoming a true craftsman.

Chapter 9

PUTTING IT
ALL TOGETHER

So far, we have been examining the pieces of the puzzle and in working through the concepts, we have begun to see how the pieces of the puzzle might fit together. It's time now to assemble the puzzle in earnest. The successful dinner is generally the product of a cook who religiously followed the recipe. The same goes for successful investing. Truly successful investors have some guidelines they adhere to religiously. I have never seen a successful investor who over time haphazardly went about this business. You must have some type of operating system or game plan. There are lots of operating systems that work in the stock market. You as an investor must find one of those systems that you believe in and can hang your hat on and then stick with it. We follow the Point and Figure method because it is based on the irrefutable law of supply and demand. It is also easy to follow as the indicators are either bullish or bearish, a stock is either on a buy signal or sell signal, the trend is either positive or negative. Unlike the bar chart which is subjective in nature, the Point and Figure chart leaves no room for subjectivity. The chart is either bullish or bearish. There is no in between. Once all the indicators are evaluated as well as the underlying stock's chart pattern, the pieces of the puzzle begin to form a picture of the overall market risk. Let's get into the program.

Guidelines for Stock Selection

We follow six steps when selecting stock:

1. Evaluate the market to determine whether it is supporting higher prices or lower prices.
2. Evaluate the sectors of the market to determine which sectors are supporting higher prices.
3. Create a fundamental inventory of stocks to work from within each sector.
4. Evaluate the technicals of each stock in the inventory to answer the question, "When to Buy?"
5. Continually monitor the position for signs of impending change in the trend of the stock.
6. There is no exception to the preceding rules!

Step 1. Evaluate the Broad Market— Who's Got the Ball?

This is the step most investors and money managers never think about. Most investors think one way—buy stocks, always play offense. Mutual funds are the same way. They are paid to keep you fully invested at all times. The problem is you don't always have possession of the football. There are times that the market has the ball, and that's perfectly fair. When the market has the ball, its job is to score against you by taking as much money away from your portfolio as it can. The market is a formidable opponent and generally takes your money away from you much faster than you can earn it. Conversely, there are also times when you have the ball. These are the times you must run plays and attempt to score against the market by having the strength in your conviction to buy stocks. Typically, the best buying opportunities come when things look the worst in the market.

Psychologically, these are roadblocks you must learn to overcome. You will invariably take possession of the ball when the news is the most bearish. The market will take possession of the ball when the news is the most bullish. This is the point where you must control your emotions. You will be forced to buy when things look the worst and forced to defend your portfolio when things look the best, a pattern that goes against human nature. It's like the edge the house has in Las Vegas—theirs is mathematical and yours is emotional. Someone always sells at the top and buys at the bottom. Who are these people? We call them the "Smart Money."

I do not belong to the select "Smart Money" group; I belong in a second group—the "Followers of Smart Money." The insiders are typically contrarian investors. They have the discipline to buy when things look the worst and sell when things look the best. When they begin operating in the market, they cast their vote by buying stock. This in turn causes the supply-demand relationship of these stocks to change, which clearly shows up on a Point and Figure chart. This is why I say the Point and Figure chart is as good as inside information. With the new Full Disclosure laws by the Securities and Exchange Commission (SEC), it makes learning about what the insiders are doing all the more important.

As the chart patterns form, they give buy and sell signals. A positive change will take place in the NYSE and OTC Bullish Percent Indexes when enough buy signals are given to cause 6 percent of the stocks on the New York Stock Exchange (or Nasdaq) to change from bearish to bullish (sell signal to buy signal). At this point, the NYSE Bullish Percent Index changes from a column of O's (market has the ball) to a column of X's (you have the ball). This is when you must have the intestinal fortitude to run plays although everything you read suggests otherwise. The opposite takes place when the Bullish Percent turns negative. Flip back to the NYSE Bullish Percent chapter and take a look again at how the NYSE Bullish Percent had you turn to a defensive mode when the financial media would have had you investing and mortgaging your house to put more money in the market. It also had you go to an offensive mode when the financial media was scaring the living daylights out of you. I know after reading this book, you will have the conviction to do the right thing.

Remember the first line of defense is knowing who has possession of the ball. When the index is declining in a column of O's, the market has the ball. When the index is rising in a column of X's, you have the ball. You must then determine your field position. Bull Confirmed at 70 percent has very little value, whereas Bull Confirmed at 30 percent has an abundance of value. The opposite is true with the bearish side of the coin. A Bear Confirmed status at 68 percent suggests higher risk than a Bear Confirmed status at 26 percent. Your best buying opportunities come when the NYSE Bullish Percent is on a buy signal and near the 30 percent level or lower. Your best selling opportunities come when the NYSE Bullish Percent Index is on a sell signal near the 70 percent level. Keep field position firmly in mind. Once you get the hang of this, you are going to love it. You will join the select few on Wall Street who understand these principles.

You need to take into account the short-term indicators and some of the very long-term Relative Strength indicators. The High-Low and Percent of Stocks above Their 10-Week Moving Averages are very good indicators for short term swings. To see if the market is supporting higher prices longer term, we look at Percent Positive Trend, Percent Relative Strength Charts in X's, and Percent Positive Relative Strength. We use the chart shown here to ascertain whether the broad market is supporting higher prices or not. Take the following form and evaluate each indicator for the NYSE and the Nasdaq market, then see if the majority of indicators are positive or negative. The chart starts with the longest term indicator and works down to the shorter term indicators. If the majority are positive, then you have stacked the odds in your favor and the market is telling us that buying pressure is outstripping supply pressure. The risk is low and you can take new positions. When the market is not supporting higher prices and wealth preservation strategies should be employed, you will see week by week more and more of the indicators flip to the bearish sign telling us risk is high:

Market Being Evaluated: NYSE or Nasdaq

Indicator	Positive	Negative
Percent of Stocks with RS Charts on Buy Signals		
Percent of Stocks with RS Charts in X's		
Percent of Stocks with Positive Trends		
Bullish Percent		
Percent of Stocks Above Their 30-Week Moving Average		

Indicator	Positive	Negative
Percent of Stocks Above Their 10-Week Moving Average		
High-Low Index		
Advance-Decline Line		

Step 2. Evaluate the Sectors

Once you have a good handle on the risk in the overall market, you are ready to evaluate the sector. Sector rotation plays a key role in the success of your investing endeavor (see Chapter 7). Proper sector selection can make the difference between success or failure. I have repeated often that about 75 percent of the risk is in the market and sector. Most investors focus their research on the underlying stock's fundamentals and place little emphasis on the sector and the market. When evaluating a sector for investment, try to select sectors that have good field position on their sector Bullish Percent charts, about the 50 percent level or lower and in a column of X's, along with combining strong Relative Strength readings for the group. It simply doesn't make sense to buy stocks in a sector that is on a sell signal because it reduces your odds of success. Once the sector rises much above the 50 percent level, the field position moves closer to the overbought side of the ledger. The higher the sector moves, the less aggressive you should become with it. You must be prepared to take advantage of sectors that move below 30 percent and then reverse up from that level. These sectors are about as washed out as they will be for years to come. Opportunities to buy stocks in such a sold-out condition do not happen very often. When such a situation occurs, take advantage of it. One of the beauties of this methodology is that once you have learned the buy and sell signals, the Relative Strength calculation, and the Bullish Percent concept, you can apply them to different markets and sectors. You don't have to learn a new set of rules for each type of market or sector. All the Bullish Percent concepts discussed in Chapters 6 and 7 and in Step 1 of this chapter apply here.

Just as with evaluating the overall market, we look to the Relative Strength and positive trend indicators for sectors. The premise behind these indicators is that when we evaluate a stock, in general we try to buy those stocks which are in a positive trend (above their Bullish Support Lines), and have strong Relative Strength. In the same way when we invest in a particular sector, we want the number of stocks with strong Relative Strength and positive trend charts to be rising. This tells us the underlying components of the sector are getting stronger technically. The indicators I am referring to here are the Percent Positive Trend (PT), Percent Positive Relative Strength (RSP), and Percent Relative Strength Chart in X's (RSX). These are used in conjunction with a Relative Strength reading for the sector and its Bullish Percent. The more of these five indicators I have positive, the stronger the sector. For new positions, I look to those sectors where the majority of the five previously mentioned indicators are positive.

In this summary, we are taking some of the basic concepts of buy and sell signals, Relative Strength, support and resistance lines, and Bullish Percents and combining them with innovative ways of evaluating these important concepts. To determine which sectors have the majority of these attributes as positive, I have a sheet on my desk that was printed from our Internet site summarizing the indicators for each sector. I can quickly glance down and see which sectors have more sectors positive than negative:

Sector Being Evaluated: _____

Indicator	Positive	Negative
Sector Bullish Percent		
Sector Relative Strength		
Percent RS Buy Signal (RSP)		
Percent RS in X's (RSX)		
Percent Positive Trend (PT)		

Step 3. Select a Group of Fundamentally Sound Stocks from the Chosen Sector

The other weekend I took a break from working on this book to see a movie at the local mall. As I was walking through the mall, I saw some Christmas promotional merchandise being pulled out—and Thanksgiving was barely upon us. As I was shopping, the thought occurred to me that being a manager of an investment or trading account is a lot like being an inventory manager. Stores like Nordstrom, Macy's, or Target own the store and the merchandise, and they are constantly rotating the inventory based on the season and consumers' demands. At the first of August, stores are having back-to-school promotions—specials on jeans, book bags, notebooks, and so on. An effective inventory manager will bring out the merchandise before the season, not at the end. When Halloween is over, then the Thanksgiving and even some of the Christmas promotional items begin to come out. The inventory manager will know what items are likely to be the "hot" gifts for the holiday seasons, whether they are toys, electronic games, outdoor toys, or clothes. Furthermore, a good inventory manager will make sure to have plenty of the popular items in stock. Something may be flying off the shelves but if Target doesn't have any in its store, it's not going to help it's bottom line.

The first step is to determine what season it is by evaluating the market and the sectors, which you have done in Steps 1 and 2. Those sectors coming into season are indicated by a Sector Bullish Percent in X's and a good field position. Furthermore, the real leaders, or hot items of the season, will be those sectors having the majority of the following positive: Sector Bullish Percent, Sector Relative Strength, Percent of Stocks Whose RS charts Are in X's, Percent of Stocks Whose RS Charts Are on Buy Signals, and Percent of Stocks with Positive Trend charts. The next step is deciding which items to place on the shelves. This is where individual stock selection comes into play. The catalog to order from, so to speak, is the fundamental list of stocks. Two great sources are Value Line ranked 1 and 2 stocks as well as S&P ranked 4 and 5 stars. As you continue to move through this four-step process, you narrow the acceptable stocks down to a smaller number with each step. By the end of Step 4, you will have refined it down to the crème de la crème.

Since the first edition of this book, the Internet has proliferated and the job of creating and maintaining an inventory of fundamentally sound stocks is much easier. When we first started in this business, we had chart books that we tossed to one another in the office as they were needed. There was no easy way of keeping and maintaining a fundamental inventory other than on paper. Today, the time it takes to keep an inventory is just a fraction of the time we spent 10 years ago, even 5 years ago. For me, I keep an inventory of S&P ranked 4 and 5 Stars and Value Line ranked 1 and 2 stocks that I update each week in our Internet System. It takes just a second to remove stocks that fall off the list and add those coming onto the list. With the completed list, I can use the Search/Sort function to filter that portfolio of stocks, or inventory, to find those that also have the best technical information. Steve Einhorn, the former director of equity research at Goldman Sachs, said about his fundamental research team, "If the market goes down, that's not their call. Their call is 'What's the best stock in my group?' and in my opinion their advice is good." We couldn't agree with Mr. Einhorn more. Wall Street has some of the smartest minds out there. When investing, however, you have to understand the job of the fundamental analyst. His or her job is just to say whether Nokia or Motorola is more fundamentally sound. It has nothing to do with whether the wireless telecom stocks will do well. The fundamentalist job addresses only 20 percent of the risk in a stock. The other 80 percent of the risk is addressed by identifying the market and sector. So whose job is it to determine that part of the equation? It is your job to do that, and following Steps 1 and 2 just outlined here will address the majority of risk in any particular issue. When reading the fundamental reports, always remember that the job of the fundamental analyst is to answer the question "what to buy" but not the question "when to buy." Step 3 of the process answers the question "what to buy."

Step 4. Evaluate When to Buy Stocks with Point and Figure Technical Analysis

Now, comes your finesse as the inventory manager. This is where you determine which items will fly off the shelf that season. For this, we look to find those stocks within the catalog inventory, the fundamental list, that have strong technical features. As mentioned, the proliferation of the Internet and its capabilities makes this job much simpler. Today, with the click of a few buttons, we can narrow down a universe of 8,000 stocks to 50 names in a matter of seconds. When we first started this company, this process would take hours, even days. When a sector changed status, we would take a chart of stock in the sector and update it by hand to bring it up to date. After that was done, we could begin to tell whether that stock was a buy. How do we determine if the stock is a buy? Let's cover some of the technical attributes that we look for in an individual security we want to consider buying.

We emphasize three long-term aspects when identifying the stocks we want to put into our portfolio. Those three aspects are trend, Relative Strength versus the market, and Relative Strength versus peer group. When looking to purchase a stock, whether for a long-term investor or a short-term trade, you greatly increase your odds of success if you focus on buying those stocks that are in an overall uptrend, have positive Relative Strength, and are in X's versus the market and the peer group. Stocks with these attributes are usually the market leaders. One question we often get is, "Well, doesn't this limit you to just the momentum stocks? I am a value buyer." My answer to that is yes, it does focus your attention on the momentum stocks but isn't that what you want? Don't you want to buy those value stocks that are ready to go up now, not six or eight months later? There are two problems with buying value stocks and not evaluating the technicals. First, the stock can stay a great value for the next decade and not move up in price. Or worse, the stock can become an even better value by continuing to decline in price. The best situation is to find a value stock that has turned the corner and is beginning to show signs that demand is taking control and the stock has momentum to move forward in price. These situations have presented themselves numerous times since I began practicing this methodology. Examples are Bank stocks in 1990, Bank stocks in March 2000, Oil and Oil Service stocks in March 1999, Technology stocks in the summer of 1994, Technology stocks in September 1998, Drug stocks in May 1994, Utility stocks in February 2000, and Food stocks in March 2000.

So once we have identified those stocks with positive trend and positive Relative Strength as the stocks we want to focus on, then we fine-tune the entry point. This is especially important for the short-term trader. For the investor, a stock that is good at

54 will be good at 55, and 56 and still at 60. However, that move of 6 might be all the trader is looking for before moving on to another idea. This brings us to some other attributes about the chart that we want to talk about.

Risk-Reward

First, let's review the chart patterns and how they can help you determine the risk-reward ratio, which is extremely important to success for both traders and investors. Risk-reward is just what the name implies. It is the process of evaluating how much risk you will take on compared with how much reward you can expect to have on any given trade. Or said another way, how many points could the stock fall if the trade doesn't work out versus how many points could you expect to see the stock rise if the trade does in fact go in your favor. Typically, when evaluating risk-reward, we like to see a two-to-one ratio, at a minimum. For every point at risk, we want to have 2 points of potential reward.

So as the preceding sentences suggest, you need to be able to figure out the expected reward, and the potential risk. How do you do that? Well, you need a few things to calculate this:

- Determine where significant resistance lies, or where the stock would be overbought on its trading band (bell curve).
- Determine where significant support resides.
- Calculate the price objective for the stock, using either the vertical or horizontal count.
- Determine your stop-loss point—where the stock will break a significant bottom or trend line, the point at which you no longer want to own the stock. You must be able to handle the worst-case scenario—that of the trade not working, and therefore being stopped out.

So that is the data you must ascertain when evaluating the risk-reward to determine whether you should buy a stock. Again, you must know where you are stopping out if the trade doesn't work out—you must be able to handle the worst-case scenario, that of being stopped out. Remember, you are only at this step in the process by already having examined the market, the sector of the stock, and its overall trend and Relative Strength. So now let's go through a couple of examples of evaluating risk-reward using XYZ Technology (XYZZ), shown in Figure 9.1, on page 258.

Example 1

XYZ Technology has rallied up to 33, breaking a double top at 29 after finding support at 21. The stock has rallied to a new high and has no overhead resistance. The (incomplete) bullish price objective is 58. The stop-loss point is 19½, which would be a violation of the Bullish Support Line; 18 could have been chosen as a stop if an investor, as that would break a spread quadruple bottom. Support lies at 20 to 21 initially, then 18½. The top of the 10-week trading band is 39.

Risk-Reward Calculation

Reward = 25 points to the upside
(58 price obj – 33 current price)

Risk = 13.5 points to the downside
(33 current price – 19½ initial stop-loss point)

$$\text{Risk-reward ratio} = \frac{25 \text{ points reward}}{13.5 \text{ risk}} = 1.85 \text{ to } 1$$

(This ratio would be worse if you used the 18 stop, or used the top of the trading band at 39 as your objective)

Example 2

XYZ Technology rallied up to a new high of 33 then pulled back to 23. It remains on a double top buy signal and has initial support at 20 to 21; below that is notable support at 18½. There is minor overhead resistance at 33 and the top of the 10-week trading band is 39. The bullish price objective is 58 using a vertical count. The stop-loss point is 19½, which would be a violation of the Bullish Support Line. Those longer term in nature can choose to use 18 as the stop point.

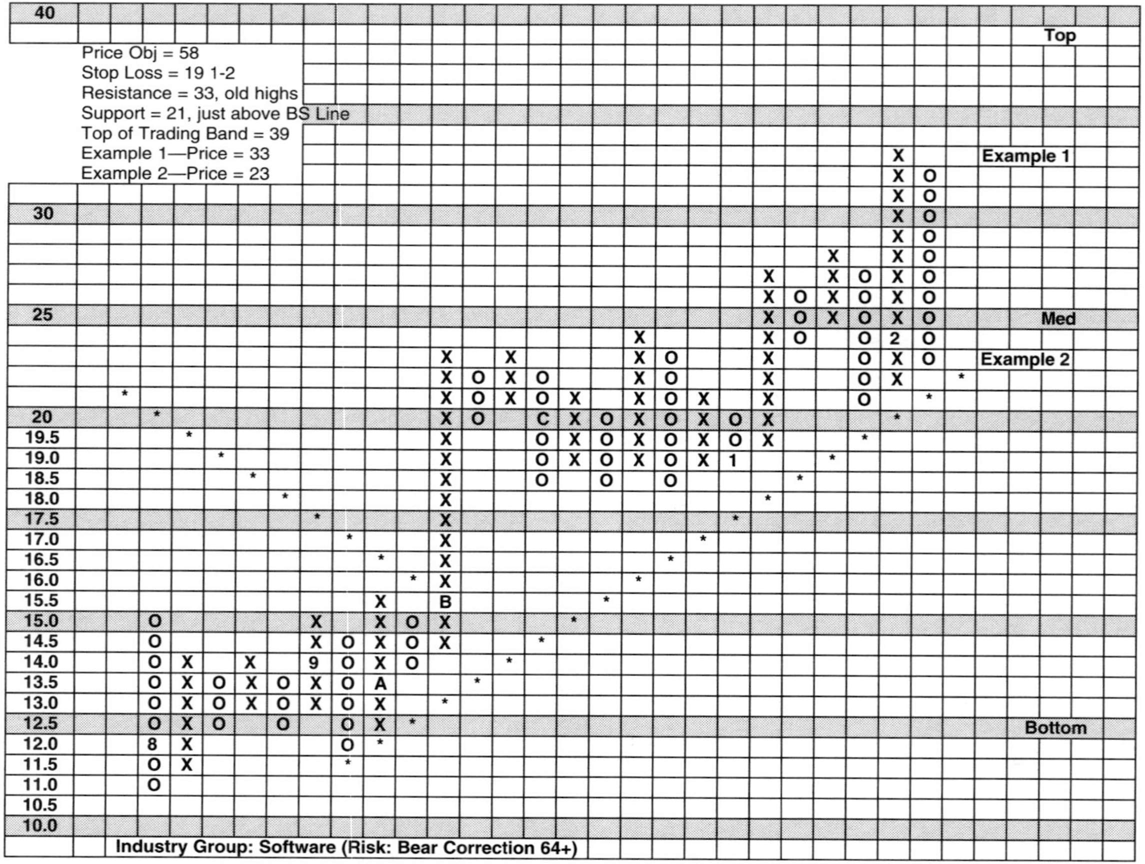

Figure 9.1 XYZ Technologies Inc.—XYZZ trend chart.

Risk-Reward Calculation

Reward = 35 points to the upside
(58 price obj − 23 current price)

Risk = $3\frac{1}{2}$ points to the downside
(23 current price − $19\frac{1}{2}$ initial stop-loss point)

$$\text{Risk-reward ratio} = \frac{35 \text{ points reward}}{3\frac{1}{2} \text{ points risk}} = 10.0 \text{ to } 1$$

Risk-reward if you use either 33 initial resistance, or 39 top of trading band:

$$\text{Ratio} = \frac{10 \text{ points reward}}{3\frac{1}{2} \text{ points risk}} = 2.85 \text{ to } 1$$

or

$$\frac{16 \text{ points reward}}{3\frac{1}{2} \text{ points risk}} = 4.57 \text{ to } 1$$

As you can see, buying XYZ Technology on a pullback greatly improved your risk-reward situation. Buying this stock as laid out in Example 1 was unacceptable on a risk-reward basis, but buying this stock as laid out in Example 2 was very attractive on a risk-reward basis, even if you were only looking to trade it back up to the initial resistance of 33. When you are going through and trying to decide which stocks to buy and where, be sure to evaluate the risk-reward characteristics. It is a very important component to overall success in the stock market. This is especially true in markets of great volatility and choppiness. Be willing to wait for that stock you want to buy to pull back closer to support. Waiting for a pullback greatly improves the "Reward" part of the equation, and reduces the "Risk."

Momentums and Trading Bands

There are two other tools that we look at for short-term trading especially but also for investing and helping us to determine, along with the chart pattern itself, when a stock might be ready for a pullback or when the pullback might be done. These two tools are Momentum and Trading Bands, both proprietary calculations of Dorsey, Wright & Associates.

Momentums

We have three different momentum calculations: daily, weekly, and monthly. Daily momentum is a very short-term trading tool. Following weekly momentum is very helpful when timing trades as well, but it gives a bit longer horizon. It is a more intermediate tool as changes to positive or negative weekly momentum last seven weeks on average. The monthly momentum is used more to highlight or signify a longer-term turnaround. Weekly momentum is the one we use most often.

Weekly momentum is basically a one-week (or day, or month) moving average compared to a five-week (or day, or month) moving average. The moving average is exponentially weighted and smoothed. When the one-week moving average crosses above the five-week, we say the weekly momentum is positive. This would suggest a bounce in the stock. When the one-week moving average crosses below the five-week, we say the weekly momentum is negative. This would suggest a pullback in the stock.

The weekly momentum calculation was created well before computer graphics became as sophisticated as they are today. At that time, it was difficult to draw two lines (1-week and 5-week) and see where they crossed one another. Therefore, we turned to the actual calculation and created two columns. One column is labeled "Top," which is the positive column, and the other column is labeled "Bot," which is the negative column. As a visual, think of the line between the Top and Bot columns as the five-week moving average. When the calculation (or the numbers) "moves" from the Bot column to the Top column, the one-week has crossed above the five-week. Likewise, when the Top column prints zeros and the Bot column has a negative calculation, the one-week has crossed below the five-week moving average. The same premise applies to the daily and monthly calculations. It is simply a different time frame.

Momentum calculations are used as a supplement, not a substitution for, the Point and Figure chart. When we get down to evaluating the individual stock chart, the three most important parts are the Relative Strength versus market and peers, and trend. In addition, before even evaluating the momentum, we would want to ascertain the risk-reward ratio and the individual patterns on the Point and Figure chart. Once we have determined that those things are positive, then we look at the short-term timing tools like weekly momentum before purchasing a stock. Let's say that we have a stock that is bullish on everything, but the weekly momentum has flipped negative. That tells us to put our order in for new positions on a pullback. Again, the momentum doesn't change our opinion of the stock, but rather it helps us time the trade.

Let's look at weekly momentum on Nextel (NXTL) and also use it as an example of some of the things we look for in a short position. First we will examine the Point and Figure chart of NXTL. This is seen in Figure 9.2. Let's evaluate the stock on August 30, when the stock is trading for $56. The Point and Figure chart tells us quite a lot about the stock. I think one of the best ways to learn how to evaluate a stock on a Point and Figure basis is to sit down with a pen and paper and just write down what you see. This is how we teach our interns as well. If I were to start writing down what I saw on the chart up to August 30 (reading from the left to the right of the arrow at August 30), the first thing I would write is a series of lower tops and lower lows from the high in July at 73. I would write down four consecutive double bottom sell signals, the first at 65, the second at 62, the third at 52, and the fourth at 51. I would also write down that the stock has violated its Bullish Support Line changing the trend to negative.

Next, let's look at the Relative Strength information. In Figure 9.3, we see that the Relative Strength chart of NXTL versus the market has just reversed down into a column of O's, which is a negative for the stock. It is still on a buy signal, but short term this reversal into O's is another red flag for the stock. Looking at the Relative Strength chart of NXTL versus its peer group, which is shown in Figure 9.4, we see here that it, too, is in a column of O's. Given all the information so far, we can say the NXTL is controlled by supply.

Now that we have established that NXTL is in a downtrend and controlled by supply, we might consider this one for a short

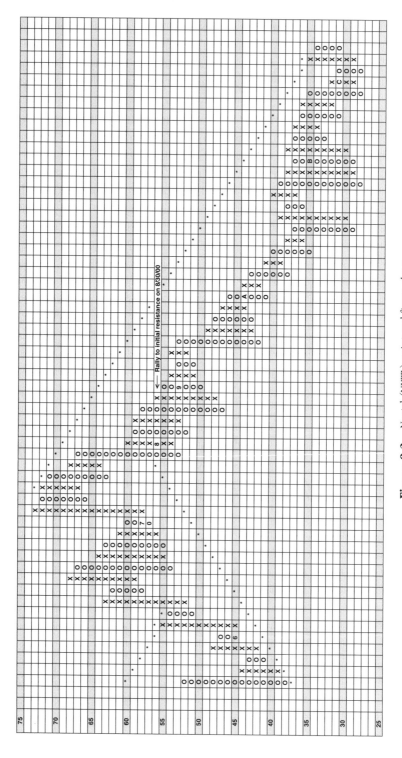

Figure 9.2 Nextel (NXTL) point and figure chart.

8.5	I	I	I	I				
8.0	I	I	I	I				
7.5	I	I	I	I				
7.0	I	I	I	3				
6.5	I	I	I	X	O			
6.0	I	I	I	X	O	X		
5.5	I	I	I	2	4	X	O	
5.0	I	I	I	1	5	X	O	
4.75	I	I	I	C	O	X	8	Reversed down on 8/29/00
4.5	O	I	I	X	O	6	O	
4.25	5	I	I	B	O	X	9	
4.0	7	I	I	X	O	X	A	
3.75	O	I	I	X	O		O	
3.5	8	I	I	A			O	
3.25	9	I	I	X			O	
3.0	O	I	I	X			B	
2.75	A	I	I	9				
2.5	B	I	I	X				
2.25	O	I	I	7				
2.0	C	7	I	6				
1.75	1	X	O	9				
1.5	O	X	O	X				
1.25	2	I	B	X				
1.0	I	I	C	I				
.75	I	I	I	I				
.50	I	I	I	I				
.25	I	I	I	I				
.00								
	9	9	9	9	9	0		
	4	5	6	7		0		

Figure 9.3   NXTL RS versus Dow (Market RS).

position. We have a close buy stop point at 60, the next potential time the stock could go on a buy signal, and there is no strong support on the chart. The weekly momentum comes into the fine-tuning of whether we should put the short position on here or wait for a further bounce. Or, if you owned the stock, should you sell it here or wait and try to get a couple more points out of it before cutting the position? Figure 9.5 shows a weekly momentum table. If you imagine drawing a line between the "Top" and the "Bot" column, that would be your five-week moving average. The numbers would be the one-week moving average. On August 4, the numbers switched from the "Top" column to the "Bot" column. That means the weekly momentum switched from being

20										
19.5										
19.0										
18.5								X		
18.0						3		X	O	
17.5						X	O	7	O	
17.0						X	O	X	8	
16.5						2	4	X	O	
16.0				X		1	O	X	O	
15.5				X	O	X	O	X	O	
15.0				X	O	X	5	X	O	
14.5				A	C		O	X	9	
14.0				X			O	6	A	
13.5				X			O	X	O	
13.0				X			O	X	O	
12.5		9		9			O	X	O	
12.0		X	O	8			O	O	X	
11.5		8	O	X				O	X	O
11.0		X	B	X				O	X	O
10.5		X	C	7				O		B
10.0		X	4	6						
9.5		X	5	X						
9.0		7	O	3						
8.5			7	2						
8.0			9	X						
7.5			A	1						
7.0			C	X						
6.5			O	X						
6.0			O							
5.5										
5.0										
4.75										
4.50										
4.25										
4.0										
3.75										
3.5										
3.25										
3.0										
2.75										
2.50										
2.25										
2.0										
1.75										
1.5										
1.25										
1.0										
.75										
.5										
.25		9		9		0				
.00		7		9		0				

Figure 9.4   NXTL RS versus DWA (Peer RS).

Date	Top	Bottom	Last	Cross	
12/11/2000	0.102	0.00	31.56	22.505	
12/08/2000	0.063	0.00	32.44	26.379	
12/01/2000	0.020	0.00	29.13	27.061	
11/24/2000	0.033	0.00	34.88	31.220	Weekly momentum turns positive.
11/17/2000	0.00	-0.007	33.563	34.377	Weekly momentum close to turning positive.
11/10/2000	0.00	-0.060	30.063	37.388	
11/03/2000	0.00	-0.084	33.063	44.801	
10/27/2000	0.00	-0.085	34.875	47.240	
10/20/2000	0.00	-0.090	37.875	51.571	
10/13/2000	0.00	-0.099	38.250	53.780	
10/06/2000	0.00	-0.076	39.125	51.078	
09/29/2000	0.00	-0.024	46.750	50.515	
09/22/2000	0.00	-0.042	47.938	54.968	
09/15/2000	0.00	-0.016	50.875	53.588	
09/08/2000	0.00	-0.033	53.688	59.518	
09/01/2000	0.00	-0.067	53.500	66.167	
08/25/2000	0.00	-0.137	51.125	80.694	Weekly momentum is getting more negative.
08/18/2000	0.00	-0.119	57.250	82.308	
08/11/2000	0.00	-0.087	54.188	70.428	
08/04/2000	0.00	-0.049	57.000	65.849	Weekly momentum turns negative.
07/28/2000	0.005	0.00	55.875	54.944	
07/21/2000	0.041	0.00	69.813	62.256	Weekly momentum begins to get less positive with
07/14/2000	0.157	0.00	72.313	47.978	the decreasing numbers.
07/07/2000	0.194	0.00	62.438	36.067	
06/30/2000	0.264	0.00	61.188	28.352	
06/23/2000	0.176	0.00	53.688	29.413	
06/16/2000	0.126	0.00	67.750	38.677	
06/09/2000	0.025	0.00	57.375	53.139	Weekly momentum turns positive.
06/02/2000	0.00	-0.019	50.657	53.701	

Figure 9.5 Nextel (NXTL) weekly momentum.

positive to negative. The numbers under each column don't have meaning to them. However, we do look at whether that number is increasing or decreasing. From August 4 to August 25, we see that the number is getting larger and that tells us the weekly momentum is getting more negative for the stock. Typically, a stock will have a positive or negative weekly momentum reading for an average of six to eight weeks so you can see this is a shorter term timing tool. With the momentum also just recently turning negative for NXTL, it would tell us we are not likely to get much more out of the stock on the upside and a short position should be taken at the market. If that weekly momentum had just turned positive, we might try and squeak 58 out of the stock to try and short it there. The fact that the weekly momentum was positive would not have changed our overall view that supply was in control of the stock; our only question is do we short it here or try to get a couple points' better execution?

If you fast-forward to December 2000 in Figure 9.2, the far right-hand side, you will see that NXTL had fallen to 28 for a low in the technology bashing of 2000, which hit telecom stocks particularly hard; NXTL was no exception. How do I know when to take a profit in the short position? There are several different answers, all of them right. One strategy would be to begin peeling off your short position once you had a 30 percent profit. Cover a third when you are profitable by 30 percent, and then cover another third of the position when you have 50 percent profit. As long as the trend is negative, hold the last one third of the short. A short-term trader might choose to lock in a profit when the stock gets down to the bottom of the ten-week trading band (which we will cover next). Another viable strategy would be to hold onto the short position until the first buy signal is given, in this case at 39. Yet another strategy would be to hold the short position until the bearish resistance line is violated. This brings us to December 2000 in the chart, which presents an interesting situation worthy of discussion.

Notice how NXTL has held support at 28 three times. This is telling us that every time the stock hits 28, supply dries up. Now the stock has set up for an interesting potential breakout at 36. A move to 36 would break a second consecutive double top and violate the Bearish Resistance Line. This would be the place you would certainly cover any short positions because the move to 36 would change the stock back to a positive for the first time since July 2000, almost six months. So NXTL would be a stock I would want to keep on my watch list for a potential buy on the breakout at 36. Take the time while the chart is still developing to check out the fundamentals to see if it is a stock that meets those criteria. You would also want to watch and see if the stock's Relative Strength charts shaped up and reversed at the same time the stock got through the trendline. That would be an aces back-to-back situation if they did. See how you can think a couple of moves ahead in the chess match? You don't make a move until the action point is hit but by watching the chart develop, you are not like a deer in the headlights when the time to act comes. If NXTL doesn't ever hit 36 and then just continues lower, so be it.

Trading Bands

Regression to mean is a natural process that we all go through in our lives. Have you ever driven down a highway early on a Saturday morning? There is virtually no traffic and no police out. You want to get to your destination quickly and decide that if there was a time to speed it was now. You pick up your speed and are actually exceeding what would be called reckless driving. All of a sudden, the traffic light ahead of you turns red. Damn, foiled again. You were just regressed to mean. Have you ever gotten too big for your britches? Come on, be truthful. At times, we become too full of ourselves and all of a sudden we get figuratively slapped down. We get regressed to mean. Something happens to make us aware we are getting a little out of control and we settle back to normal.

It is life's way of keeping nature in the center of the curve. In a particular meadow there might be a certain number of rabbits. As they begin to reproduce, their numbers grow geometrically. More rabbits in a particular field means the available food supply decreases as a percentage for each rabbit. The rabbits reproduce until starvation kills some off. This is life's way of regressing the rabbits back to normal for this field. As well, the rabbits in the field attract more wolves to the area. The wolves in the area could cause the population to regress past mean to the endangered side of the equation. The wolves leave because their food supply is gone and the cycle begins again. This is how the stock market works.

One of the best ways to graphically represent this movement back and forth to mean is with the 10-week trading band. We all remember the bell curve concept from our college Stats 101 class. Given a set of data, one can construct a range that is depicted as a bell curve. There are six standard deviations to the bell curve. Three standard deviations to the left is considered 100 percent oversold. Three standard deviations to the right is considered 100 percent overbought. The middle of the curve is normal and most of the time, stocks reside within one standard deviation of normal. For each stock and index, we can take 10 weeks' worth of data and create a bell curve. When a stock gets to the overbought side of the curve, it will typically move back to the middle. There are two ways a stock or index can get back to the middle of the curve. First, the stock can fall in price and move back to the middle of the curve. Second, as time passes, the stock can stay relatively the same in price and the curve shifts. Conversely, when a stock or index gets oversold, you will typically see it move back to the middle in one of the two ways. Most of the time, you will see strong Relative Strength stocks trade between the middle and the top of their trading bands, whereas weak Relative Strength stocks trade between the bottom and the middle of their trading bands.

Now that you have an understanding of the bell curve, it brings us to the application of the concept. For every stock on our Internet system, we put a "Top," "Med," and "Bot" designation on the chart, on the right-hand side. This lets us quickly see when evaluating a position where it is on that trading band. Look at the chart of Cooper Industries (CBE) in Figure 9.6. The sector is positive; the Relative Strength chart of the stock reversed up from a long tail of O's; the trend just recently turned positive for CBE after breaking a spread triple top at 38. Now the stock has rallied to 44 on the chart. Notice that this is near the top of the 10-week trading band denoted by the "Top" on the chart. You can also see this in graphical format in Figure 9.7. As for a stop-loss point, one could easily justify using 29, a violation of all near term support on the chart, as a stop-loss point. At 44, however, that stop is a bit far away and with the stock near the top of the 10-week trading

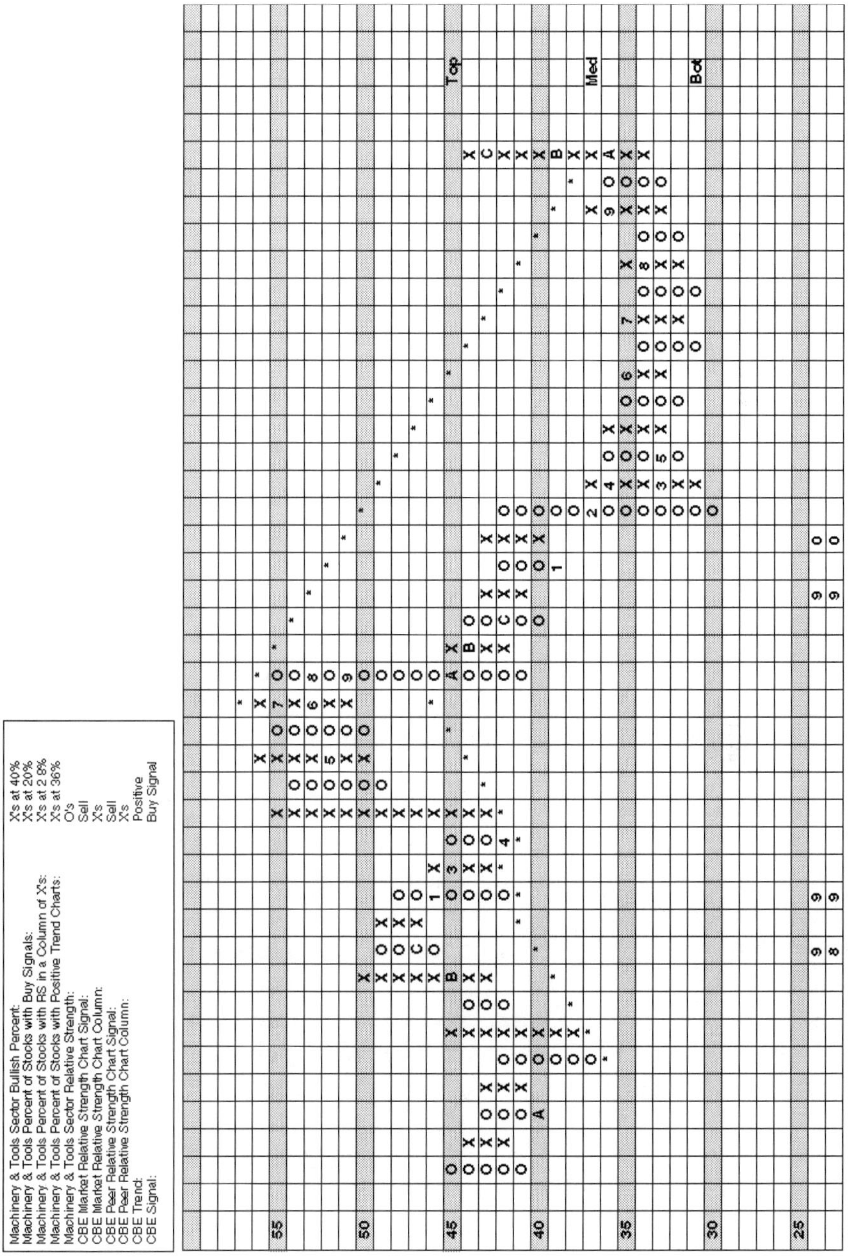

Figure 9.6 Cooper Industries (CBE).

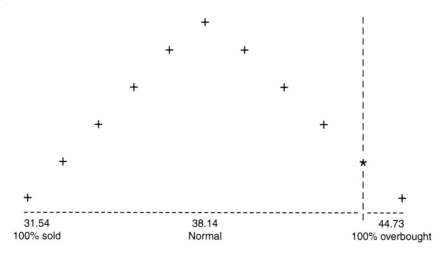

Figure 9.7 Cooper Industries (CBE) 10-week trading band.

band, the likelihood is that you will see the stock pull back. But how much of a pullback? Again, typically strong stocks trade between the middle and the top of their 10-week trading bands. Therefore, it would logical to expect to see CBE pull back to the upper 30s (the middle of the 10-week trading band is 38.14). If you were to wait for a pullback to the bottom of the trading band at 32, you probably wouldn't get that in a strong stock. Conversely, if you were to wait for a stock in weak hands to rally up to the top of the 10-week trading band, you probably wouldn't see it. Use rallies to the middle of the trading band as opportunities to lighten up, sell the position, or hedge. Over time, these trading bands will shift as you are constantly re-evaluating the most recent 10 weeks' worth of data. We have also found that the trading band tend to work really well with broad market indexes like the Dow Jones, Nasdaq Composite, and S&P 500.

Practice Examples

One of the best ways to learn how to use the Point and Figure method is to practice with real examples. Whenever we conduct our Point and Figure Institutes, we always teach a section then do some practice examples. We culminate the seminar with several practice exercises, and in some instances a full case study, incorporating all the concepts taught. Therefore, as you finish reading this book, which is like attending a Dorsey, Wright Point and Figure Institute, it is fitting to do some practice examples that bring all the information together. One of the things I recommend is that you get a sheet of paper and just write down the pros and the cons for the stock. Create a checklist with two columns, one Positive and one Negative, as well as a Comments column. Then as you examine each of the attributes of the market, sector, and stock, put it in the Positive or Negative column. Your evaluation sheet would look like the one in Figure 9.8. Continue to do this exercise whenever you evaluate a position. The DWA Internet site makes this easier because you can click a button and see an evaluation sheet just like the one in Figure 9.8, filled in with all the information available.

Practice Example 1

For the first practice example, we have given you all the technical data you would need to evaluate the position in Figure 9.9. You

Stock:			Date:
	Positive	**Negative**	**Comments**
Market			
Sector			
Sector RS			
Trend			
Rel Str			
Peer RS			
Pattern			
Price Obj.			
Risk-Rewd			
Momentum			
Trading Bd			

Figure 9.8   Stock Evaluation Checklist

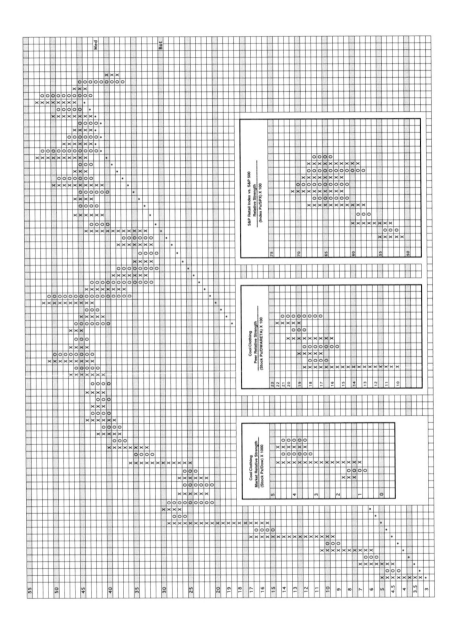

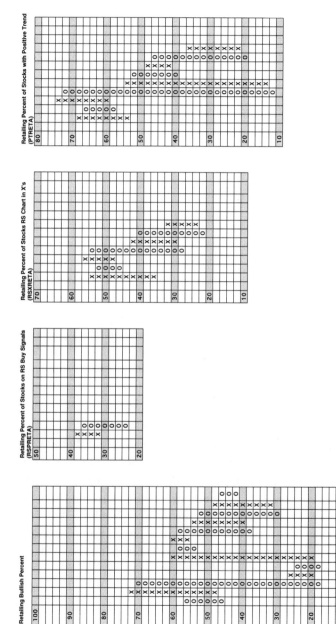

Figure 9.9 Cool Clothing Inc.—weekly momentum negative (1 week), monthly momentum negative (1 month).

273

will notice that we use a fictitious name for the stock and omit the time period. This is so you are not unduly influenced by the name. When conducting case studies like this at our Broker Institutes, we found that not knowing the name of the stocks helped immensely in the evaluation. You won't "fall in love" with the stock. Remember, stocks are only lunch dates, not marriage candidates. Take your time and study each chart given. Make a copy of Figure 9.8 on your notepad and then fill it out. Make comments on your observations. Once you fill out this form, pieces of the puzzle will fall into place to give you a clear picture of what you should do.

After evaluating Figure 9.9, here is what my evaluation sheet looked like (see Figure 9.10). Looking at this sheet, you can see that most of the indicators are marked off in the "Negative" column. This suggests that the odds would be stacked against me if I were evaluating this stock for purchase. If I owned this stock, I would have a stock in my portfolio with the probabilities of

Stock: Cool Clothing

	Positive	Negative	Comments
Market		X	NYSE Bullish Percent in O's
Sector		X	Retail Bullish Percent in O's & RS Buy Signal in O's RS in X's & Positive Trend in X's
Sector RS		X	On a Sell Signal and in O's
Trend		X	Violated a very long term trend line
Rel Str		X	On a Buy Signal but in O's
Peer RS		X	On a Sell Signal and in O's
Pattern		X	Violated major support in the 40–42 area and has started making lower tops
Price Obj.			Next support on chart is 31 which is near bottom of 10-week trading band
Risk-Rewd		X	Resistance at 46—Support at 31 6 upside and 9 downside
Momentum		X	Negative weekly & monthly
Trading Bd		X	At the middle of the trading band

Figure 9.10   Stock evaluation checklist.

lower prices. Therefore, if I owned "Cool Clothing" I would want to begin taking some type of defensive action. This could range from selling all of the position, selling part of the position, buying protective puts, and so on. The point is I know that because the risk is high in this stock, I should employ a strategy to reduce that risk.

Now flip to Figure 9.11. The stock we were evaluating was The Gap (GPS). From April 2000 to December 2000, the stock took a major hit falling from the 40 area down to 26. That's a loss of 35 percent. Had you not taken any defensive action, that sell-off in just one stock could have been a killer to your portfolio. A loss of 35 percent means you need to see that stock rally by 55 percent just to get back to even. Considering the average return for equities is about 12 percent, it would take you four years at 12 percent to get back to even. The lesson here is when the odds are stacked against you, take action to preserve wealth. You can always make up opportunity but it is hard to make up money. Be willing to accept a small loss while you let your profits run. Small losses are more manageable.

Practice Example 2

Just as you did for the first practice example, make a copy of Figure 9.8 on your notepad and then use Figure 9.12 to gather the technical information. We will assume that the stock is recommended by a firm on a fundamental basis. Again here we have given the stock a fictitious name so as not to influence your decision. As well, we haven't told you what time period this is as that is not important to your decision-making process. The only thing that is important is to make a list of Positive features and Negative features of Sage Software on a technical basis and then see which one has the most. After you do this exercise, the picture should make very clear what your strategy should be.

After evaluating Figure 9.12, here is what my evaluation sheet looked like (see Figure 9.13). Wow! This is an aces back-to-back hand. The only negative I could really find was that the weekly momentum had not turned positive yet. The OTC Bullish Percent was in O's but the majority of OTC indicators were positive,

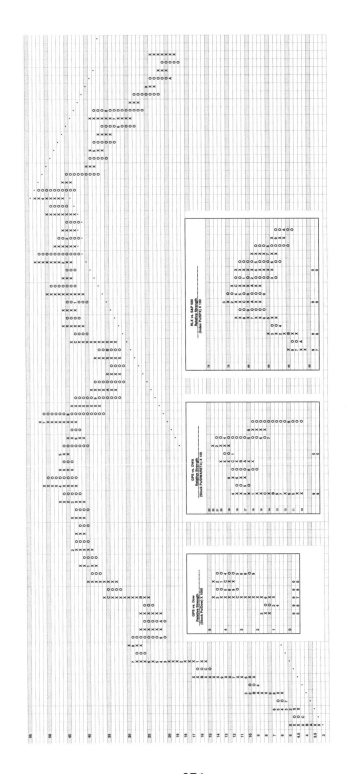

Figure 9.11 The Gap (GPS).

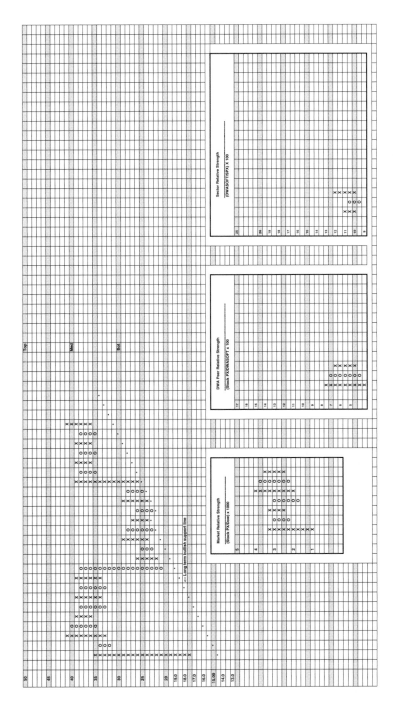

Figure 9.12 Sage Software—daily and monthly momentum positive, weekly negative for 6 weeks.

277

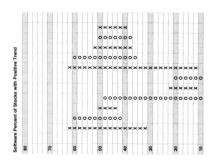

Software Bullish Percent

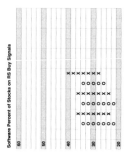

Software Percent of Stocks on RS Buy Signals

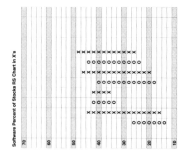

Software Percent of Stocks RS Chart in X's

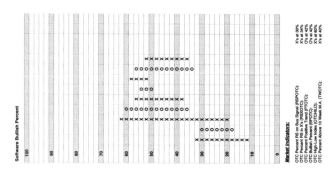

Software Percent of Stocks with Positive Trend

Figure 9.12   (Continued)

278

Stock:			Date:
	Positive	Negative	Comments
Market	X		The majority of the OTC Indicators are Positive
Sector	X		All the Software Indicators are in X's
Sector RS	X		In X's and on a Buy Signal
Trend	X		Long-Term Bullish Support Line was strong support
Rel Str	X		On a Buy Signal and in X's
Peer RS	X		In a column of X's
Pattern	X		"Big Base Breakout" at 40
Price Obj.	X		Horizontal Count is 84
Risk-Rewd	X		Stop = 31; 43 pts upside & 10 pts downside
Momentum	X	X	Dly & Mnthly Positive; Wkly Negative
Trading Bd	X		Middle which is a good pullback for strong RS stks

Figure 9.13 Stock evaluation checklist.

like the Percent of Stocks with Positive Relative and RS in X's. As well, the short-term indicators for the OTC had reversed up. All of that suggested the OTC Bullish Percent would reverse up into a column of X's soon. Everything for the sector was bullish too. The Software sector Bullish Percent was at 52 percent, still not too extended. By knowing that the market and the sector were in our favor, we had covered 75 percent of the risk in this stock. Now for the stock specifics, the Relative Strength of Sage Software was positive versus both the market and its peer group. The trend chart was positive too, with the long-term Bullish Support Line being just like a brick wall in the mid-20s. Even though the stock had rallied up to 39 and had already had a nice run, that doesn't mean the stock can't go further. The breakout at 40 suggested that after a period of consolidation, demand was once again in control. In determining our price objective, we looked at the horizontal price objective counting from the first time Sage hit 39 to the most recent breakout to get 21 columns. From there, we multiplied by 3 to 63 and then added to the lowest point of that whole base we counted across, which was 21. This gives us a price objective of 84. For short-term traders, a stop could have been placed at 34, but investors would give the stock room to 31 initially, a violation of the Bullish Support Line. Of course, as the chart developed, you could continue to raise that stop-loss point. Typically when a stock breaks out of such a strong pattern, you would want to take at least a partial position and then add on any pullback.

Well, have you figured out what stock this is? It is Oracle Systems (ORCL) and the breakout at 40 was in September 1999 (on a presplit basis). Figure 9.14 shows a chart of ORCL a mere three months later. The stock has rallied to 90, a double.

This brings us to another important part of managing the trade, where should you take profits? Taking profits can be one of the hardest things investors do. As the stock moves up, hope springs eternal. Each point rise is accompanied by the hope of another point rise. We tend to fall in love with stocks. Eventually the stock tops out and supply overtakes demand. The first few points' retracement is viewed as a mere pullback in an otherwise strong uptrend. The next few are viewed with shock and disbelief as all the news is still bullish on the stock. The expected earnings are coming onstream, new products are coming to market, and the fundamental analysts are falling all over themselves raising earnings expectations. *Time* might even have had a cover story on the company. These are the things tops are made of. At this point, everyone who wants to buy has bought. The supply-demand relationship of the stock shifts decidedly to the supply side of the equation. A lack of buyers augmented by a handful of sellers causes stiff declines in the stock. Once the move is on, concern changes to fear and the decline accelerates. One analyst then reduces earnings estimates, which creates panic. The Wall Street herd follows the first analyst, not wanting to be left in the stampede, and more earning estimates are lowered. Before you know it, the investor's profit turns into a loss. After you have studied this book closely (and if you adhere to its principles), you are likely to be faced with the question of "where do I take profits?" quite often. Here are some alternatives you might want to consider when the trade goes in your favor:

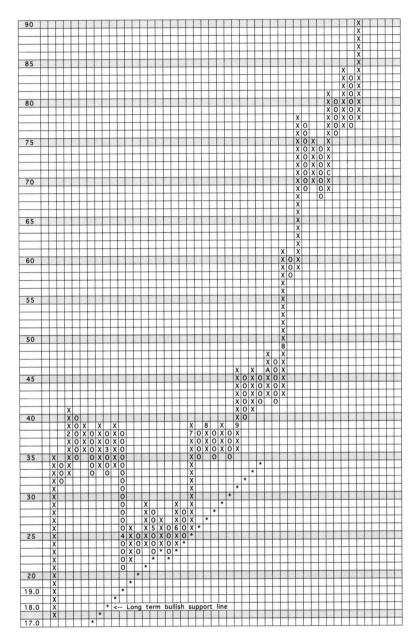

Figure 9.14 Oracle Systems (ORCL).

- Use a stop of the Bullish Support Line. As long as the stock is above the Bullish Support Line, the main trend is positive. You may have to draw subsequent Bullish Support Lines if the stock gets too far above the main trend line. You could also use a stop on the violation of an important support area if that is applicable.
- Take at least partial profits off the table if the sector Bullish Percent goes above 70 percent and reverses down. This suggests at a minimum that the sector is ready for a breather. If the Relative Strength readings of the sector are also negative, then expect more downside than if the Relative Strength readings are positive for the sector.
- Take profits if the majority of indicators for the sector turn negative. Now you don't have the odds in your favor anymore.
- If you have profits in the stock, take those profits and buy calls or leaps. Don't overleverage here. Let's say you have a stock that moves up from $40 to $60. You have 500 shares. One strategy would be to sell the 500 shares of stock at $60 booking the profit. Now, take some of those profits and buy six-month or more in-the-money calls. Only buy five calls; otherwise it is abuse of the strategy. Put the rest of the money in a money market account. This allows you to still participate in the upside yet you know your risk—the cost of the calls.
- Begin selling calls against part of your position at a higher strike price, provided the chart still looks good. This helps take the sell decision away from you and put it to the Options Clearing Corp. Let's say again that your stock has risen from 40 to 60. You could sell 2 calls struck at 60 or 65, three to six months out. The premium you take in helps offset declines in the stock and if you get called away, great. That means the rest of your position is rising too.
- Sell one third of the position if the stock rises 30 percent. Sell one third of the position if the stock rises 50 percent. Hold the last one third of the position until the stock declines to the first level where you took a profit or the Relative Strength chart turns negative. This will ensure you get the most out of stocks that just keep going. One reason I like this alternative method to taking profits is that it forces you to take some money off the table when things are looking good. It is much

easier to sell stock when things look good than it is to sell stock when everyone is scrambling for the door. Conditions change rapidly in the market and it is better to be in control. As well, this method will keep one position from becoming too large a percentage position in the portfolio (i.e., too many eggs in one basket).

Conclusion

I hope you now have an operating system that allows you to keep the odds stacked in your favor. Using an operating system based on the irrefutable law of supply and demand will make you just as good, if not better than, any other professional on Wall Street. Above all, keep it simple. If the simple evaluation charts we have shown you in this book have more indicators in the "Negative" column than the "Positive" column, then you have a situation where the odds are not in your favor for making money. If most of the indicators are in the "Positive" column, then play offense and manage the position using your play book. The guidelines outlined here will help you develop confidence in your convictions and allow you to buy when the news media are saying the worst is upon us. You will also be able to sell when the news is great and things have never looked better from the media's perspective. We have been applying these simple principles in the market with great success for 20 years now, and the Bullish Percent concept is 45 years old. It has been through bullish markets, bearish markets, and neutral markets and has guided us successfully through each one. These indicators and guides are there for the taking. By reading this book, you are on the path to becoming a craftsman in this methodology. Now that you have religion, go to church!

INDEX